Modernism between
Benjamin and Goethe

Modernism between Benjamin and Goethe

Matthew Charles

BLOOMSBURY ACADEMIC
LONDON • NEW YORK • OXFORD • NEW DELHI • SYDNEY

BLOOMSBURY ACADEMIC
Bloomsbury Publishing Plc
50 Bedford Square, London, WC1B 3DP, UK
1385 Broadway, New York, NY 10018, USA
29 Earlsfort Terrace, Dublin 2, Ireland

BLOOMSBURY, BLOOMSBURY ACADEMIC and the Diana logo are trademarks of
Bloomsbury Publishing Plc

First published in Great Britain 2020
This paperback edition published in 2021

Cover design: Catherine Wood
Cover image © Boaz Balachsan

A catalogue record for this book is available from the British Library.

A catalog record for this book is available from the Library of Congress.

ISBN: HB: 978-1-3500-1397-1
PB: 978-1-3502-6737-4
ePDF: 978-1-3500-1394-0
eBook: 978-1-3500-1395-7

Series: Walter Benjamin Studies

Typeset by Newgen KnowledgeWorks Pvt. Ltd., Chennai, India

To find out more about our authors and books visit www.bloomsbury.com
and sign up for our newsletters.

Contents

Acknowledgements

The central ideas discussed in this book draw on research originally conducted for a doctoral thesis, undertaken between 2004 and 2009 at the Centre for Research for Modern European Philosophy (CRMEP), based then at Middlesex University but now at Kingston University, and made possible through the award of Research Student Tutorship funding. The time necessary to undertake additional research and make significant revisions to the original thesis for this book was made available by a sabbatical for research granted by the University of Westminster in the spring of 2018. Only in the course of rereading and rewriting the original thesis, reframing it around the literary antimony between romanticism and classicism, did it become apparent to me that some of these ideas first surfaced in a dissertation I had written in 2001 on the concepts of genius in Benjamin's work, as part of a master's in philosophy and literature at the University of Warwick. This book has, then, been developing for nearly two decades, and there are a number of people without whom it would not exist: Andrew Benjamin, who stands at the beginning and end of this project as supervisor for the MA dissertation and as series editor for this book; Peter Osborne, who supervised the doctoral thesis at the CRMEP; and my current colleagues at the School of Humanities, University of Westminster, most notably Alex Warwick and David Cunningham. This book is dedicated to my parents, Brenda and Terry; my children, Benjamin and Finley; and above all my wife, Michele, whose encouragement and patience has supported me through its long gestation.

Introduction: Perverse antiques

The opening vignettes of Walter Benjamin's *One-Way Street* – 'Filling Station', 'Breakfast Room', 'Number 113' – traverse a backward passage from the petrol station to No. 113 of the Palais-Royal, from the present of 1920s Berlin to the Paris arcades of the early nineteenth century, and from a constructivist praxis of writing via a Surrealist preoccupation with the narration of the dream to the 'house of dream' itself. If these preoccupations are familiar aspects of Benjamin's writing, the destination is more surprising: the cellar of this dream-house leads up into Johann von Wolfgang Goethe's study. When the 'house of our life . . . is under assault and enemy bombs are taking their toll', Benjamin exclaims, 'what enervated, perverse antiquities do they not lay bare in the foundations!'[1]

This book seeks to rescue some of the seemingly perverse antiques that lie at the foundation of Benjamin's thought. Specifically, it seeks to unearth the presence of Goethe's scientific, artistic and historical writings as a strange kind of classicism buried within the modernist theory and practice of criticism that Benjamin develops. In doing so, it challenges a dominant understanding of Benjamin's philosophy as *essentially* romantic based on the significant role that Early German Romanticism plays in his early writings, particular in the wake of Philippe Lacoue-Labarthe and Jean-Luc Nancy's *The Literary Absolute: The Theory of Literature in German Romanticism* (1978, trans. 1988), which broadly suggested affinities between German Romanticism and French post-structuralism, and so as a consequence the possibility of recuperating Benjamin's thought for a 'postmodern' moment in the 1990s and early 2000s.[2] Other commentators have emphasized Benjamin's neo-romanticism as a way to enlist his thought into a revolutionary romanticism that embraces the anti-capitalism of utopian socialism, Marxism, anarchism and other contemporary political movements.[3]

At the same time, this book seeks to answer the question as to what value an aristocratic figure whose thought had been influential on a range of conservative and reactionary figures, albeit against Goethe's own self-declared liberalism, including members of the George Circle assembled around the poet Stefan George and the Cosmic Circle assembled around the mystic Alfred Schuler, could hold, given Benjamin's radical commitments to anarchism, Marxism and the artistic avant-garde. Yet Goethe's thought exerted such an influence not merely on Benjamin's philosophizing but on a range of early-twentieth-century thinkers, including Georges Simmel and Georg Lukács, whose ideas were taken up by Benjamin and critical theorists more generally, and even, as the final chapter of this book suggests, on the artistic theories and practices of the Soviet avant-garde themselves.

Although the aesthetic theory and artistic style that Goethe develops after 1788 is described as Weimar Classicism, it is an unstable and perverse kind of classicism, formed in very close proximity to the proto-romanticism of Goethe's earlier *Sturm und Drang* and simultaneous with the new generation of Romantics writing in the wake of Kant's Copernican revolution. The significance of Goethe's classicism for these writers, it will be argued, is connected to its movement away from and opposition to romanticism and therefore as a corrective to deficits of romanticism, specifically associated in Benjamin's writing with formalism, affirmationism and singularity that provide a fertile cultural ground for nationalist political movements. Even where the significance of Goethe's writings for Benjamin's thought is recognized, such as across Esther Leslie's important attempts to develop a Marxist poetics of science, there tends to be a reluctance to conceptually differentiate Goethe's thought from that of romanticism and so to historically flatten out the antinomical tensions that Benjamin grasped as productive.[4]

Benjamin's modernist concept of criticism, it will be argued, is constituted not by any classical reaction to romanticism but within the very movement between the polarities of romanticism and classicism. Modernism is, therefore, not conceived here as another reaction to – the acceptance or refusal of – the phenomenological experience associated with modernity, nor some progressive overcoming of previous literary or artistic perspectives, but rather as a critical deepening of a philosophical conception of literary criticism achieved through the alternation or oscillation between the opposed viewpoints of romanticism and classicism. In positing the existence of a classical Goethean moment in Benjamin's concept of literary criticism, we should conceive this as the antinomy to romanticism in a constellation of extremes whose tension generates its modernist depths. Conversely, placing Goethe's classicism in relation to Benjamin's literary criticism reveals the historical tension with romanticism that constitutes its untimely – indeed, it will be argued in the final chapter, cinematic – modernism.

The relationship between Benjamin and Goethe constructed here is, therefore, a transcritical one, a term that the literary critic and philosopher Kojin Karatani uses to emphasize both a transcendental critique and a transversal movement of parallax. The chapters in this book therefore alternate in a transcritical fashion between the writings of Benjamin and Goethe, mediated through a constellation of other philosophical figures, including Immanuel Kant, Friedrich Nietzsche, Hermann Cohen, Ludwig Klages, Salomo Friedländer, Gilles Deleuze and Reinhard Koselleck, and across three paradigmatic kinds of experience: the content of colour given expression in the paintings of Matthias Grünewald, Hans von Marées, Paul Klee and J. M. W. Turner; the destructive negation of language as bodied forth in the poetry of T. E. Hulme; and the vision of technology found in the artistic practices of F. W. Murnau, Sergei Eisenstein and Sergei Tretyakov.

The transcritical modernism that is produced in this interstice is nominated in what follows as 'Expressionist'. It should be noted that Goethe's work predates Expressionism by nearly a century and although Benjamin belongs to the Expressionist milieu of early-twentieth-century Germany, he carefully distances himself from the perceived excesses of most of their art. Yet, as Andreas Kramer observes, Expressionist artists and writers sought to transform Goethe into a 'living pre-image [*lebendiges Vorbild*]' of the 'modernist cultural project' of their generation,[5] and Benjamin's writings are not immune to such influences, revealing what Lisa Marie Anderson describes as the 'thematic and structural correspondences between philosophy and literature in the Expressionist era' and a messianic 'openness to the possibility of apocalypse and redemption *at any moment*' that bears a close affinity with the Expressionist ethos.[6] What is termed 'Expressionism' in this book is therefore utilized as a fertile and not unproblematic medium to connect the polarities of Benjamin and Goethe (as well as Kant and Nietzsche, Cohen and Deleuze, and so forth). It is posited as an excessive and unstable kind of modernism, encapsulated in the paintings and films of Klee and Murnau discussed, but expanded to incorporate the colours of Grünewald, Marées and J. M. W. Turner, the language of T. E. Hulme and the biomechanical effect of technology in Eisenstein and Tretyakov.

The first chapter of this book explores how Benjamin's desire to be the foremost critic of German literature necessitated a recovery and renewal of an inherently transdisciplinary concept of criticism (*Kritik*) inherited from the German tradition of critical theory that runs through the philosophical criticism of Kant, the literary criticism of Early German Romanticism and the economic criticism of Marx. Benjamin regards this renewal of criticism as necessitating a philosophical redevelopment of the Kantian system that had been partially initiated by the neo-Kantianism of Hermann Cohen. Although consideration of Benjamin's metacritical transformation of Kantian and neo-Kantian criticism has been well established in the philosophical reception of his thought, this chapter offers a distinctive understanding of such a project by emphasizing the transdisciplinary nature of this concept of criticism.

This transdisciplinarity pertains not just to Benjamin's (and, as the second chapter examines, Early German Romanticism's) attempt to transpose the Kantian concept of critique into the realm of literary criticism but to Kant's concept of criticism itself, which is borrowed from the British tradition of literary criticism. In reconnecting Kant's concept of criticism to this original tradition of literary and, specifically, journalistic criticism, Benjamin's 'philosophizing beyond philosophy' sought to develop a mode of judgement capable of criticizing the aesthetic and ephemeral content of experience. This involves a radical transformation of the relation between the Aesthetic, the Logic and the Teleological within Kant's architectonic, which is reconstructed in this chapter via Benjamin's disagreement with Hermann Cohen. As a consequence, the transcendental and transversal *movement* associated with the Kantian antinomy, in distinction to both an emphasis on Benjamin's concept of the *Stillstand* or a more Hegelian-Marxist understanding of dialectic, is expanded beyond the realm of the a priori conditions of experience to encompass the content of biological, historical and artistic experience itself.

The latter grounds the basic principle examined in the subsequent chapters of the book: that Benjamin's concept of criticism is developed from within the antinomical movement – the parallax – between romanticism and classicism, and it is this that constitutes its specific modernity. The second chapter investigates the first pole of this antinomy by examining how Benjamin's subsequent attempt to investigate the philosophical history of the problem of criticism (*Kritik*), announced in his dissertation 'The Concept of Art Criticism in German Romanticism', transforms the philosophical concept of criticism in Kant by examining it from the transdisciplinary perspective of Romantic literary criticism. In doing so, Benjamin sought to restore a messianic relationship between particular and the Absolute in history, albeit one that is differentiated from Cohen's neo-Kantian messianism in terms of its focus on the aesthetic and contingent content of historical experience within the ethical-historical medium of theoretical teachings (*Lehre*). In contrast to most one-sided interpretations of Benjamin's romanticism, this chapter places a greater emphasis on the epistemological and political deficiencies that he ambiguously characterizes in terms of a weak messianism, identified as its formalism, affirmationism and singularity. These necessitate the transversal movement towards the antinomical extreme of classicism, which is explored in detail in relation to Benjamin's thought through the remaining four chapters of this book.

Chapter 3 carefully delineates Benjamin's recuperation of a Goethean concept of negative criticism, distinct from that of romanticism, and identifies the philosophical basis of the former as the tender, delicate or fragile version of empiricism (*zarte Empirie*) found in Goethe's natural philosophy. This tender empiricism is reconstructed, with the aid of Arthur Schopenhauer and Friedrich Nietzsche, in relation to an alternative development of Kant's critical philosophy from that of German Romanticism, emphasizing how Goethe's critique of sensibility involves an aesthetics of science that focuses not on the form but rather on the pure content of nature, experienced as Ideals of sensibility associated with Goethe's notion of exact sensorial phantasy (*exakte sinnliche Phantasie*). Goethe's natural philosophy simultaneously places an emphasis on multiplicity rather than singularity that involves the pessimistic rejection of teleological judgements concerning natural-historical progress.

These characteristics of Goethe's natural philosophy are fundamental to his concept of literary criticism and account for the classical features of his artistic works associated with the period of Weimar Classicism. These features are explored across subsequent chapters in terms of an alternative relationship between the particular and the Absolute, one that is examined in Chapter 4 in terms of a sphere of pure content, in Chapter 5 as a medium of destructive refraction and in Chapter 6 as a plurality of discontinuous archetypes.

Chapter 4 expands upon Howard Caygill's claim in *Walter Benjamin: The Colour of Experience* that an original experience of colour permitted the speculative recasting of Kant's philosophy. For Benjamin, unlike Kant, colour is a transitive, shifting, contingent and formless content of intuition and yet no mere auxiliary to aesthetics but constitutive of the highest kind of metaphysical experience. The latter is identified with the content of pure seeing or pure perceptibility and with the ephemeral temporality of pure transience, following Esther Leslie's recognition that this theory of colour is grounded not in the scientific doctrine of Newton but the spiritual and artistic *Lehre* elaborated in the philosophy of Goethe. The latter, and its connection to Kant's concept of experience, is explained through a Deleuzian interpretation of Goethe's tender empiricism, drawing on the work of Eric Alliez. For Benjamin, this perception of the pure, ephemeral content of experience is realized not directly in the colours of nature, however, but in the Expressionist paintings of Matthias Grünewald, Hans von Marées, Paul Klee and, it will be added, J. M. W. Turner.

Chapter 5 examines how this understanding of the experience of colour becomes transposed into the linguistic sphere as the correlating notion of the expressionless as the pure linguistic content of language, identified with an Adamic original speech or 'pure noncommunicative language' of silence. Although the corresponding conception of all expression as a practice of translation evokes the Early German Romantic idea of perfecting criticism, contrasting this view with Goethe's own theory of translation draws out a number of essential differences, most notably the transformative aspect of translation as akin to a refractive medium of chromatic differentiation, whose totality lies in a harmonic multiplicity.

A consideration of Benjamin's essay on Goethe's *Elective Affinities* elaborates on such translation in terms of the critical violence specifically involved in literary expression, in which the symbolizing activity of language becomes symbolized itself as the allegorical. This is exemplified through a closer analysis of Benjamin's own criticism of Goethe's *Elective Affinities* but also through consideration of the poetry of T. E. Hulme, whose cinder theory and imagist poetry is shown to share a comparable allegorical viewpoint to that of Benjamin and is similarly situated, in a Nietzschean transformation of Kantian aesthetics, in the movement between romanticism and classicism.

Having examined this aesthetics of expression, Chapter 6 develops Benjamin's transdisciplinary conception of literary criticism in relation to a pragmatics of history that transposes Goethe's description of tender empiricism from the realm of nature to that of history. As this chapter demonstrates, Nietzsche also invokes the same transposition as the foundation for his own pragmatics of history in the *Untimely Meditations*, and the recent work of Reinhard Koselleck provides a fuller understanding of why Goethe's untimeliness, which presents a multiplicity of relations between the present and the sedimented experiences of the past that is rooted in his own natural philosophy, was so influential for Nietzsche, as well Salomo Friedländer and Benjamin himself. Whereas Nietzsche's pragmatics of history is devoid of any reference to a messianic relation between the particular present and the redemptive Absolute, conflating this with a Judaic and socialistic conception of now-time (*Jetztzeit*), Benjamin's own historical reconstruction of Goethe's life, written from the perspective of post-revolutionary Moscow, aims at rescuing – against the grain – precisely these theological and political dimensions from within his thought.

While Chapter 5 examines how Benjamin's critical violence liberates a moment of radical theological hope within Goethe's pagan aesthetics, Chapter 6 broadens this viewpoint to consider how a similar act of criticism liberates a cosmopolitical conception of technology from out of the pagan conception of history. This will connect Benjamin's critical engagement with Ludwig Klages's Goethean theory of primal images to a Marxist conception of the collective liberation of nature through technology via the revolutionary aesthetics of the Soviet avant-garde, in which Benjamin found the model for his own messianic revisioning of Klages, Nietzsche and Goethe. The now-time of this historically expanded and cosmopolitical conception of technology is subsequently retrieved as the modernist moment within the 'Classico-Romantic Phantasmagoria' of the second part of Goethe's *Faust*. Conversely, these Goethean motifs play across Benjamin's late essays on Baudelaire and on 'The Concept of History', specifically in relation to the Goethean refrain, 'All that is ephemeral / Is only an allegory [*Gleichnis*]; / The inadequate / Here becomes an Event'.[7] In contrast to the demonic belief that 'All that exists deserves to perish' (Mephistopheles) and its derivations in the materialism of Marx and Engels and the idealism of Hermann Cohen ('All that is ephemeral . . . perishes'), Goethe's refrain, it is argued, constitutes the critical violence of a messianic intersection of the empirical contingency of nature and a theological contingency involved in historical redemption.

1

Criticism, transdisciplinarity and transcriticism: Walter Benjamin and the Kantian tradition

Walter Benjamin desired, at the outset of his career, to be the 'foremost critic of German literature'; a century later, he is regarded as one of the foremost cultural critics of European capitalist modernity.[1] The writings he produced at the beginning of the twentieth century, and indeed the subsequent reception of his work in the intervening period, involved a series of translations of ideas between disciplines, genres and modes of writing (in print as well as for radio), which oscillate between cultural, political and religious perspectives as Benjamin himself travelled between Germany, France, Russia, Denmark and Spain. This shifting of ideas, perspectives and experiences was central to the transdisciplinary nature of Benjamin's 'philosophizing beyond philosophy',[2] characterized in terms of a dynamic movement across existing disciplinary boundaries that is pragmatically rooted in a problematizing – and simultaneously aimed at the transformation – of everyday experience.[3]

This transdisciplinary impulse is inherent to the internal dynamics of the concept of critique (*Kritik*), which is so central to the German tradition of critical theory that Benjamin inherited, indebted as it is to the philosophical criticism of Kant, the literary criticism of Romanticism, and the economic criticism of Marx. Confronted with the metacritical problem of its own self-sufficiency, the practice of critique – whether philosophical, literary or economic – is driven beyond the conventional borders of its own disciplinary constitution, drawing on the content of experiences paradigmatic for other – whether past, current or future – fields and disciplines.[4]

Benjamin's aim to be the foremost critic of German literature necessitated, he believed, a philosophical-historical reconstruction of the practice of literary criticism itself, one that he developed from within the context of Kant's philosophical method of critique. In his early writings associated with 'On Perception' and 'On the Program of the Coming Philosophy', Benjamin regards the redevelopment of the Kantian system as a task which, having been partially initiated by neo-Kantianism, was to be completed by the 'coming philosophy'.[5] His subsequent attempt to investigate the philosophical history of the problem of criticism (*Kritik*), announced in his dissertation on 'The Concept of Art Criticism in German Romanticism', transforms the philosophical concept of criticism in Kant by examining it from the perspective of literary and art criticism, most notably in his writings on German Romanticism and Goethe.

In particular, it will be argued, the philosophical concept of criticism is examined from the perspective of journalistic criticism, implied in the centrality of the journal (most notably the *Athenaeum*) to the philosophical form of Early German Romanticism, but explicit in Benjamin's reflections on journalism and the crisis of literature in his announcement for the journal *Angelus Novus*, where 'both critical discourse and the habits of judgement stand in need of renewal' in order to 'restore criticism to its former strength' through a journal characterized by translation, discontinuity and ephemerality,[6] as well as in his writings associated with Karl Kraus's journalism and with the work of art in the age of its technological reproducibility. Whereas Friedrich Nietzsche had identified the debasement of genuine culture with modern journalism, characterized by its ephemeral politicality (literally *du jour*), levelling down of aristocratic distinctions and barbaric corruption of artistic style,[7] Benjamin suggests that 'it is at the scene of the limitless debasement of the word – the newspaper, in short – that salvation is being prepared'.[8]

Although Kant's dense philosophical writings appear to be a strange starting point for the reconstruction of journalistic-literary criticism, the central argument of this chapter is that the notion of philosophical critique (*Kritik*) that Benjamin develops from Kant, and that Kant introduces into the German language, was already an inherently transdisciplinary one, to the extent it was inherited from the British tradition of literary criticism that emerges in response to a crisis – one connected to the rise of public exhibitions and public journalism – concerning the standards of the judgement of taste in the mid-eighteenth century. The concept of critique that Benjamin utilizes is inherently transdisciplinary in this double sense: it possesses its own inner dynamism, a conceptual impulse to movement that stems from the negative moment of criticism itself, and this transdisciplinary impulse is evident in the history of the concept itself.

The present chapter elaborates on this recovery of a transdisciplinary concept of criticism in Benjamin's early engagement with Kant and the neo-Kantianism of Hermann Cohen by expanding on three central features: first, the association of philosophical criticism with the experience of aesthetic judgement (literary criticism) and, second, the emphasis on the transversal movement associated with the antinomical (transcriticism). What Benjamin's transformation of the Kantian concept of criticism sought to do in renewing its literary and journalistic potency, it will be argued in this chapter, was to reconnect 'critique' to its origins in a mode of judgement capable of criticizing, indeed characterized by, aesthetic sensibility and specifically the spatial movement of parallax. This includes a third moment, or movement, involving the dissociation of criticism from all modes of teleological judgement, which leads to an emphasis on the contingency of the ephemeral (contingent criticism). This provides the framework for the chapters that follow, which specifically locate the modernism of Benjamin's philosophical concept of criticism in the contingent interstice opened up in the transversal movement between romantic and classical literary criticism.

Literary criticism and aesthetic judgement

In Benjamin's early writings, the malign influence of the modern state upon institutions of education is regarded as having transformed them into primarily professional apparatuses in which the 'community of learning' and the 'original unity' of the disciplines in the 'idea of knowledge' have been abandoned.[9] Benjamin regards the possibility of a liberation from such deformed existence to be 'the exclusive task of criticism [*Kritik*]'. As his subsequent essays 'On the Program of the Coming Philosophy' and 'The Concept of Criticism in German Romanticism' make evident, the concept of criticism that he evokes here is that which becomes prevalent in German Idealism in the wake of Kant and is taken up in various forms by Early German Romanticism in the late eighteenth century and by neo-Kantianism in the late nineteenth century.

As the Kant scholars Hans Vaihinger and Norman Kemp Smith have both observed, however, Kant's introduction of the term 'critique' (*Kritik*) into German, most likely from his reading of *Elements of Criticism* by Henry Home (Lord Kames), derives from the common use of the term 'criticism' in eighteenth-century English to denote the standards of taste in literary and artistic judgement, as earlier used in the poetry of John Dryden and Alexander Pope.[10] Kant's delineation of an aesthetic kind of judgement in the *Lectures on Logic* links it specifically to what, Kant says, Home more correctly called criticism, understood as providing the 'norm (model or standard for passing judgement), which consists in universal agreement', but which can never become, as the German philosopher Alexander Baumgarten attempted, a science.[11] Logical judgement, conversely, is founded not on mere criticism but on 'a science or doctrine, provided that one understands by doctrine a dogmatic instruction from principles *a priori*' as a 'canon (law)' that subsequently serves for criticism 'as the principle for passing judgement on all use of the understanding in general . . . in regard to mere form'.[12] Science provides the canon for epistemological criticism, as a set of laws for judging the correctness of logical kinds of judgement, whereas, as Home correctly observed, criticism is a kind of judgement that itself provides the standards for taste.

Home's concern with deducing the rules of taste, despite the fact that taste seemingly involves subjective feelings of pleasure or displeasure and is prone to cultural and historical change, is perhaps reflected in his insistence on speaking not of *the* elements of criticism but of *elements* and his writing a chapter that is not 'Of the Standard of Taste', as his cousin Hume would do, but is devoted to some 'Standards of Taste', emphasizing the partiality of his project. In his *Elements of Criticism* from 1762, Home emphasizes the cultivation of judgement in accordance not merely with the external standards provided by nature or the classical poets, as Pope and before him Dryden had done, but with the inner standards provided by a common sense.

Significantly, establishing the elements of criticism had acquired a vital significance for Home and Kant because the emergence of journalistic criticism for guiding a new public judgement of taste coincided with the simultaneous disintegration of the relevance and standards inherited from classicism, usually associated with Aristotle's *Poetics*, rediscovered in the Renaissance and evinced in Dryden and Pope's use of the term to insist on a return to nature and the ancients. This crisis took place within the context of the emergence of often anonymous journalistic art criticism in the exhibition pamphlets, newspapers and magazines that accompanied the 'development of regular, public exhibitions of contemporary art in Paris and London in the mid-1700s'.[13] Home himself had, in the late 1730s, planned a literary and political periodical with his distant cousin, the philosopher David Hume.

Home's *Elements of Criticism* had argued that although it is generally accepted that there is no disputing about taste because it concerns that which is subjectively agreeable or disagreeable, we nonetheless speak equally of the existence of good and bad taste as the universal basis of criticism in the arts, and so the universality of taste must have a foundation in a providentially given human nature, upon which the conviction of a common standard or common sense must be based. Although Kant's transcendental account of a *sensus communis* in the third *Critique* is in part indebted to this British tradition, his critical version moves beyond Home's idea of a shared 'good taste' in deducing a notion of universal assent as a necessary condition for the judgement of beauty itself. For in assuming a providentially given foundation for judgement, Home's concept of criticism becomes dependent on a 'crude teleological naturalism', which 'does not direct individual judgement through reason, but nevertheless determines it according to rational ends', providing a standard for taste that is 'felt but not known in the act of judgement'.[14] Consequently, Kant 'denied the title of philosophy to the British theory of taste because it did not properly account for the universality and necessity of its judgements', equivocating between 'sense' and 'reason' in 'dissolv[ing] reason into the unknowable yet unnegotiable conviction behind the discrimination of sense'.[15] This not only confused 'the sensible and intellectual capacities, committing in Kant's eyes the amphiboly of sensualizing the concepts of the understanding', but in doing so unphilosophically relied on a providential teleology of the human constitution.[16]

The antinomy of taste that Kant eventually develops in the *Critique of the Power of Judgement* is therefore situated between this British tradition of the criticism of taste and the German science of aesthetics inaugurated by Alexander Baumgarten, distinguishing the reflective kind of judgement identified with criticism from the logical kind identified with science and in its two distinct parts systematically distinguishing and addressing the relationship between aesthetic judgement and teleological judgement. Kant's solution reveals how the discrimination of perfection or lack of perfection involved in aesthetic judgement cannot concern the spatio-temporal intuitions of sensibility itself but rather the 'form' of accord between intuitions of sensibility and concepts of cognition in judgement that Home left unresolved. Yet the basis for this accord between sensibility and understanding, those 'two stems' of human cognition, 'which perhaps spring from a common root, though one unknown to us', remains, notoriously, a fundamental problem within Kant's system as well.[17]

However, this entangled problem of the various standards of judgement and the crisis induced by criticism is not confined to the special case of aesthetic judgement of taste in the third *Critique*, Howard Caygill argues, but is present from the outset and has 'worked through in all of Kant's texts'.[18] Similarly, extending Vaihinger's observations on the aesthetic origins of Kant's concept of *Kritik* in Home's literary criticism, Kojin Karatani argues – against interpretations that emphasize how Kant's system is brought to completion with the transcendental deduction of the judgement of taste and the critique of aesthetics in his third *Critique* – that 'from the beginning, the Kantian critique had been derived from the problem of artistic experience' and that Kant had 'sought to reconsider all problematics through "criticism" in the judgment of taste', which 'is also to say, criticism in a journalistic sense'.[19] The central problem of judgement, and with it the question of the relation between the Aesthetic (criticism) and the Logic (scientific/scholarly doctrine), is consequently to be extended to the whole of Kant's critical philosophy, beginning with the first *Critique*.

It is this problem that animates Benjamin's own critique of Kant's philosophy in his early writings, notably in 'On Perception'. Benjamin argues that the required transformation of Kantianism must address this central problem within the architectonic of the critical system, starting with a 'confrontation' with the 'stumbling block' of Kant's isolation of the Transcendental Aesthetic from the Logic.[20] As an effect of this separation, Kant's system separates theoretical reason from practical reason, and therefore, ultimately, nature from history. This follows from the fact that Kant's 'Copernican revolution', the method of transcendental deduction, permitted him to produce what he regarded as the only valid 'metaphysics of nature', in which he 'described that part of the natural sciences which is pure – that is, proceeds not from experience but simply from reason *a priori*', that is, from the structure of knowledge itself.[21] With the certainty achieved through this theoretical knowledge of nature, Kant subsequently hoped to secure the integrity of a distinct, practical experience of ethics that might found a critical metaphysics of history. But the continuity between the thought and the experience of nature established through this procedure entailed the risk that 'the *metaphysics* of nature … could easily collapse into the concept of experience', because the form of experienced nature is necessarily structured by our thought.[22] This raises the blasphemous notion that not just the form but also the content of experience might be deducible from certain necessary principles of knowledge possessed by a subject implicated in actively producing such a world.

Benjamin maintains that 'Kant feared nothing so much as this abyss', and his 'method' for avoiding it 'was not only to relate all knowledge of nature, as well as the metaphysics of nature, to space and time as constitutive concepts, but to distinguish these concepts absolutely from the categories'.[23] Kant posits the faculty of the understanding as providing the formal, pure a priori concepts – the Aristotelian categories – through which the content of 'experience' is schematized, distinct from the pure a priori intuitions of space and time through which the manifold given to sensibility is synthesized, by systematically distinguishing the Transcendental Aesthetic of the first *Critique* from the Transcendental Logic. This dichotomy structurally corresponds to, and is the systematic legacy of, Kant's pre-critical distinction in his *Lectures on Logic* between aesthetic kinds of judgement of taste, found in the act of mere criticism, and logical kinds of judgement of knowledge, founded on canonical laws of doctrine.

This, in Benjamin's view, unjustified distinction of the a priori intuitions of sensibility from the a priori categories of understanding 'artificially distanced' the a posteriori material of sensation or 'given' 'from the animating centre of the categories by the forms of intuition by which it was only imperfectly absorbed'. Fearing the continuity between the knowledge and the experience of nature, Kant had artificially separated the contingently given material of experience from the pure concepts of the understanding by interposing between them sensibility's pure intuitions of space and time.[24] This meant 'from the outset he avoided a unified epistemological centre whose all-too-powerful gravitational force might have sucked all experience into itself'.

As Benjamin notes, it was the neo-Kantian school, and Hermann Cohen's philosophy in particular, that both recognized and systematically sought a confrontation with Kant's separation. Astrid Deuber-Mankowsky has pointed out the extent to which Benjamin's terminology of the Kantian 'abyss' and the neo-Kantian 'task', here – as well as in his essay on language where he similarly speaks of 'the great abyss into which . . . all philosophizing . . . threatens to fall' and the 'task' of such philosophizing as 'to survive suspended precisely over this abyss' – are indebted to Cohen's neo-Kantianism.[25] As this brief discussion of Cohen's philosophical engagement with Kant will show, the concept of Origin (*Ursprung*), developed in Benjamin's 'Epistemo-Critical [*Erkenntniskritisch*] Prologue' to his book on German *Trauerspiel*, is also a legacy of this decisive encounter with Cohen.

What Cohen termed his 'epistemo-critical idealism [*Erkenntniskritisch Idealismus*]' was preoccupied with recognizing the proper meaning of Kant's transcendental method by starting out from '*scientific facts* as its objects, not things and not events, *not even those of simple consciousness*'.[26] The epistemological certainty of such facts of science must be dependent on some 'foregoing rational structure', Cohen argues, that should be reclassified as an a priori 'productive synthesis', establishing 'Kant's theory of *a priority* on a new basis', that of a reason that *produces* its experience.[27] It was before the spectre of such a productive reasoning, it should be recalled, that Benjamin believed Kant had shrunk back. For Cohen, in contrast, the a priori does not simply precede objects but constructs them according to a principle of synthesis in which 'the conditions of the *possibility of experience* in general are likewise conditions of the *possibility of the objects of experience*, and that for this reason they have objective value in a synthetic *a priori* judgement'.[28] The a posteriori material content of cognition is 'from the beginning only present in us ourselves – as the entirety of a phenomenon', Cohen argues, and the content is 'inherently united in and with the form' in the 'whole phenomenon', and 'only analysed afterwards out of the effect on our senses'.[29]

Cohen calls this unity an Origin (*Ursrpung*), one that cannot be conceived as some 'first' act, akin to the temporality of the initial suggested in the standard notion of synthesis, because it is immanent in every act and the a priori ground of knowledge itself. As a consequence, the 'logic of origin becomes the logic of pure knowledge': that of an 'originative' production which is both 'the necessary beginning of thought' and 'the moving principle in every development'.[30] What, in the *Logic of Pure Reason*, Cohen describes as *Ursprungdenken* – thinking based on the principle of origin – is a pure, generative activity which has no beginning but is a primal leap, an act of origination.

This pushes consideration of the first *Critique* away from the 'reality' of that which is 'given' to sensibility, towards the 'lawfulness' of that which is 'synthesized' in the relation between sensibility and understanding. 'The synthesis is the common tie',[31] Cohen maintains, 'which guarantees the same *a priority*, in the forms of intuiting and thinking.'[32] Consequently, 'one can start off from the physiology of the senses, or from pure psychology, from metaphysics in its ancient meaning, or from *that* metaphysics which is known as the theoretical science of nature', Cohen points out, but anyone 'who does not feel at home in Kant's Transcendental Aesthetic will lose his bearings at speculative crossroads'.[33] For Cohen, then, a transcendental justification of the possibility of metaphysics itself within Kant's philosophy – as the scientific cognition of lawful facts – points to the implicitly scientific theory of experience underlying Kant's idealism.

As a result, Cohen argues, the Transcendental Aesthetic of Kant's first *Critique* already points towards the importance of the Transcendental Logic in deducing the formal a priori elements of experience, demanding a rethinking of structural separation of the Transcendental Aesthetic from the Logic, and so the intuitions of sensibility from the categories of understanding. Philosophical reflection on experience identifies the purely formal elements of experience, a method explicitly established in the Transcendental Aesthetic, which deduces space and time as the pure intuitions of sensibility. This methodology, Cohen argues, is present but hidden in the Transcendental Logic, which moves from judgement to the categories, and then to the purity of the principles. However, it is only in the Transcendental Logic, with its deduction of ideality of the principles of experience, that the phenomenal-noumenal distinction that characterizes Kant's transcendental idealism becomes properly clarified. The Aesthetic therefore presupposes the Logic for the clarification of the empirical reality and transcendental ideality of the pure intuition – space and time – discovered there.

Cohen's argument that an implicit theory of experience lies at the heart of Kant's transcendental idealism and, moreover, that it is a specifically scientific concept of experience that animates the critical philosophy is significant for Benjamin's project of undoing Kant's artificial separation between the Aesthetic and the Logic. Agreeing with Cohen that Kant's philosophy takes as 'immediate and natural experience' what is already structured and synthesized under the model of unity and continuity offered by scientific 'knowledge', Benjamin concurs that what counts in the general 'concept of experience that Kant relates to knowledge' is a 'concept of scientific experience'.[34] He notes that the 'outlines of a development of the transcendental philosophy of experience into a transcendental or speculative philosophy' can therefore be discerned in the efforts of the neo-Kantian school's 'abolition of the strict distinction between the forms of intuition and the categories'.[35]

Cohen's recognition of an underlying, originative relationship between what Kant had divided into the Transcendental Aesthetic and the Transcendental Logic provides the background for Benjamin's critical engagement with Kant, but Cohen is able to overcome the arbitrariness of Kant's narrowly scientific concept of experience by expanding the Logic, and the scientific model of knowledge it contains, to such an extent that the Aesthetic is enveloped into a purely mathematical-logical medium of knowledge. The result is a fully scientific or logical idealism, which disposes of the materiality given to sensibility to the extent that the a posteriori of experience is transformed into an underlying logical structure original to knowledge. Hence, 'in the neo-Kantian rectification of one of Kant's metaphysicizing thoughts . . . a modification of the concept of experience occurred', which involved 'the extreme extension of the mechanical aspect of the relatively empty Enlightenment concept of experience'.[36] The neo-Kantian school is therefore 'distinguished by the fact that it continued to use the battle plan set out in Kant's thought', and while the 'positivism' of 'the exact sciences' had 'nurtured the growth of critical thinking', it is also responsible for its limitations.[37]

Benjamin does not seek to embrace this concept of knowledge as originative of experience, as Cohen's idealism had done, but rather to reject it as a 'metaphysics that has become rudimentary'.[38] In contrast to Cohen, Benjamin insists there 'is no doubt that Kant does *not* intend to reduce all experience so exclusively to scientific experience, no matter how much it may belong, in some respects, to the training of the historical Kant'.[39] This inherited concept of experience, 'whose best aspect, whose quintessence, was Newtonian physics', had, Benjamin argues, 'a restricting effect on Kantian thought'.[40] Where pre-Kantian philosophers, such as Leibniz, 'sought to establish the closest possible continuity and unity [between experience and knowledge] . . . through a speculative deduction of the world', Kant instead sought to keep them distinct. The 'scientific' conceptions of space and time become valid as the legitimate forms of experiential intuition, while all other forms of intuition become 'illusory' (*scheinbaren*).[41] In this way, Kant mistook his Newtonian 'phenomenal' as the only one, and implicitly excluded all other conceptions of phenomenal experience.

While Cohen subsequently sought to resolve the Aesthetic entirely into the Logic in order to provide a logical foundation for scientific experience, Benjamin refused such a move on the basis that the Logic is constituted in advance according to a merely 'mechanical' exploitation of the Aristotelian categories. In general, this involves the expansion of the limited spatio-temporal forms and essentially causal-mechanistic categories of Kant's philosophy through the integration of, for example, religious, historical, linguistic, psychological, biological and, importantly, aesthetic and artistic experiences. With this the Aristotelian table of categories will be 'completely revised' to permit the 'knowledge of an experience which is multiply gradated and nonmechanical'.[42]

Benjamin's appeal to a 'theory of orders', founded upon 'primal concepts' and comprising 'that which Kant discusses in the transcendental aesthetic, and, furthermore, all the basic concepts not only of mechanics but also of geometry, linguistics, psychology, the descriptive natural sciences, and many others',[43] effectively seeks to 'invert' Cohen's idealist move beyond Kant by placing the 'known experience' appearing within the Logic into a mediated relationship with the Aesthetic, as a deeper and more fundamental level of transcendental experience.

This can be seen in notes associated with Benjamin and Gershom Scholem's 1918 reading group of Cohen's *Kant's Theory of Experience*, where Scholem summarizes the 'main objections' that had been raised 'against the metaphysical exposition of space' in Kant and Cohen's work: that 'Kant mixes up perception and intuition', mixes 'concept and intuition through false terminology' and 'equivocates between "representation" and "thinking"'.[44] Benjamin's transformation of Kantian philosophy can be seen as seeking to distinguish and emphasize those confused elements in the Transcendental Aesthetic's exposition of space and time by separating out 'thinking' from 'representation' through the delineation of 'concept' from 'intuition' and 'intuition' from 'perception'. Benjamin seeks to dissociate language from the epistemological context of knowledge – the logical judgements, concepts and principles of understanding in the consciousness of a knowing subject – and associate it instead with the aesthetic context of perception as a kind of reading. He insists on distinguishing between the knowledge (*Erkenntnis*) and the perception (*Wahrnemung*) – as a sensory representation – of truth. This kind of perception is related to an intuition of the readability of symbols – which cannot themselves be read or written – that acquire a coherence (*Zusammenhang*) in their aesthetic configuration in the absolute surface.[45]

'On Perception' reconfigures the relationship between experience and knowledge in terms of that between a painting and the landscape it depicts. While the painting of the landscape is a construction, arrangement or configuration of the real landscape, because it must always emphasize but omits particular details of the view before it, it is nonetheless impossible to speak of such a landscape independently of the painting and thus its inherent possibility for artistic configuration. Describing what might be termed this potential for portrayal in the landscape as the 'symbol of its artistic context', Benjamin compares this to 'experience' as the 'symbol of this context of knowledge'.[46] The knowability of experience 'therefore belongs in a completely different order of things from knowledge itself', resulting in a necessary distinction between the spheres of experience as it appears for knowledge (known experience) and experience when it is postulated outside the context of knowledge (experience as such). In contrast to what might be termed Cohen's scientific sphere of 'experienced knowledge' within the medium of 'knowledge', Benjamin's reversal of this relationship posits 'known experience' within the broader medium of 'experience' in general, or a transcendental concept of pure experienceability.

Transcriticism and non-synthetic judgement

Benjamin's 'coming philosophy' resists privileging any single discipline of knowledge or necessary methodology of representation, preserving the multiplicity of experiences that implicates truth in the aesthetic problem of perception. Rather than being divided, Benjamin combines Kant's exposition of the pure intuitions of space and time in the Aesthetic and the pure concepts of the understanding in the Logic into a unified a priori of the mechanical spatio-temporality of the Newtonian categories. But unlike Cohen, Benjamin simultaneously posits a host of other spatio-temporal intuitions, allied with an additional set of conceptual categories, which therefore introduces an alternative dissensus into the heart of Kant's epistemology.

Benjamin believes that this more speculative metaphysics would necessitate the abolishment of the sharp distinction between Nature and Freedom – or causal mechanism and moral willing – in Kant's architectonic. Since it is a specific understanding of 'dialectic' which mediates between these two spheres in Kant's critical system, Benjamin's rethinking of the Kantian dialectic suggests that new possibilities of syllogistic logical relations might themselves be opened up, including what, in addition to Kant's delimitation of three basic kinds of logical judgement (categorical, hypothetical and disjunctive), he proposes as a 'certain non-synthesis of two concepts in another', developing upon the speculation, in an earlier fragment, of an 'a-identical' infinity pertaining to a non-reversible relation of potential or virtual metaphysical identity.[47] One important influence for this idea of criticism in Benjamin's thought is the concept of creative indifference, developed in the work of the Expressionist philosopher and writer Salomo Friedlaender as a gap or non-place, but not synthesis, between original polarities. Friedlaender's amalgamation of Kant, Schopenhauer, Bergson and Nietzsche was combined with an artistic interest in and close acquaintance with German Expressionism.

To emphasize this point is to affirm and develop Paul North's tentative, and ultimately disavowed, suggestion that Benjamin's 'strange mode' of criticism is 'closer to "transcritique" perhaps'.[48] The latter is Kojin Karatani's portmanteau to characterize his interpretation of Kantian critique as simultaneously transcendental and transversal: Kant's transcendental inquiry elucidates a structure of which we are unaware not from any 'stable third position' but only from within the dynamic, transpositional movement between alternate positions.[49]

The Copernican turn of Kant's transcendental idealism, Karatani argues, involves not a turn towards subjectivity as such (of the self or of the other) but rather a transcendental deduction produced through the difference between the objectivity of the thing-in-itself (the perspective of that which is other to subjectivity) and the subjective perspective. Methodologically, this involves a movement between epistemological domains, domains that are constituted through the act of temporarily 'bracketing' other domains, and so a dynamic process of bracketing and unbracketing. The partiality and incompleteness of Home's *Elements of Criticism*, where the objective universality sought for criticism is problematized by its basis in the judgement of taste as a particular and subjective pleasure and resolved through the teleological assumption of a 'common sense', becomes for Kant 'a problem of communication . . . among others'. In this way, Karatani argues, Kant encountered 'the very problem of the other' that is generalized across Kant's critical system into that of the 'thing-in-itself'. For 'in seeking universality, Kant had to introduce the other . . . [who] is not one who can be identified with the self in any sense of intersubjective or common sense' but must include the possibility of all 'others living today', 'the future other' and 'the otherness of . . . the dead . . . from whom one can never evoke mutual consent'.[50] Karatani generalizes the problem of communication at the heart of the judgement of taste into the characteristic methodological feature of Kantian critique.[51]

In particular, Kant's analogy of the parallax, the angular displacement produced by the movement or oscillation *between* the subjective and the objective viewpoints, expresses this attempt not to see things only from his own subjective viewpoint, nor to try and see things from the point of view of others, but rather to hold on to both positions at once and grasp the reality exposed *through the difference* between discursive systems and epistemological perspectives. Caygill explains how in Kant's writing the need for a 're-orientation of the scales of judgement' – discussed earlier in relation to the judgement of taste – 'merges into the second analogy of the parallax',[52] a trigonometrical technique used in astronomy that involves the calculation of the distance of a star based on the angular displacement between two different viewpoints (it also forms the normally unnoticed basis of depth perception in human vision, where the slight difference in perspective between two eyes produces our cognition of spatial three-dimensionality).

Kant's analogy proposes moving between two viewpoints: that of his own, subjective judgement and that of another 'strange and external' to it, the objective judgement of the common sense of others. The comparison of these two perspectives upon an object 'may produce a strong parallax', but this allows judgement to judge *itself* and so preserve against optical illusion.[53] The same analogy is used in Kant's discussion of the fourth antimony in the *Critique of Pure Reason*, where he notes how common human reason 'falls repeatedly into the trap of disagreeing with itself when it considers its object from two different standpoints' and illustrates this through the astronomer Jean Jacques d'Ortous de Mairan, who 'took the controversy between two famous astronomers', Newton (represented by Cassini) and Kepler (following Copernicus), concerning the rotation of the moon on its axis, 'arising from a similar difficulty in the choice of a standpoint to be a sufficiently strange *metabasis eis allo genos* [the Aristotelian fallacy of a shift of principles and causes from one field or *genus* of conceptual reasoning to another, namely, transdisciplinarity]'. Newton and Cassini explained the librations of the moon, the appearance of small horizontal and vertical rocking motions of the hemisphere of the moon as observed from Earth, which otherwise does not appear to rotate in its elliptical orbit, as a parallax effect caused by the moon's rotation and orbit *relative* to the movement of an observer on Earth, with its own rotation and orbit.

Caygill compares this to Kant's analogy, in the *Critique of Pure Reason*, by which reason's interest in continuity 'forms the [common] horizon within which the bias [between two conflicting interests, each with their own horizons from their narrower viewpoints] may be exhibited' and which allows reason to be 'led from the higher to the highest genus which is the universal and true horizon, one that is determined by the viewpoint of the highest concept'.[54] What 'is most significant here is the passage *between* the horizons: it is the journey which is essential, not the horizons through which it travels'.[55] In this way, Kant's methodological critique is *transveral* in the sense of its oscillation or movement of parallax produced by antinomy and *transcendental* in the sense of designating a structural depth of which we, without the dynamism involved in parallax, would remain unaware.[56]

As Slavoj Žižek summarizes, 'We should renounce all attempts to reduce one aspect of [an antinomy] . . . to the other (or, even more, to enact a kind of "dialectical synthesis" of the opposites) . . . [but] conceive the point of radical critique not as a determinate position as opposed to another position, but as the irreducible gap between the positions': a 'new dimension', within the structural gap, 'which cannot be reduced to either of the two positive terms between which the gap is gaping'.[57] The topos from which transcritique operates is, consequently, distinct from that of any single domain or position; it is, rather, the interstice or depth between them made possible only through this parallax.[58]

Samuel Weber claims that 'all of Benjamin's writing and thinking can be productively studied in light of the task' to practice a certain kind of non-synthesis of the a-identical, including his mature concept of the dialectical image, which 'heightens precisely what Hegelian dialectics seek to over-come: the "disjunctive relation" of the "synthesis"'.[59] The non-synthesis of concepts suggested here can be seen to inform Benjamin's understanding of the 'Idea – or, to use Goethe's term, ideals' – becoming perceptible through a 'synthesis of extremes': the conceptual act of reconfiguring phenomena such that 'the unique and extreme stands alongside its counterpart' and represents 'the sum total of all possible meaningful juxtapositions of such opposites'.[60] The methodological practice that Benjamin characterizes as the representation of Ideas through the encircling movement of phenomena derives its depth from what, in his discussion of the allegorical imagination of baroque 'modernism', he calls the 'movement between [antinomical] extremes'.

What results from Benjamin's trandisciplinary renewal of the Kantian concept of criticism is an aestheticization of concepts that substitutes for the latter, in accordance with the practice of constellation, the spatialized image. It is important to emphasize, however, that this constellation also involves a dynamic temporalization, one described as being visualized only in 'the *encircling dance* of represented Ideas'.[61] This transformed concept of (trans)criticism contains the seeds from which Benjamin's later concept of the dialectical image, developed in relation to the *Arcades Project* from the late 1920s onwards, grows. Hence, while Rolf Tiedemann has seized upon the notion of standstill in the following passage, it is also important to recognize the very movement of thought that generates the productive tension: 'To thinking belongs the movement as well as the arrest of thoughts. Where thinking comes to a standstill in a constellation saturated with tensions – there the dialectical image appears . . . It is to be found, in a word, where the tension between dialectical opposites is greatest'.[62]

Contingent criticism and teleological judgement

If the space of the dialectic image is interstitial, however, its temporality involves the radical contingency of ephemerality: it is 'an image that emerges suddenly . . . flashing up in the now of its recognizability' and the 'rescue that is carried out by these means . . . can operate solely for the sake of what in the next moment is already irretrievably lost'.[63] As already discussed, in his 'Program for the Coming Philosophy', Benjamin argues that every 'demand for a *return to Kant* rests upon the conviction that this system . . . has, by virtue of its brilliant exploration of the certainty and justification of knowledge, derived and developed a depth that will prove adequate for a new and higher kind of experience yet to come'.[64] The problem, Benjamin argues, is that this only enabled Kant's epistemology to 'give a valid explanation' regarding 'the question of the certainty of knowledge that is lasting' and to do so only for a reality of 'a low, perhaps the lowest, order', without being able to link this to 'the question of the dignity of an experience that is ephemeral [*der Dignität einer Erfahrung die vergänglich war*]'.[65]

Benjamin's sees the task of the coming philosophy to recover a concept of criticism from Kant's philosophy that is capable of justifying not only the validity of timeless knowledge but also the contingency of experience. An adequately higher sphere of experience must phenomenologically incorporate the most diverse kinds of intuitions, including the 'spirituality' of youth, the 'irrationality' of the supposedly primitive and the 'mysticism' of the paranormal into 'a pure and systematic continuum of experience'; most importantly, criticism must also incorporate experience of the most contingent, transitory and ephemeral content of history.[66] At the heart of such a task is the attempt to transform Kant's system in such a way as to relate aesthetic judgement not, as Cohen's idealism had done, to the logical judgement of scientific knowledge, grounded in canonical laws of doctrine (*Doktrin*), but rather to the ethical-historical experience of *Lehre* as an alternative notion of doctrine, understood in terms of artistic and linguistic expression as an ephemeral and contingent medium of theoretical teachings.

Here, once again, Benjamin's philosophizing touches upon Cohen's own attempt to delineate what, in the context of Kant's philosophy of history, he regards as Kant's replacement of eschatology with 'prophetic Messianism'.[67] As with his speculative recasting of Kant's critical metaphysics of nature, Cohen sought to secure a more certain and necessary basis for the metaphysics of history than Kant's merely regulative experience of the historical sign. Kant had argued that when the discipline of history attempts to find a regularity, lawfulness and necessity in human affairs that would ground the possibility of practical ethical experience, it discovers only the senselessness of a farcical comedy. The philosophical historian must, therefore, 'attempt to discover a purpose in nature behind this senseless course of human events', and in line with the Copernican revolution of his critical philosophy Kant therefore proposes the supposition of a transcendental standpoint for history.[68] In 'The Conflict of the Faculties', Kant therefore takes the phenomenon of the French Revolution as an 'historical sign [*Geschichtszeichen*]' that would represent the regulative idea of 'the tendency of the human race viewed in its entirety', which 'points to the existence of such a cause and to its effectiveness . . . undetermined with regard to time, and which would allow progress toward the better to be concluded as an inevitable consequence'.[69]

For Cohen, the contingency of history must be oriented towards the messianic eternity of the future, which – like Noah's covenant with God – secures 'nothing other than the *preservation*, i.e. the future, of the human race' and this can be located in the pure will, which 'wants nothing but the eternal and only it can produce the eternal'.[70] An orientation to the past only connects desire with ephemeral pleasures and so seeks to eternalize merely ephemeral values.[71] The 'point of view from which the world is now seen' in Kant's historical idea of perpetual peace 'no longer lies in the present but in the eternity of the future'.[72] Deuber-Mankowsky has argued that this '"rejection of the transitory" is the secret motive that guides Cohen's determination of the moral ideal', for 'all that is ephemeral, all that is selfish perishes [*Alles Vergängliche, alles Selbstische geht unter*], becomes invalid [*wird hinfallig*], and disappears in the self-consciousness of eternity [*und verschwindet in dem Selbstbewusstsein der Ewigkeit*]'.[73] By withdrawing the moral ideal from the 'inventory of aesthetics', Cohen obtains against the ephemerality of history a counter-concept of eternity.

To understand the significance of this for the messianic reconstructions of Kant's philosophy of history, it is important to recognize what Cohen regarded as the 'abyss of intelligible contingency' over which 'the whole of experience [now] hangs' after Kant. For Cohen, the 'inevitable *task* of reason' – the *telos* bequeathed to a neo-Kantian philosophy that recognizes the logic of pure knowledge as that of originative production – is specifically the 'covering' over of this abyss of intelligible contingency that threatens to engulf experience.[74]

The idea of intelligible contingency, introduced by Kant in the fourth antinomy of the first *Critique* in relation to the idea of an absolutely necessary being, concerns a purely logical rather than aesthetic, that is, spatiotemporal or sensory, kind of contingency. 'Alteration', the temporal change of state of objects of experience, that is, from existing to not existing, 'proves only empirical contingency, i.e. that the new state could not have occurred on its own, without a cause belonging to the previous time, in accordance with the law of causality' and this 'cause, even if it is assumed to be absolutely necessary, must yet be of such a kind as to be encountered in time and belong to the series of appearances'.[75] Intelligible contingency, in contrast, involves objects whose contradictory opposite is possible not at another time but at the same time, that is, that it could also *logically* not exist and so 'cannot produce any synthetic proposition, such as that of causality'.[76]

Kant uses this distinction as part of his refutation of the cosmological proof of God's existence, associated with Leibniz's proof *a contingentia mundi* or argument for the existence of an absolutely necessary being from the contingency of the world itself. In contrast to Spinoza's pantheistic insistence that all things, partaking of a necessary substance, are themselves necessary, Leibniz's cosmological proof emphasized the contingency of this world, as the most perfect of an infinite number of possible worlds: since, Leibniz's various versions of the cosmological proof go, there must be a sufficient reason for the sequence or series of particular contingent things in the world, in other words for why there should be a world at all – something rather than nothing – and why it should be such as it is, this reason must lie outside all such contingency in a necessary substance or God, who freely acts in accordance with the principle of perfection.

Kant, in his pre-critical writings such as his 'Attempt at Some Reflections on Optimism', is largely sympathetic to Leibniz's cosmological argument, agreeing with the claim concerning this as the best of all possible worlds, although disagreeing with Leibniz's belief that the flaws of the world are the result of God's free – albeit morally necessary – choice. Kant insists on the metaphysical necessity of such flaws as part of even the most perfect possible world, which are due 'not to the choice of God's positive approval, but to the inescapable necessity that finite beings will have essential defects'.[77] 'To all creatures, who do not make themselves unworthy of that name, I cry,' he concludes: ' "Happy are we – we exist!" . . . the whole is the best, and everything is good for the sake of the whole.'[78] Although Kant appears to later repudiate this 'Attempt',[79] its deviation from Leibniz prepares the ground for his later critical distinction between an empirical and intelligible concept of necessity and of contingency.

Part of Kant's critical objection to Leibniz's cosmological argument is directed against 'the transcendental principle of inferring from the contingent to a cause, which has significance only in the world of sense', and so applies only to possible objects of experience within the spatio-temporal world of appearances (such as the causal alterability of appearances) but not to any intelligible contingency or necessity outside of time, or vice versa.[80] As Philippe Hunemann points out, these 'metaphysical issues about contingency and necessity' resurface in the discussion of teleology in the third *Critique*, where Kant criticizes the appearance of natural purpose as proof of the intelligent design in the world.[81]

A natural purpose is that which appears to be '*both cause and effect of itself*' because 'the possibility of its parts (as concerns both their existence and their form) must depend on their relation to the whole', and furthermore, 'the parts of the thing [must] combine into the unity of a whole because they are reciprocally cause and effect of their form'.[82] In Kant's example, a tree considered as the cause of its species in reproduction, of itself in growth and of its organs in preservation seems to involve an idea of a final cause, in order to explain the ultimate self-organization of, respectively, the reproductive processes, formless plant material and interdependent organs. This purposiveness concerns the 'lawfulness that [something] contingent [may] have [insofar] as [it] is contingent', a lawfulness that concerns the contingency of the particular left undetermined by logical judgement and so one that cannot be accounted for as necessary a priori because the absence of a cognizable concept indicates it has not been determinately supplied as a pure form of reason.[83]

Kant resolves this problem by introducing a reflective power of judgement, which, when 'only the particular is given' to sensibility with no universal – 'the rule, principle, or law' – provided by the understanding, reflectively seeks out an appropriate one.[84] It is reflective judgement that ascribes a regulative purposiveness to the diversity of the forms of nature by viewing them 'in terms of such as unity as [they would have] if they too had been given by an understanding (even though not our own) so as to assist our cognitive powers'.[85] This resolves the problem of the contingent appearance of natural purpose without undermining the Newtonian necessity of a mechanistic world of forces contained in the critical metaphysics of nature or speculatively utilizing them in teleological variants of the cosmological argument to demonstrate the necessary existence of a rational purpose to the world (preserving the possibility of a critical metaphysics of history). It nonetheless raises the possibility of another kind of intelligence – one that, unlike ours, 'does not (by means of concepts) proceed from the universal to the particular and thus to the individual' but is able to represent the particular parts and their relation to the formal whole from an 'intuition of the whole as a whole' (what Kant calls an 'archetype' or 'synthetical universal') – and so highlights the contingency of human subjectivity itself.[86]

The first *Critique* singles out the cosmological proof as 'the great possible transcendental illusion', 'in which an entire nest of dialectical presumptions is hidden'.[87] It is founded on a speculatively deployed transcendental Ideal of unconditioned necessity – the intelligible necessity of God – that Kant describes as making 'such a dizzying impression on the mind' that 'everything gives way beneath us, and the greatest perfection as well as the smallest, hovers without support before speculative reason': it is 'for human reason the true abyss'.[88] While the transcendental Ideal of unconditioned necessity leads the theoretical use of pure reason into speculative flights of fancy with its cosmological proof of God, it nonetheless possesses a 'practical power (as regulative principles) ground the possibility of the perfection of certain actions'.[89]

In *Kant's Theory of Experience*, Cohen suggests that the critical narrowing of the concept of contingency to that of empirical contingency – temporal alterability – threatens to undermine the distinction between necessity and contingency and so the scientific status of the laws of nature.[90] Cohen reverses the usual approach to this problem by arguing that the 'meaning and value of the Kantian doctrines of space and time' provide 'another way of enquiring into the principle of knowledge' that now begins with the question: 'must and can our thought be confirmed by the laws of nature?'[91] For Cohen, though, the whole of experience – the world itself – still hangs over this 'abyss of intelligible contingency', and he sought to bridge this – the possibility there could be nothing rather than something, the possibility that the laws of the world might also *not* exist – by reconceptualizing the contingency of possible experience as an 'inevitable *task* of reason': 'an *infinite task* of producing possible experience in its totality and this means the totality of possible knowledge'.[92] If 'the abyss of intelligible contingency confronts thought with its inability to found the existence of the universe', writes Deuber-Mankowsky, 'the same limit turns out, in relation to ethics, to be the seam where history arises' in Cohen's neo-Kantian philosophy of history. Cohen's *Ursprungsdeken* is therefore bequeathed the messianic task of rationally producing this ethical-historical experience through the overcoming of the transitory and ephemeral in the eternal.

Benjamin believed that the problems he discerned in the Kantian system could be fully exposed and challenged by investigating, as the topic of his doctoral dissertation, Kant's philosophy of history; Philippe Lacoue-Labarthe has characterized Benjamin's envisaged philosophical transformation of this system as the construction of a 'messianic Kant'.[93] In contrast to Cohen's messianic neo-Kantianism, however, Benjamin's 'deeper motive', Deuber-Mankowsky argues, is 'precisely . . . to *save* the transitory' and so remember and redeem the contingency of the past.[94]

In contrast to Cohen's efforts to replace eschatology with a prophetic messianism based on the infinite and future-oriented task of reason, Benjamin rejects 'a view of history that puts its faith in the infinite extent of time and thus concerns itself only with the speed, or lack of it, with which people and epochs advance along the path of progress'.[95] The higher concept of experience Benjamin sought is therefore one that returned the aporia of natural and historical contingency to the heart of philosophy by connecting the question of the empirical alterability or transitoriness of experience to a criticism of the contingency of the given, exemplified, as we have seen, in the apparent natural purpose associated with the experience of living – but also artistic – things.[96]

Literary transcriticism as modernism

At the time Home and Kant were writing in the second half of the eighteenth century, the conflict between two fundamental principles of taste was beginning to be dramatized in the pages of literary periodicals and journals: the emerging movement of romanticism and classicism, which, in 'extrapolating normative rules from works that had been given the designation "master-pieces" ', posited 'a certain empirical norm in art and literature'.[97] Samuel Taylor Coleridge's *Biographia Literaria*, for example, is specifically targeted at the anonymous criticism of himself, William Wordsworth and Robert Southey practiced in reviews, magazines and news-journals for nearly twenty years.[98] Coleridge argues that the criticism of Romantic poetry requires a romantic taste just as rare as romantic talent, associated with the immanent standard of imaginative genius that he characterizes as 'genial criticism' and a 'genial Judgement' able 'to distinguish accurately the character and characteristics of each poem, praising them according to their force and vivacity in their own kind – & to reserve Reprehension for such as have no character'.[99]

Karatani emphasizes how 'Kant existed in a transitional moment from classicism to romanticism' or, more specifically, 'operated in critical *oscillation between* romanticism and classicism, assuming the same . . . stance that he took, in a different dimension, between empiricists and rationalists'.[100] Moving between the external standards of criticism sought in the objectivity of classicism and the internal standards of subjectivity pursued by romanticism, for Kant, 'beauty comes into existence only by way of the subjective act' of bracketing other concerns, a stance that 'is not classicistic or romantic'.[101] Kant's transversal movement between classicism and romanticism transcendentally deduces 'the modern problematic of art lying beneath both', argues Karatani, and Clement Greenberg is therefore correct in identifying Kant as 'the first modernist critic',[102] since the 'new kind of criticism' that Greenberg associates with modernism – the intensification of the self-critical tendency that uses the 'characteristic methods of a discipline to criticize the discipline itself' – is founded in Kant.[103]

If, as suggested, Kant's epistemological notion of critique is itself precipitated by the eighteenth-century problem of taste – the problem of the conditions of possibility of literary criticism following the journalistic and aesthetic crisis of judgement *between* classicism and romanticism – it is possible to reformulate Karatani and Greenberg's position. If Kant's philosophical concept of criticism develops in response to the – journalistic and aesthetic – crisis of art criticism, in the transition between the classicism of Pope and the romanticism of Coleridge, then the system of transcendental idealism, which moves between the perspectives of empiricism and rationalism in its attempt to address the aporia of judgement, could be said to originate not so much philosophically as aesthetically. Kant's inauguration of modern criticism, rooted in the transversal oscillation between the antinomies of classical and romantic criticism that transcendentally deduces the conditions of possibility of judgement, exposes a new dimension of depth within the structural gap that will come to be defined as modernism and characterized here in terms of a literary transcriticism, constituted not as a *position* but as a movement or oscillation between the poles of romanticism and classicism.

Following Kant, Benjamin's own analysis of and contribution to this transformation proceed by way of a similar and largely unremarked upon movement between the perspectives of romanticism and classicism that constitute the modernist depth of his transformed concept of criticism. Indeed, Benjamin's anticipation of a 'coming philosophy', characterized by Nickolaus Lambrianou as a 'post-metaphysical metaphysics' that rediscovers its relationship to 'pre-modern dimensions of experience', can be seen to mirror modernism's own critical recovery of a future rescued not from out of the present but the otherness of the past.[104] Key to Benjamin's critical project, and an additional characteristic of its modernism, is the attempt to rescue the transitoriness of the past in such a way as to preserve its contingent character: this will provide the theoretical lens through which his engagement with, critique of and movement between romanticism and classicism will be examined in the chapters that follow.

2

Weak messianism in German Romanticism

Benjamin believed that the problems he discerned in the Kantian system, discussed in the preceding chapter, could be fully exposed and challenged by investigating, as the topic of his doctoral dissertation, Kant's philosophy of history.[1] Kant's attempt to avoid the abyss of a speculative metaphysics of nature, into which the a posteriori content of experience might collapse, necessitated the distinction between the Transcendental Aesthetic and Transcendental Logic – between the a priori intuitions of sensibility and the a priori concepts of understanding – from which followed the sharp distinction between Nature and Freedom, and the subsequent 'dialectic' between causal mechanism and moral willing, that both Kant and Cohen had sought to address in differing ways in their critical metaphysics of history.

While Benjamin subsequently felt it necessary to change this dissertation topic to the Early German Romantic philosophy of art, crucial features of the proposed project survive in the final work and astute readers would, he says, still discern in it an 'insight into the relationship of truth to history'.[2] Specifically, the concept of art criticism operating in Romantic aesthetics rests upon epistemological presuppositions that reveal the 'messianic' essence of romanticism.[3] Benjamin's engagement with romanticism in his dissertation therefore constitutes part of a project, in these early writings, to construct what Philippe Lacoue-Labarthe calls a 'messianic Kant'.[4]

Central to this messianic reading of Kant lay a transdisciplinary concept of criticism that connected the aesthetic judgement of the sensibly given not to the canonical laws of scientific Doctrine but to the contingency of *Lehre*, conceived as the ethical-historical medium of theoretical teachings. One resource for doing so was to model the ethical-historical relationship between the contingency of the particular and the Absolute on that between the particular artwork and the

Absolute of art in Early German Romanticism. In this way, a 'romanticized' literary criticism might constitute one moment in the transdisciplinary reworking of Kant's philosophy of history into a messianism capable of rescuing the radical contingency and multiplicity of the historically given by establishing its relationship to the truth of the historical Absolute. As this chapter seeks to emphasize, however, Benjamin's critical engagement with the Romantic position also raises a number of deficiencies, ambiguously characterized in terms of a weak messianism, which necessitate a transversal movement towards romanticism's opposite extreme: the antinomical pole of classicism. Benjamin's concept of criticism therefore develops, it will be demonstrated in subsequent chapters, in the interstitial movement between romanticism and a classicism, a parallax that constitutes the basis of its modernism.

Literary criticism as messianic reflection

As 'soon as the philosophy of history, in Kant … still explicitly and emphatically affirmed both the possibility of thinking an intellectual intuition and its impossibility in the realm of experience', Benjamin argues, 'a manifold and almost feverish endeavor emerged to recover this concept for philosophy'.[5] This is most obvious in the work of Friedrich Hölderlin; Fichte, however, sought to ground the possibility of a certain and immediate type of cognition without recourse to the problematic notion of an intellectual intuition. For Fichte, reflection indicates the free activity of consciousness taking itself as its own object of thought: its capacity for thinking of thinking. In doing so, the initial form of thinking is transformed into its content. In such reflection, thought seems capable of immediately grasping itself as a thinking subject and therefore of possessing a certain kind of immediate and foundational knowledge.

In his doctoral dissertation, Benjamin argues that the philosophical relationship between the Idea of art and particular artworks posited in Early German Romantic literary criticism must be understood in relation to Fichte's theory of reflection. When Benjamin suggests that 'Kant's aesthetics constitute the underlying premise of romantic art criticism',[6] this notion of aesthetics should therefore be understood in its earlier and broader connection with the relation between the sense experience of perception and metaphysical knowledge, taken up in the consideration of the cognition of natural objects in his dissertation on German Romanticism. If the 'theory of natural knowledge is indispensable' both as the basis of and for the exposition of a Romantic concept of criticism, it is here that the problem of experience – specifically Benjamin's attempt to overcome the artificial division interposed between aesthetic sensibility and logical understanding – might be exploited to overcome the critical reservations of Kant's own architectonic.[7]

The central feature of Romantic science is the overcoming of the absolute dualism between subject and object by the insistence on reality as a medium of perception in which the 'subject-object correlation is abrogated'.[8] The immediacy of perception therefore 'proceeds from a medium common to the perceiver and the perceived', Benjamin explains, 'as the history of philosophy shows in the case of Democritus, who describes perception on the basis of a partly material interpenetration of subject and object'.[9] As a consequence of this account, the Romantic conception of criticism is seen to correspond to their scientific understanding of the 'experiment [*Experiment*]' as a 'magical observation' in which 'the experimenter is capable ... of getting nearer to the object and of finally drawing it into himself'.[10]

Benjamin's investigation of the theory of reflection in Romantic practice of art criticism, with its focus on the particular work as a fragment, sought a comparable model for a messianic and redemptive relationship between the contingency of possible historical experience and the idea of the historical Absolute. This conception of a fulfilled infinity constitutes the messianism that Benjamin claims is essential to Early Romantic epistemology, and which he had sought to develop in his programmatic rethinking of Kant's critical metaphysics of nature and history. His reconstruction of the concept of criticism in Early German Romanticism is therefore intended to aid his construction of a messianic Kant, one that – in contrast to Cohen's neo-Kantian reconstruction of Kant's messianism – develops a concept of criticism able to take the contingency of particular experience as its object. The messianic conjunction between the highest metaphysical state of history and the ephemerality of each particular moment is here seen as theoretically determining the Romantic relationship between the artistic Absolute – or what Benjamin defines as the Idea of art – and each particular artwork. In this way, Benjamin's transformation of Kant's transcendental idealism would, via a critical engagement with Romantic messianism, simultaneously permit the sought-for revival of German art criticism.

Benjamin values the Fichtean concept of reflection for providing the epistemological foundation of Friedrich Schlegel's and Novalis's understanding of the metaphysical function of art criticism. Unlike in Fichte, here immediacy and infinitude are not mutually exclusive aspects of cognition. The uniqueness of the Romantic concept of the Absolute resides in the fact that the Romantic conception of infinitude regards it not as empty but as 'substantial and filled'.[11] Benjamin argued that the Romantics specifically identified this structure of the Absolute with the Idea of art, and in particular with artistic form.

For Friedrich Schlegel, in the *Athenaeum* fragments, 'Romantic poetry is a progressive, universal poetry' that 'hover[s] at the midpoint between the portrayed and the portrayer ... on the wings of poetic reflection, and can raise that reflection again and again to a higher power, can multiply it in an endless succession of mirrors'.[12] For this reason, while other 'kinds of poetry are finished and are now capable of being fully analysed', romantic poetry 'is still in the state of becoming; that, in fact, is its real essence: that it should forever be becoming and never be perfected ... It alone is infinite'.[13] Although Schlegel had, in his essay 'On the Study of Greek Poetry', originally made a distinction, in a way similar to Schiller's distinction in 'On Naïve and Sentimental Poetry', between ancient poetry that strove for an ideal and was objective and modern poetry that strove for a subjective originality that was 'individual' or 'mannered', he came to regard the origins of the novel (*Roman*) in medieval literature as a dividing line between what he now more specifically terms the classical and the romantic. For Schlegel, romantic poetry now acquired a positive meaning to describe the modern, and previously derided, features of a non-classical art: '*lack of character* seems to be the only characteristic of modern poetry; *confusion* the common theme ... *lawlessness* the spirit of its history'.[14]

Schlegel's aesthetic theory is in part indebted, Hans Eichner demonstrates, to his successive readings of Kant's *Critique of the Power of Judgement* and its stress on the impossibility of judging beauty according to empirically given, external rules.[15] Art criticism becomes central to this concept of infinite fulfilment because, like the epistemological relation between reflection and thought in Fichte, criticism both consummates the finite and particular work by raising it to a higher level – in which the form of the work is transformed into content as the object of criticism – and simultaneously connects the work's particular artistic form with the continuity and unity of absolute form in the Idea of art.

Whereas the 'ordinary critic' breaks the work down 'into its original constituents, which in respect of the work are dead things, because their elements are no longer of the same nature as the whole', in seeking to 'represent the representation anew, and form once more what has already been formed' a Romantic criticism that has itself becomes poetic 'will add to the work, restore it, shape it afresh';[16] Schlegel's review originally ended with the words 'to be continued', Sofie Kluge notes, as 'an invitation to posterior critics to take up the lead' and continue the critical process of the infinite perfectibility of the work in relation to Schlegel's own criticism.[17] Criticism is, for the Romantics, the continuation and ongoing completion of the particular work through its infinite connection with other art works and works of criticism.

This is elaborated in his essay 'On Goethe's *Meister*', where Schlegel insists that the novel 'is absolutely new and unique' and so 'our feelings … protest against an orthodox academic judgement of this divine organism'.[18] In particular, 'our usual expectations of unity and coherence are disappointed in this novel as often as they are fulfilled'. 'Driven by the punning conviction that the novel, for which German uses the word "Roman", is paradigmatic for a *roman*tic era', Artnd Bohm writes, 'Schlegel sees Wilhelm's essence in "Streben, Wollen und Empfinden" (striving, wanting and sensing) and the world of the novel as a fantastic realm.'[19] The novel therefore seems to possess a 'personality and living individuality … an indwelling genius', which overrides any sense of superfluity and discontinuity'.[20] In accord with his theory of romantic poetry, therefore, Schlegel insists that we must not judge it 'according to an idea of genre drawn from custom and belief' but 'only on its own terms', for Goethe's novel 'carries its own judgement within itself … not only does it judge itself; it also describes itself'.

For German Romanticism, the artwork provides the immanent criterion for critical reflection, which in turn completes the work by raising it into an autonomous and higher existence. In doing so, 'Schlegel seems to have set himself the heroic task of eliminating once and for all unreflexive habitual thinking and common misunderstandings of contemporary literary criticism, proving its lack of theoretical foundation',[21] arguing in particular 'against the classicist idea of timeless artistic rules and norms'.[22] It 'appeared quite plausible' to the Early German Romantics that the overcoming of the philosophical extremes of dogmatism and scepticism could be carried out in aesthetics 'under the same name by which Kant had arbitrated that conflict in epistemology', that is, criticism, and moreover that 'higher criticism' could even prove more important than Kant's own epistemological critique.[23] This Romantic conception of criticism rejects both the dogmatic imposition of external rules, such as those of classical aesthetics, and any dissolution of all aesthetic criteria, which would lead to aesthetic nihilism. It was the Early German Romanticism of Schelling, Novalis and the Schlegels that therefore raised Kant's concept of criticism to a higher power, Benjamin claims, through which it acquires 'an almost magical meaning' for speculative philosophy as an 'objectively productive' thought in which 'the knowledge of truth sprang forth magically, as it were, from insight into the falsehood' of the restrictive conditions of thought.

In the version of the dissertation formally submitted to the university, Benjamin concludes by identifying the Romantic theory of art criticism with 'the consummation of the work', one that constitutes, he thought, one of the fundamental legacies for a modern concept of art criticism.[24] By conceiving the Idea of art as a 'medium of reflection', the early Romantics dissolve the Enlightenment worldview of the positive sciences that Fichte inherited from Kant, and in doing so overcome the critical injunctions placed upon the experience of the infinite.[25] This provides the resources for Benjamin's own attempt to rethink the relation between the Aesthetic and the Logic in Kant's system, in terms of a connection between literary criticism and not scientific doctrine but ethical-historical *Lehre*, conceived in comparable terms as a medium of tradition. It is in this sense that Benjamin defines the 'essence of Romanticism' as 'messianism', exemplified in Friedrich Schlegel's claim that the 'inception of modern history' is found in the 'revolutionary desire to realize the kingdom of God on earth'.[26]

Weak messianism: formalism, affirmationism, singularity

Marcus Paul Bullock has argued that 'the concept of *Reflexion* does not have such a high priority in Schlegel's thinking as Benjamin assumes' and is 'distinctly secondary to *produktive Fantasie* ("productive imagination")', concluding that the religious function of the latter is a major contradiction to the messianic order which Benjamin attempts to ground in the former.[27] 'Indeed it can be shown that there is an immediate contradiction of the Messianic idea necessitated by Schlegel's position here', Bullock continues, because the 'never-ending progressivity of imaginative production precludes any image of redemption in finality or completion'.[28] Similarly, Sofie Kluge has highlighted the ambiguity of Schlegel's position regarding the poetic work's need for 'the *Ergänzung* of the critical interpretation', which indicates 'completion and supplementation, both closure and infinite addition', and how Benjamin resolves the critical *Ergänzung* of the literary text into a completive act, regarding 'Schlegel as a systematic and idealistic thinker, whose concept of criticism is said to be completive and almost apotheosizing' (against 'the poststructuralist and deconstructivist tendency of recent Romantic scholarship, notoriously appalled by idealism and metaphysics', who prefer to emphasize it as 'a supplementary, principally endless rewriting of the text').[29] Winfried Menninghaus has likewise criticized Benjamin's characterization of Fichte and his influence on Early German Romanticism: rather than 'guaranteeing immediate cognition', reflection 'produces a reversal in its relation to what is reflected, an "ordo inversus"; it guarantees precisely that the absolute "can never be obtained from within itself"', but this circumvents the unconscious capacity of the productive imagination that the Romantics valued so highly as a 'hovering between being and not-being'.[30]

The version of Benjamin's dissertation circulated among friends and colleagues, however, does not conclude with a complete affirmation of German Romanticism, but contains a critical afterword that renders explicit critical objections and disagreements, connected to the objections raised earlier, that Benjamin had carefully inserted into the text. Rodolphe Gasché has highlighted 'Benjamin's repeated, if not systematic criticism of Romantic philosophy', demonstrating '[a]t times … little sympathy, or even direct hostility toward the Romantics' insights'.[31] These suggest that the Romantic theory of literature, and by implication the structure of the Absolute it is grounded upon, is problematically one-sided and incomplete with regard to its formalism, affirmationism and singularity. These epistemological problems are implicated, it will be argued, in the problematic nationalism associated with later romanticism.

Formalism

When Benjamin criticizes German Romanticism for inheriting the Fichtean concept of reflection in his essay on 'The Concept of Criticism', he notes how the 'Fichtean "I" signifies for Schlegel and Novalis only an inferior form among an infinite number of forms of the self'.[32] The beginning of the 'I' – the point in which reflection arises from nothing – was for Novalis 'merely ideal … [and] arises later than the "I"; therefore the "I" cannot have begun. We see from this that we are here in the domain of art'.[33] The Romantic conception of the medium through which the object penetrates the observing subject in artistic criticism is that of a Fichtean 'medium that shelters in itself and builds out of itself the context of forms'.[34] This indicates 'a continually more comprehensive unfolding and enhancement of poetic forms' in transcendental poetry, in which the work undergoes 'an infinite process of fulfilment' through progressively intensifying reflection.[35] At the heart of Romantic reflection is a theory of pure form which problematically reasserts the Fichtean idealism of cognition through self-knowledge, in which the content of thought is conceived as the 'form of the form' of thinking. Hence, in Benjamin's reading, at the basis of the Romantic philosophy of science lies the belief that there is 'in fact no knowledge of an object by a subject', only a 'self-knowledge' in which the 'subject-object correlation is abrogated' entirely at the expense of the object.[36]

As Gasché explains, the Romantic infinitizing of the Fichtean form of reflection beyond reflection itself, which culminates for Fichte in the 'I', such that it becomes 'not only the form of intuitive cognizing par excellence but, in its universality, it comprises all other forms of thinking as well', entails that the 'strict form of reflection is … shaken and assaulted by' problems in its ambiguous role as both the object and subject of thinking. As a 'disastrous consequence of directing the illimited, and hence formless form of the strict kind of reflection upon the Absolute itself', the Romantic conception of the Absolute 'becomes characterized by increasing ambiguity', resulting in the 'mysticism' of the Romantic position.[37] What Benjamin characterizes as the 'radical, mystical formalism' of the Romantic theory of cognition therefore effectively ends up jettisoning a theory of experience altogether for an idealism of intuitive knowledge, from which all content has been effaced.[38] Partly as a consequence of this, the Romantics are forced to turn to religion to attain the semblance of content within their work.[39]

While Benjamin protects the correlating Romantic notion of progressive, universal poetry from any 'modernizing misunderstanding', he does so only by invoking what he calls Schlegel's fundamental error.[40] Since 'Schlegel strove for the determinacy, the individuality of the idea', the endlessness of this progression should not be interpreted as indicating 'a mere function of the indeterminate infinite of the task' within the 'empty infinite of time'. The task is a determinate one, Benjamin reminds us: 'the ever more exact and thorough regulating and ordering of that medium [of forms] the continually more comprehensive unfolding and enhancement of poetic forms'. With this, Benjamin joins together his criticism of German Romanticism with the first section of his essay, concerned with Fichtean reflection. For Schlegel's mystical thesis of individuality 'stands in exact correlation with the principle which asserts the indestructibility of works that are purified in irony'.[41] That is, the principle of the indestructibility of works – their progressively higher, reflective unfolding and determining of lawfulness in the continuous medium of forms – is equally mystical.

This leaves the Romantic Absolute, with its emphasis on self-knowledge through reflection, as a medium of progressive ascent through the pure forms of knowledge towards the ultimate Idea. Although Romantic criticism 'in its central intention is not judgement but … the completion, consummation, and systematization of the work', this completion coincides with its 'resolution in the absolute'.[42] Such a vision of consummation means that German Romanticism eschews any judgement of the work according to prior models, instead performing an immanent criticism which takes as the only standard of the work 'the reflection … imprinted in its form'. Since the content of each, successive, level of reflection is supplied by the form of its object, criticism unfolds the germ of immanent criticizability contained in each particular artwork's form, leading to a formalism that precludes any serious discussion of the artwork's specific content. Specifically, Benjamin describes the Romantic concept of prose as the 'creative ground' of poetic forms manifested in the Romantic privileging of the novel as the 'comprehensive manifestation' of the continuum of forms, as prosaic: 'indistinct … equivocal … transparent and colourless'. Indeed, as we shall see in the next chapter, Benjamin seeks to rescue a metaphysical experience of colour, in opposition to the colourlessness of empty Romantic form, precisely as the exemplar of the pure content of aesthetic experience.

Affirmationism

If anything immanently uncriticizable cannot constitute a true work of art, Romantic criticism is unable to differentiate between good or bad artworks, since its only criterion is whether a work *is* or *is not* art. Such criticism is entirely positive or affirmative in its evaluation, lacking the important negative moment essential to judgement. Romantic 'judgement' therefore eliminates any moment of negativity, since the only criterion against which the work may be negatively judged concerns its original status as a work or not. In Romantic criticism's perfecting 'intensification of the self-consciousness of the work, the artwork becomes transported, or converted into Art itself', Gasché concludes,[43] rendering the finite absolute: a translation of the 'necessarily incomplete … in relation to its own absolute idea'.[44]

The Romantic philosophy of art culminates in a concept of criticism that demanded the consummation of the work through its 'distinct unfolding and articulation within the totality of art': the artistic Absolute.[45] If the unity of the particular artwork is only relative to that of the unity of the Idea of art itself, and so 'burdened with a moment of contingency', Romantic criticism must be 'the *regulator* of all subjectivity, contingency, and arbitrariness in the genesis of the work', 'irrevocably and earnestly dissolv[ing] the [work's contingent] form in order to transform the single work into the absolute work of art, to romanticize it'.[46] This 'romanticizing' therefore raises the essence of the work – its form as the 'germ cell of reflection' – nearer to indestructibility.[47] In this way, this 'basic mystical conviction of early Romanticism' in the 'infinite process of fulfilment' (as a qualitative progredibility and not quantitative progress) approaches messianism.[48]

This posits the genuine work as a fragment in relation to the absolute whole, necessarily incomplete but involved in an infinite and continual process of completion. Criticism becomes 'the medium in which the restriction of the individual work refers methodically to the infinitude of art and finally is transformed into that infinitude [*Unendlichkeit*]'.[49] Novalis compares this to certain 'mythical' translations of works which, Benjamin explains, represent 'a medial, continuous transposition of the work from one language into another'.[50] Lacking any dialectical moment of completion or fulfilment, 'romanticizing' – as the immersion of the 'central, that is, universal – moment of the work' in the medium of art becomes, in Novalis's words, an 'absolutizing, universalizing, classification of the individual moment'.[51] The complete positivity in the 'intensification of the consciousness of the work through criticism' excludes from theoretical consideration what Benjamin calls the necessary, negative 'moment of self-annihilation'.[52] As a consequence, Romantic criticism is 'exercised for its own sake': it refuses 'to assess or judge the work' and has 'no pedagogical aim', either in terms of moral instruction or cultivation of the judgement of taste.

The 'complete positivity' of their resulting concept of criticism – criticized by Benjamin for occluding the 'necessary moment of all judgement, the negative' – results in Schlegel's concept of the 'symbolic form' or the 'imprint of the pure poetic absolute in the form itself', the indestructible aspect which endures in this infinite process of completion.[53] In doing so, Gasché argues, 'the important distinction between profane and symbolic, or absolute form, becomes blurred' since the 'latter form is only the reflectively enhanced profane form'.[54] As a result, 'the Absolute – the critical concept *par excellence* – is not only not demarcated from the profane with the necessary rigour, everything profane is drawn into the region of the Absolute, polluting what, in principle, is to be kept pure of all alien ingredients'.[55] It is in this sense that Schlegel speaks of the way in which 'the show of the finite is set in relation to the truth of the eternal and thereby dissolved into it … through symbols, through which meaning takes the place of illusion – meaning, the one real thing in existence'.[56]

Although Benjamin cites the comment that Schlegel's 'new religion' denies 'an ideal of human fulfilment that would be realized in infinity' and demands it instead 'at this very moment … at every point of existence, realized ideal on every level of life', nonetheless the positivity of Romantic judgement as the medium of messianic intensification problematizes the virtuality associated with this conception of history.[57] From the standpoint of the Absolute of Art, Benjamin argues, the elimination of the moment of negativity represented by the Fichtean check (*Anstoß*) means there is no 'not-I': 'no Nature in the sense of a being that does not become itself [*keine Natur im Sinne eines Wesens, das nicht selbst wird*].[58] The Romantic medium of reflection excludes any concept of Nature as a principle of difference, resulting in a pure virtuality of self-identity. This incompleteness of the historical object as a fragment in relation to the singular Idea removes any reference to the actuality of history from the process of completion. 'From the point of view of the philosophy of art', Benjamin says, 'the historical process is *merely* virtual'.[59] In contrast to the absolute negativity of historicism, the affirmationism of Romantic criticism culminates in a virtuality divorced from actual history content.

For Friedrich Schlegel, the work of art 'must be a mobile transitory moment in the living transcendental form' and the act of criticism directed at the overcoming of that contingency.[60] Benjamin calls this 'contingent character of individual works' their 'status as a torso' in relation to the infinitude of the absolute, and remarks that Schlegel's concept of the Absolute as a medium of the lawfulness of forms is directed against this very torso character.[61] Against this, as the next chapter will explain in detail, Benjamin will counterpose a theory of the artwork as a torso: as both contingently incomplete and necessarily finite and so incapable of completion, even through higher criticism.

Singularity

In seeking to overcome the contingency of the singular in the virtual medium of progressive determination towards the Idea, the validity of all intermediary generic or epochal structures are dissolved in the positivity of intensification. Utilizing Schlegel's conception of the essential Idea of art, Benjamin approvingly notes that in an 'effort to secure the concept of the idea of art from those who would see it as an abstraction from empirical artworks', Schlegel seeks to identify this concept with the Platonic Idea as a ground. But Schlegel 'committed the old error of confounding "abstract" and "universal" when he believed he had to make that ground into an individual'.[62] Calling this the '*mystical* thesis that art itself is one work', Benjamin notes how Schlegel 'strains his concepts and grasps at a paradox' when this progressive formalism leads him to effectively deny any intermediary structure between the particular fragment and the individual, unified Idea.[63] He therefore gave a 'false interpretation' of the unity of all works when he conceived this as pertaining to some mystical, singular and transcendental work. 'Made present as an individuality, or a work, the

Absolute is stripped of what makes it absolute … entail[ing] a loss of the force of transcendence and the relativization of difference.'[64]

Because the Romantics could not acknowledge any conception of prototypes as 'autonomous works complete in themselves, definitively fashioned entities exempted from eternal progression', they set about completely dissolving 'the ancient works, as well as the ancient genres, into one another'.[65] As a consequence, they also dissolved the temporality of art into the space of a flattened-out unity and continuity of the medium, which results in the 'the absolute identity of the ancient and modern – in past, present, or future'.[66]

A comparable moment is apparent in Benedetto Croce's 'devotion to the particular', as it is considered in the 'Epistemo-Critical Prologue', where Croce's 'concern that departure from [the particular] might mean the complete loss of the essential' results in the jettisoning of all aesthetic classification in order to preserve the integrity of the essence, turning it into a single and universal absolute. Since the originality and particularity of each artwork resists further classification according to merely abstracted common features, the result is that 'the genre or class is, in this case, a single one: art itself'.[67] Croce's concern with the individual work ends up with a total immersion in the chaotic flux of particulars, doomed to remain merely unconceptualized 'objects of vague wonder' without the possibility of transformation and therefore without history.[68]

With its mistaken emphasis on the singularity of the Idea of art, Romantic fulfilment coincides with the infinity of the unconditioned: 'Ultimately the mystical thesis that art itself is one work … stands in exact correlation with the principle which asserts the indestructibility of works that are purified in irony.'[69] Such criticism cannot be described as judgement, since all authentic judgement involves an essential negative moment of completion in 'self-annihilation'.[70] Consequently, because 'Romantic messianism is not at work in its full force' here, the Romantics were increasingly forced to turn to the 'accoutrements' of ethics, religion and politics to provide the content required to complete their theory of art.[71] This results in the 'Nazarene' characteristic of later romanticism: the Catholic affectations of the movement assembled around Johann Friedrich Overbeck in the first quarter of the nineteenth century and inspired by the style and intention of mediaeval religious painting. As Benjamin notes in a later essay, when the Schlegel brothers 'exchanged the humanistic enthusiasms of their youth' (an enthusiasm that Benjamin identifies with a sober, cosmopolitan classicism) for their later Catholicism, 'the pursuit of false riches began'.[72] They came to view 'everything past as also lost, and everything lost as unreplaced and irreplaceable'.[73]

Aestheticentricism and problems of the Romantic imagination

Karatani traces the modern development of the imagination from the moral sympathy of British empiricism, through the political sentiment of fraternity of the French Revolution, to the privileging of imagination, after Kant, in the philosophical aesthetics of German idealism and romanticism in Germany and England. The 'rise of nation and the discovery of the imagination as a mediating link between sensibility and understanding took place at the same moment', Kartatani argues, since what he characterizes as 'nationalism or romanticism' imaginarily recovers a traditional sense of 'community' based on a sentiment of solidarity – the mutual reciprocity of gift exchange and obligation characteristic of such community – felt to be lacking in the modern organization of society by the power of the state and the freedom of the market.[74]

Kant's concept of criticism emerges, it has been argued, out of aesthetic criticism concerned with the universality of the judgement of taste at a historical moment when the two fundamental principles of classicism and romanticism were coming into confrontation with the rise of public exhibitions and the market for journalistic criticism. For Caygill, the crisis of criticism and the problem of the judgement predominant in the eighteenth century were also related to an associated problem of political judgement with the emergence of modern civil society, the conditions which give rise to public criticism.[75] As discussed in the previous chapter, Home resolved the problem of judgement central to the standards of criticism by relying on a teleological appeal to the providential arrangement of human nature, in which moral and aesthetic judgement are interlinked. Like other British empiricists, Home assigns a central role to sympathy as the foundation of both human understanding and social cohesion, as a passion, aroused by human suffering and gratified by its relief, that 'invites a communication of joys and sorrows' that is 'necessarily productive of mutual good-will'.[76] Such moral sympathy can be aroused by the ideal, as well as real, presence of human suffering, and which therefore pertains not to perception (which involves a conviction of the reality of its object), nor conception (which, as in reflective remembrance, is said to be a passive conception without conviction of reality), but to an active 'sort of creative power ... of fabricating images without any foundation in reality' or (productive) imagination.[77]

Kant's concept of criticism emerges between this tradition of the judgement of taste and the scientific aesthetics of Baumgarten. For Kant, though, 'sensibility and understanding are synthesized through the imagination ... only in imagination'.[78] In contrast, the Romantic re-aestheticizing of Kant's philosophy, in rejecting the split between sensibility and understanding, also lost sight of the imagined status of the community it sought to recover in the empirical sensibility of a shared climate, language, people and literature.[79] The problematic formalism, affirmationism and singularity of the Romantic solution contains the epistemological seeds of this political conception of history.

One of the accoutrements that later romanticism turned to in order to provide content for a weak messianic form, Benjamin suggests, is that of nationalism. Although Johann Gottfried Herder had initiated their interest in folk literature, the Romantics nationalized and historicized folk poetry, eventually limiting it to German traditions and belonging to a lost age that they sought to reconstruct.[80] The Romantic attentiveness to vernacular language led to the idea of the nation as a cultural unit defined 'as groups of people identified by a common, separate language', furnishing 'a new criterion of nationality' which for Schlegel 'becomes the categorical unit for literature'. In Schlegel's Vienna lectures of 1810, for example, this idea of literature as the 'collective imagination and memory of a national community' is tied to a dynamic process of organic growth, already anticipated in Schlegel's definition of Romantic poetry as progressive-universal, through which national literature articulates itself into higher states of historical awareness and powers of cultural self-reflection. These aspects are fused in the Romantic imagination into a historicist conception of nation that helps fan the nationalist movements of the nineteenth century.

As Benjamin notes, the Romantic theory of observation reconstructed in the essay on 'The Concept of Criticism' is identical in its stance to that of the philosophy of history of the School of Law founded by Karl Friedrich von Savigny, which sought to deduce law not from universal abstract principles but from the collective *Volksgeist*. Leerssen concurs when he argues that what 'Schlegel delivers is in fact an application of Savigny's organicism to literature'.[81] In regarding the system of law as 'an historical accumulation rather than as a mere set of rules and guidelines', one that developed 'as the nation developed across the centuries', Savigny rejected the uncritical adoption of the classical rules of Roman law, formulating a link 'between national essentialism, organicism, and historicism' that Benjamin sought to reject. The notion of a *Volksgeist* as, in a national context, the 'transcendental essence which poets and historians tried to extrapolate from the transient incidents of material reality ... originated in the legal arguments of ... especially, Friedrich Carl von Savigny', who 'became the foremost proponent of an organicist notion of law ... that each nation engendered its own proper legal system – as much as it had its own language', which was like language 'the direct expression of a nation's specific mentality'.

It is observation that unites the theoretical and practical stance in the Early Romantic concept of reflection and the Later Romantic concept of love. 'For the Late Romantics, observation was a sun beneath whose rays the object of love opens up to further grow', a power of nonviolent control identical to that of 'the gaze of the father in education', which educates the behavior of the child through attentiveness and educates, more than reflection does, the attentiveness of the father who, 'from the sight of many things, 'learns to see what is appropriate to the child'.[82] Yet the ultimate sterility of this philosophy of history, as manifested in the historicism of Savigny, derives from an 'absolutism of method' that 'insists on the "growth" of history as the sole form of historical movement'.[83] The scope of the observation of the historian, in contrast to that of the father over the child, is 'incalculable' and encompasses not only 'the soil of peaceful growth' but also 'the realm of bloody conflict', a realm with its own categories that can only be grasped by a 'religious and pragmatic' system of pre-modern thought, capable of recognizing the complex ontological layers or strata, in a 'scale that advances from existence to appearance', that 'compose the world and its best features'.[84] These ontological layers are collapsed in the organic view of modern thought, preoccupied with the Romantic affirmation of the singular form, an 'ideal of an unspoiled state of nature and its belief in the "beautiful" development of a nation'.

This can be exemplified in the English Romanticism of S. T. Coleridge, whose 'politics of the imagination' consists, Nigel Leask argues, in the 'attempt to find an alternative source of value to substitute for the discredited hierarchies of the *ancien régime* against the commodification of social relations', that is, between state and capital in the people of a nation.[85] For Kir Kuiken, romantics such as Coleridge engaged in the 'task of inventing a fundamentally modern form of sovereignty ... that would no longer rely on the absolute ground of the divine' through a construction of the imagination.[86] For Kuiken, Coleridge's 'missing' deduction of the imagination as an 'esemplastic' or unifying power in the *Biographia Literaria* is crucial in this respect, since the immanent sovereignty of the subject that Coleridge seeks as the ground of 'the possibility of social cohesion' is therefore premised on the fictionalizable moment which permits it to emerge *in the imagination*.[87] In this sense, Romantic nationalism can be said to involve an inherently literary project: as with the inauguration of modern philosophy, then, so the advent of modern politics – with the appearance of the capitalist nation-state – can be seen as emerging, in the romantic imagination, from the criticism of the judgement of taste.

Karatani expands on this idea in the context of what he terms an aestheticentrism that endorses the imaginative art and culture of the Other while bracketing out the intellectual and ethical concerns of its real, living people.[88] As Karatani makes clear, the problem with aestheticism is not the act of bracketing itself – the shift in perspective is the necessary basis of parallax – but 'never unbracketing' this perspective and so discerning the metaphysical illusion.[89] Significantly, when 'this change of stance' involved in aestheticentrism – praising native cultural products while advocating anti-modernism and anti-industrial capitalism – is 'promoted within a nation, it is called modernization, and once it is applied abroad, it is called colonialism', while it is also 'at the core of fascism: appearing to be anticapitalist, it attempts to aesthetically sublimate the contradictions of the capitalist economy'.[90]

This nationalist or colonialist consequence of aestheticentrism can be compared to what Benjamin later characterizes as the aestheticization of politics, such that his later critique of fascism can be retraced to comparable moments in his criticism of certain aspects of German Romanticism in his earlier writings. The relations of mass production under industrial capitalism, which Marx understood as leading to the dominance of exchange-value over use-value, become expressed, Benjamin argues in 'The Work of Art in the Age of Its Technological Reproducibility', in the transformation of use-value from its ritual function in cult-value to that of an increasingly political function in exhibition-value. The rise of public exhibitions and of journalistic criticism in eighteenth-century Europe, discussed in the previous chapter as the context for the crisis of criticism that gives rise to the problem of the universality of the judgement of taste as the aesthetic basis for modern philosophy and politics, constitutes an early example of such a transformation. In this process, the experience of a work of art undergoes a transformation that Benjamin conceptualizes as a crisis of the 'aura' associated with the aesthetic concepts of creativity and genius, eternal value and mystery. These concepts had, in the movement away from the work's origins in ritual, become privileged as aesthetic principles connected to the authenticity of art, with the latter associated with the effects of the work's unique origin, associated with the imaginative genius of the artist, its singular history, passing down from a here-and-now of its origin to that of its present reception. At the critical moment that the technological forces of industrial production in newspapers, photography and film appear to shift aesthetic experience from these concepts, the commercial interests of the culture industry recuperated them in a commodified form as the fame of the star director, actor or writer and the singular spectacle of the product: the imaginative synthesis of the cult and the exhibition.

The recuperation of the aesthetic function of exhibition as commercial spectacle serves the interests of early-twentieth-century fascism, which is an attempt 'to organize the newly proletarianized masses' of industrial capitalism, 'while leaving intact the property relations which they strive to abolish', for it 'sees its salvation in granting expression to the masses – but on no account granting them [property] rights' and so altering the relations of production.[91] Fascism seeks to imaginarily recover the form of community, grounded in the notion of a linguistic and literary national culture, at the precise moment the movement of industrial capitalist globalization (what Goethe and Marx called a 'world literature') threatened to destroyed the traditional roots of such community.

Benjamin's link between the aura and the Romantic concept of observation hints at a cultural legacy of romanticism – by no means the only possible one – that permitted such an imaginary recovery of the lost past. The romantic valorization of a contentless imaginative creativity, of the expressive power of the individualized genius (whether artist or critic) and of a historicist and organicist notion of development that dissolves pragmatic intermediary categories into the totality of the singular Idea of the Absolute (as proxy for the Judeo-Christian God of monotheism) culminate in an aestheticizing of theological concepts, in which the critic, as the unique and authentic individual capable of giving a higher and living expression to the buried material of the work, stands in an 'auratic' and unifying relation to the fragmented mass of spectators. The 'logical outcome' of such a tension is the 'aestheticizing of political life' that culminates in imperial warfare, as the only possibility of harnessing proletarian 'mass movements on the grandest scale while preserving traditional property relations'.

Benjamin's critical engagement with Goethe will be read in the chapters that follow as part of the necessary movement of doubling back or retracing the oscillation from classicism to romanticism as a way of warding off a certain direction of modern history. 'The theory of art … formulated by Goethe' stands in opposition to that of the early Romantics, Benjamin argues, a 'problem-historical' opposition within aesthetic theory around 1800 that brings to light 'the pure problem of the criticism of art'.[92] This concerns the antinomy between the Romantic 'idea' of art and the Goethean 'ideal as the a priori of a correlative content'.[93] Benjamin defines the Ideal as the 'supreme conceptual unity of content' that is manifested only in a 'limited plurality' and 'harmonic discontinuum of pure contents', into 'which it decomposes'.[94] With this, Goethe 'makes contact' with the classical Greek notion – the polytheistic and essentially pagan notion – of *das Musische*: the 'musical' quality of the 'Muse-like'.

This is not to argue that Goethe's work can be posed in any straightforward sense as a 'classicism', nor a 'classicism' superior to romanticism, since Early German Romanticism provides a philosophically important correction to Kantian criticism, with regard to the contingency of the world, and since Goethe's work is deeply immersed in the same romantic currents; nor is it to reduce Goethe's aesthetics to 'classicism' or to disregard the problematic manner in which classical aesthetics contributed in its own significant way to a conservative and reactionary impulse evidently manifested in the rise of fascism. Rather, Goethe's movement back from *Sturm und Drang* to classicism initiates a turning whose momentum Benjamin utilizes in a transcritical manner to open up a perspective on the pure content of experience, on the necessary (rather than contingent) contingency of the finite, on a polytheistic multiplicity and discontinuity of the realm of truth, and so on the negative moment of judgement within criticism. In what follows, then, the romantic philosophical position with which Benjamin's work is largely identified is temporarily bracketed in order to expose the Goethean element of his thought, and this Goethean element is explored in relation to classicism as a way of understanding his identity as a 'conservative revolutionary' and drawing attention to Benjamin's guerilla raids on the concepts of his political opponents.

3

Strong aesthetics in Goethe's tender empiricism

In 'The Concept of Criticism in German Romanticism', Benjamin seeks to rescue the weak messianic structure of romanticism by supplementing the affirmationism of Romantic criticism with a negative, destructive moment drawn from a number of sources, including a radicalized version of their own concept of irony, Friedrich Hölderlin's principle of artistic sobriety, a concept which had already been invoked in his earlier writings to delineate a different kind of romanticism, and Goethe's contrasting thesis of the essentially uncritizable status of the particular work. What is gestured towards in each of these is a principle of destructibility, the negative movement of annihilation which proceeds not from lawful necessity but from the radical contingency of the particular.

In the formal version of the dissertation submitted, the critique of German Romanticism attempts to develop the metaphysical relation between necessary completion and contingent incompletion – the Absolute and the particular – not by drawing on Goethe directly but, for example, from Friedrich Schlegel's early work, where his Romantic understanding of criticism nonetheless 'still stood close to Goethe's conception'.[1] Schlegel gives Goethe's theory of art a 'pregnant formulation', Benjamin suggests, 'in referring to Greek art as that "whose particular history would be the natural history of art in general"'. Here, then, it is the Romantic appropriation of Goethe which proves a more useful tendency for Benjamin, who quotes Schlegel's insight concerning the 'perfect intuition' of the one 'who dedicates himself to the lawfulness of that primal image' and who gives content to an empty law by imitating 'a highest aesthetic archetype'.[2] Similarly, Benjamin notes that Novalis 'cites approvingly Goethe's opinion "that every substance has its closer rapport with itself, just as iron in magnetism"' and concurs that 'Goethe's work displays a concept of empiricism [*Empirie*] which is very close to the Romantic concept of observation'.[3]

As discussed in the previous chapter, Benjamin associated the Romantic concept of observation as an experimental stance towards the object – exemplified in the Early Romantic concept of reflection and the Late Romantic concept of love – in which the theoretical and practical were united and 'the experimenter is capable ... of getting nearer to the object and of finally drawing it into himself'.[4] This proximity between Romantic and Goethean observation is most apparent in Goethe's description of his scientific approach as a 'tender [delicate/fragile] empiricism [*zarte Empirie*] which becomes intimately identical [*innigst identisch*] with its object and thereby becomes actual theory [*zur eigentlichen Theorie wird*]'.[5] Adopting Johann Heinroth's description of his thought as a thinking objectively, Goethe describes an experience in which thinking 'is not separate from objects; that the elements of the object, the perceptions of the object, flow into my thinking and are fully permeated by it; that my perception itself is a thinking, and my thinking a perception' and how the residual traces of this encounter appear in thought as material after-images (*nachbilder*).[6] Fundamental to Goethe's concept of experience, therefore, is a similar theory of the 'experiment' as a 'mediation [*vermittler*]' in which the absolute division between subject and object is suspended.

Benjamin's claim concerning the similarity between the Romantic and Goethean theory of experiment is qualified, however, by the reservation that 'the ultimate intention of [Goethe's] regard for nature does not at all coincide with the romantic theory in question', and he concludes that he must at this point leave 'undecided' how far the Romantic 'experiment' 'actually accords with Goethe's opinion'.[7] This displays a resistance to the common predilection to uncritically conflate Goethean and Romantic science within the domain of *Naturphilosophie*, a tendency which has been challenged by R. H. Stephenson, who rejects the description of 'Goethe's Romantic approach to science' as 'still persistent "hyperbolic caricatures" of Goethe's position'.[8]

Benjamin takes up this distinction again – this time in the context of art, where the differences between Goethe's classicism and romanticism are more clearly evident – in the supplementary afterword to the dissertation circulated among friends on 'The Early Romantic Theory of Art and Goethe'. Here he is less equivocal, insisting that the important distinction between the Romantic and Goethean theories of criticism is based upon their differing conceptions of the nature of the medium of observation. The distinction drawn between a Romantic and a Goethean nature of the 'experiment' as it mediates between subject and object, and therefore the distinction between the accompanying conceptions of the Absolute, suggests that for Benjamin there is something specific about Goethean empiricism which proves fruitful for his own attempt to think beyond the narrowly scientific limitations of the Kantian theory of experience, and which is, nonetheless, distinguishable from the Romantic model of criticism so important to his philosophy.

This significance is encapsulated in Benjamin's ambiguous evaluation of romanticism in the 'Epistemo-Critical Prologue' to the *Trauerspiel* study, where he comments that the Romantic attempt to renew the Platonic theory of ideas, as a more speculative overcoming of the epistemological limitations of the Kantian concept of criticism, is frustrated by their concept of truth as one of 'reflective consciousness'.[9] To the extent that the concept of experiment in Early German Romanticism involves the dissolution of the absolute difference between subject and object, this takes place within the context of the consciousness of knowledge, specifically as a generalization of the self-knowledge of the pure form of thinking exemplified in Fichte's concept of reflection.

Benjamin does not, therefore, conclude this version of the dissertation with his positive evaluation of Romantic criticism but inserts a negative Goethean counterposition to Romantic criticism into his 'esoteric afterword', one that renders explicit the problems of Romantic criticism implied in the footnotes of the formal submission discussed in the preceding chapter. At this point, Benjamin brackets the Romantic concept of criticism, grounded in a generalization of Fichtean reflection that rehearses a weak messianism, in order to explicate more clearly what Joanna Hodge has described as Goethe's 'strong aesthetics'.[10] Significantly, there is no attempt made to synthesize these two positions: they represent the poles of the antinomy of criticism and the parallax from which the transcendental position of modern criticism becomes perceptible.

Benjamin admits in his footnote that 'no evidence' for the Goethean position he offers 'can be offered within this narrow framework' because 'the relevant passages would require as detailed an interpretation as the propositions of the early Romantics do'.[11] Although he indicates that such an exposition 'will be pursued elsewhere in the widened context it demands', no such direct discussion appears except in scattered references across his subsequent work. Goethe's continued significance for Benjamin's concept of criticism is nonetheless apparent in the oblique reference to the epistemological structure of the Goethean 'Ideal' in the 'Epistemo-Critical Prologue' to the *Origin of the German Trauerspiel*, where Benjamin claims that his concept of *Ursprung* – distinct from that of the neo-Kantianism of Hermann Cohen discussed in the first chapter – may be formulated using 'Goethe's term, ideals'. The accompanying claims that the 'Ideas … are the Faustian "Mothers" [which] remain obscure so long as phenomena do not declare their faith and gather around them' does not entail a vision – not even an intellectual vision – of the object but a 'total immersion and absorption' into truth in which the distinction between subject and object is suspended.[12]

This centrality is reaffirmed in the *Arcades Project*, where in a 'moment of belated revelation'[13] he claims that, 'in studying Simmel's presentation of Goethe's concept of truth, I came to see very clearly that my concept of *Ursprung* in the *Trauerspiel* book is a rigorous and decisive transportation of this basic Goethean concept from the domain of nature to that of history'.[14] This revelation follows his stay in Moscow in the winter of 1926–7, during which Benjamin wrote a biography of Goethe intended for the *Great Soviet Encyclopaedia* alongside an essay on Moscow that took Goethe's empiricism as a model for historical criticism that recognized the radical contingency of the historical situation there. His final theses, 'On the Concept of History', in which the concept of history informing such a practice of criticism is famously expounded, is similarly replete with Goethean allusions.

This chapter therefore seeks to begin an investigation into Benjamin's 'Goethe' by reconstructing this missing Goethean concept of criticism, identified with the idea of observation and presented as an antithesis to that of romanticism, as Benjamin had done within the widened epistemological context of natural philosophy. As a development of the claims made in the earlier discussion of Kant's concept of transcriticism and its relationship to aesthetic and teleological judgement, it will be suggested that the significance of Goethe's concept of criticism involves an emphasis on the experience of the pure contents of nature, associated with the development of an aesthetics of science and tied to archetypes or Ideals of sensibility associated with an exact sensorial phantasy. Accompanying this is an emphasis on multiplicity, rather than singularity, that is tied to the pessimistic rejection of teleological judgements concerning progress. These will provide the context for the subsequent discussion of Goethe's artistic turn from the quasi-romantic striving of his earlier *Sturm und Drang* towards the modern classicism of his later work.

Aesthetics of science: critique of sensibility

While Kant's *Critique of the Power of Judgement* is regarded by Timothy Lenoir as the 'definite analysis' of the 'difficulties and intricate problems' relating to the emergence of the science of biology, Goethe – whose *Metamorphosis of Plants* was published the same year as the third *Critique* – is acknowledged as 'one of the most distinguished co-workers in this enterprise'.[15] Goethe's scientific writings remain unsystematic, however, offering a blend of original empirical research in geology, comparative anatomy, plant morphology, colour and the weather with isolated philosophical reflections influenced by Spinoza and Kant, and filtered through his aesthetic sensibilities as a poet, dramatist and novelist. While his early morphological account of science retains much in common with romanticism in opposing any conception of nature as static and fixed, indeed, with the dynamic view of the world emerging, evident from Hegel to Darwin, the influence of his scientific writings on Schopenhauer and Nietzsche also testifies to a distinctive understanding of such dynamism.

Goethe's lifelong engagement with science should be understood as an intellectual struggle against both theological conceptions of nature as unchanging and hierarchically organized from the outset and the mathematization and quantification of scientific empirical inquiry, which results in an artificial nature. His research into the presence of a metamorphosized intermaxillary bone in the human skull, for example, is directed against the theological insistence on the absolute and fixed distinction between humans and other creatures; the *Metamorphosis of Plants* takes aim at the rigid and essentialist classificatory system of Linnean taxonomy, whose 'conceptual approach [was] more suited to the spirit of the time' which favoured preformation theory as the 'successive development undergone by things dating from the time of Adam'; and the *Theory of Colours* against the 'pathological' artificiality of the Newtonian experiments upon colour which imprisoned phenomena in a 'gloomy empirical-mechanical-dogmatic torture chamber'.[16] His other investigations into the weather and geology are similarly motivated by the desire 'to banish mathematical philosophical theories from those area of physics where they only hinder insight instead of furthering it, and where mathematical treatment has found such a wrong-headed application by the one-sidedness of the development of scientific education'.[17]

For Goethe the dominance of the mathematical approach to empirical science, particularly within biology, depends upon a reification of form which ends up mistaking exactitude for truth.[18] This obsession with quantity and formal exactitude leads the mathematical scientist to attempt to 'include the immeasurable world together with the measurable and calculable world' so that 'everything appears tangible, within reach and mechanical'.[19] For the mathematical approach, then, 'nothing is of value … except form: content is a matter of indifference'. Goethe opposes those concepts which offer a purely formal solution because 'there is always a material quality about such an organic substance'.[20]

Against this, Goethe insists that 'quantity and quality must be looked upon as the two poles of visible being'.[21] The orientation of such a perspective can be seen in Goethe's description of his morphological approach to nature as 'a science new not because of its subject matter … but because of its intention and method, which lend its principles their unique form'. This intention, he adds, is 'to portray rather than explain'.[22] For whenever a 'corpus of knowledge is ready to become a science', Goethe argues, it undergoes a crisis as it is torn between two conflicting 'ways of representing [*Vorstellungsweisen*]'.[23] Those characterized as Universalists seek to 'separate what is particular and give a separate account of it', and are therefore 'convinced and imagine that everything is always and everywhere there, even though in infinitely varied and manifold shape, and is also discoverable'.[24] In contrast, the Singularists 'keep the general in view while wanting to add and integrate what is particular'; they 'concede the main point' to the Universalists, but 'always want to find one exception where type [*Typus*] is not particularly marked'.

This is represented in the natural sciences when biology, specifically 'comparative anatomy' in one of Goethe's earliest example, finds itself split between the distinct disciplines of 'natural history' and 'natural philosophy'. The former remains Universalist in assuming that 'the variety of forms in the organic world is a known phenomenon', and arranges phenomenon 'according to the forms that are observed and the characteristics that are sought out and recognised' and 'eliminating all that is arbitrary insofar as possible'.[25] The fruitfulness of such an approach lies in the value of a fixed standard for comparison between the diverse and complex transformations of phenomena. The 'type' for the Universalist is therefore a universal and fixed form. But this is effective only to the extent that it eliminates the contingent and the arbitrary in its analysis of the structural interrelationships of chemical compounds and physical forces, the 'inner structure' beyond the 'surface appearance of forms'.[26] In contrast, Goethe praises the Singularists for seeking out the contingent, arbitrary and the exceptional, but he criticizes their approach for jettisoning the type altogether, based upon their misunderstanding of its character as a basic form (*Grundgestalt*) and for denying its existence when it is hidden. Osteology, for example, is deprived of a 'promising approach' with its 'indirect denial of the type', which accounted for its previous incapacity to perceive physiological similarities between humans and apes.[27]

Because breaking down its object into constitutive parts is less problematic for what Goethe calls 'unorganized matter' in chemistry than for the organized interrelationships of living organisms, this knowledge of inner structure is even more problematic for biology as the science of life. As Kant's third *Critique* makes clear, attempting to build upwards from the part to the whole fails to capture – indeed, in the process of analytically breaking down into parts, it destroys – the special unity of the living thing. His attempt to develop a morphological appreciation of organic nature is intended to grasp, preserve and represent its dynamism, its particular content and its specific quality. Since what has been formed is instantly transformed, to obtain any 'vital intuition of Nature, we must strive to keep ourselves as flexible and pliable as the example she herself provides'.[28] One fundamental issue at stake in Goethe's philosophy might therefore be characterized, with its attentiveness to the intuitive stance of the subject towards the object, as the development of an appropriate aesthetics of science.

In 'wonder[ing] if another path – a better one – might not open up for me', Goethe sought to ground his new science of morphology in a concept of type that transcends the limitations of the Universalist and Singularist approaches. For while a use of a type is necessary for grasping the 'constructive interrelationship' of parts that so troubled Kant's concept of natural purpose, this concept should not be understood as some fixed and universal form. Goethe's appeal to the type or the archetype (*Urbild*) should therefore be understood in the context of his preference for speaking of formation (*Bildung*) rather than structured form (*Gestalt*), the former describing 'the end product and what is in process of production as well', capturing that which 'has been brought forth and likewise what is in the process of being brought forth' and not 'exclud[ing] what is changeable and assum[ing] that an interrelated whole is identified, defined, and fixed in character'.[29] The introduction of the 'leaf' as a protean organ in *The Metamorphosis of Plants*, for example, is 'only an abstract idea or concept, or something which in actuality is held fast but for an instant', and is meant to express an underlying schema or process of transformation.[30]

The concept of form (*Gestalt*) as something that is 'made fast, is cut off, and is fixed in its character' is associated with the mechanistic categories of the Kantian understanding by Goethe and rejected for omitting 'the element of mutability'.[31] Suggesting that Kant had nonetheless adopted a 'roguishly ironic way of working', Goethe cites as 'particularly significant' the account of the *intellectus archetypus*, the archetypal rather than ectypal intellect, which Kant hypothesizes from the contingency of human understanding in the 'Critique of Teleological Judgement' of the third *Critique*.[32] This hypothetical kind of cognition, which proceeds not from parts to the whole but from an 'intuition of the whole as a whole' and consequently of grasping the particular parts and their relation to the formal whole via the synthetical universal or archetype (*Urbild*), would provide, Goethe suggests, an 'intuitive perception of eternally creative nature' that could underpin his own morphological approach.

In Kant's first *Critique*, focusing on the subsumption of the particular under the concept according to the logical use of judgement, the archetype is comparable to the Ideal as a pure – and therefore only regulative – concept but one determined in its systematic unity as something both concrete and individual.[33] The archetype of the Stoic sage, for example, provides the moral Ideal of an impossibly 'divine human being', combining both happiness and virtue, who 'exists merely in thoughts, but who is fully congruent with the idea of wisdom'. This Ideal or archetype provides a standard for judging our own conduct, even though to 'try to realize the ideal in an example, i.e. in appearance, such as that of the sage in a novel [*Roman*], is not feasible, and even has about it something nonsensical'.[34] Kant uses the Ideal in a similar sense when he defines philosophy, 'the system of all philosophical cognition', as an objective archetype, one that serves for judging any subjective philosophizing 'whose edifice is quite often diverse and changeable'.[35] The Ideals of sensibility, in contrast, as unattainable models for empirical intuition undetermined by any intelligible concept, are 'creatures of the imagination': a monogram, 'wavering sketch' or 'incommunicable silhouette of their products or even of their critical judgements' that painters and physiognomists say they have in their heads.[36] That Kant's analogies for the Ideals of reason and sensibility are drawn from literature and painting might appear odd unless we recall the ground of his concept of criticism in the crisis of aesthetic judgement.

In the *Critique of Practical Reason*, Kant claims that a moral Ideal for practical reason can be felt in experience, if not become an object of appearance, as the *factum* – the fact or deed – of freedom. When he came to deal with artistic and biological kinds of experience in the third *Critique*, however, Kant was required to introduce a reflective role for judgement, capable of finding hypothetical laws for the subsumption of particular sensible intuitions not themselves determined by the understanding by indirectly borrowing principles of pure reason to stand in for concepts within the understanding. In the biological experience of living organization, the receptivity of our merely 'ectypal' or derivative understanding is dependent upon the images supplied by sensibility, meaning our cognition of the organism involves a form derived from the spatially unified image of the whole in relation to the parts. Because this contradicts any mechanical explanation, and because we are not supplied with any other adequate concept of form, we can only judge in accordance with regulative principle of purpose supplied by reason and understood as a formal and final cause.[37] Since this is only an appearance of form for us, however, Kant insists that our need for such a teleological explanation does not logically contradict the simultaneous possibility of a mechanical one: we can negatively posit an intuitive type of understanding as a power of complete spontaneity, which is capable of an intellectual intuition of the thing-in-itself outside of the spatial form supplied of our sensibility, and therefore hypothetically capable of proceeding directly from the intuition of a determinate universal to the particular parts.

When Goethe sought to sketch an image of the primal plant (*Urpflanze*) for Schiller, he understood such an archetypal plant as a concrete convergence of idea and sensible experience. It involves the portrayal of that 'unknown [*unbekanntes*] quality of lawfulness in the object' – that lawful contingency apparent in natural purpose which Kant had sought to explain from a reflectively borrowed concept of subjectivity – 'which corresponds to the unknown quality of lawfulness in the subject'.[38] This objective lawfulness of natural organisms is not, for Goethe, to be conceived teleologically, reflectively borrowing from an Idea of moral freedom to explain the purpose of nature and so associated with an Ideal of the highest good. The freedom of nature so problematic for Kant's account of natural purpose is not simply imposed upon the organism as a consequence of the empirical contingency of its indeterminate particularity but rather understood by Goethe as an objective fact of experience given as the determined content of experience itself.

Goethe therefore speaks of the necessity for a 'Critique of the Senses [*Sinne*]' in the manner of Kant's *Critique of Pure Reason* and describes this as entailing 'a higher empiricism [*höhere Empirie*]', one which relates to nature 'as human reason relates to practical life', that is, through an Ideal (of sensibility).[39] When Goethe delineates what he calls 'pure intuition [*reines Anschauen*]' from 'ordinary intuition [*Gewöhnliches Anschauen*]', the former must be distinguished from Kant's own essentially mathematical-geometrical exposition of the pure intuitions of space and time, associated with the productive imagination, in the Transcendental Aesthetic of the first *Critique*. In contrast to Kant's use of the term, this pure experience is pure *not* of intuition but of concepts. Goethe's higher empiricism, elsewhere characterized by Goethe as a tender or delicate (*zarte*) empiricism, is instead concerned with the kind of 'pure experience [*reinen Erfahrung*]' that would derive from a transcendental deduction of ordinary experience in a critique of pure sensibility.[40]

Goethe's description of his capacity to 'imagine a flower in the centre of my visual sense', whose 'original form never stayed for a moment; it unfolded, and from within it new flowers continuously developed', indicates that such products are not 'natural flowers' but 'phantastic [*phantastiche*]' ones, insisting however that they are 'as regular as rosettes carved by a sculptor'.[41] The use of the term 'phantasy' here likewise indicates an involvement of the imagination, in the sense that Goethe elsewhere speaks of an 'exact sensorial phantasy [*exakte sinnliche Phantasie*]', indispensable to art and serving a fundamental role in his own scientific attempt to render contingent content perceptible through its aesthetic and image-creating function.[42]

For Kant, reflective judgement is at work not only in subsuming intuitions of living organization under borrowed teleological principles of pure practical reason, but also as the experience of beauty in the reflective judgement of taste. However, the feeling of beauty can also be reproduced by the imagination in its expanded role as a productive power capable of finding sensible expression for the Ideas of pure reason. Like judgement, therefore, Kant extends the role of the imagination in the third *Critique* through a relationship with not only the understanding but now also pure reason. The genius is able to imitate the beauty of nature through the unconscious production of artefacts which are animated by what he terms the Aesthetic Idea. Kant elsewhere speaks of how the 'imagination [*Einbildungskraft*], insofar as it produces imaginings involuntarily as well, is called phantasy [*Phantasie*]'.[43] He assigns this role to the phantasizing of the productive imagination, which he distinguishes from merely reproducing in recollection, but which he insists is incapable of creating a 'presentation of sense that was never before given to our power of sense'.[44] In calling the products of such presentations Ideas, Kant also makes it clear that by 'striv[ing] toward something that lies beyond the bounds of experience', they 'hence try to approach an exhibition of rational concepts', that is, concepts of pure reason.[45] Because such 'Ideas' are nonetheless sensibly exhibited, Kant calls them Aesthetic Ideas, defining them as a 'presentation of the imagination which compels much thought, but to which no determinate thought whatsoever, i.e., no [determinate] concept, can be adequate': an unexpoundable 'intuition (of the imagination)' for which the understanding can find no 'adequate concept'.[46]

Despite the symmetry between reflective judgements of art and science, Kant restricts the role of Aesthetic Ideas to the artist, insisting that the genius for exhibiting such Ideas is 'a talent for art, not for science', since science must 'start from distinctly known rules that determine the procedure we must use in it.[47] At the core of this distinction is the claim that Aesthetic Ideas 'cannot be brought about by any compliance with rules, whether of science or mechanical imitation, but can be brought about only by the subject's nature'.[48] Monika Klass suggests that this denial was grounded in Kant's disdain for the proto-romanticism of *Sturm und Drang* and part of his attempt to tame the theory of genius by mediating between these values and those of the Enlightenment.[49]

Goethe disagrees with Kant that scientific procedure is thoroughly determined in advance by distinctly known rules of investigation, and he does so on the basis of a rejection of Kant's claim that genius – and the phantastical presentation of sense animated by the Aesthetic Idea – belongs only to the subjective nature of the artist. According to Kant, the Aesthetic Idea is the product of the imagination when it seeks to 'give sensible expression to rational ideas of invisible beings' but also when it strives to give things 'exemplified in experience [*Erfahrung*] … sensible expression in a way that goes beyond the limits of experience, namely, with a completeness for which no example can be found in nature'.[50] In the former a Rational Idea becomes sensibly animated through its imaginative conjunction with an aesthetic attribute, effectively serving as the symbolic expression of the transcendental and otherwise inexpressible Idea of pure reason. This would seem to be exemplified slightly later on in the poetic lines, 'Thus the sun, his daily course completed, / Spreads one more soft light over the sky; / And the last rays that he sends through the air / Are the last sighs he gives the world for its well-being'.[51] Here the poet is 'animating his rational idea of a cosmopolitan attitude, even at the end of life, by means of an attribute which the imagination … conjoins with that presentations'. In light of Kant's description of supplying an Idea with an analogous sensible intuition through symbolic hypotyposis, this practice might be called 'symbolic', with the Aesthetic Idea a symbol in the sense of an indirect exhibition of a transcendental and otherwise inexpressible Idea of pure reason.[52]

But another kind of expression occurs when the imagination poetically expands that which is exemplified in nature towards a supersensible completeness. In the lines 'The sun flowed forth, as serenity flows from virtue', the experience of sunlight is animated and expanded through the practical rational principle of virtue. These two poetic applications of the Aesthetic Idea and its attributes also seem to mirror structurally the different relations between nature and freedom in the two parts of the *Critique of the Power of Judgement*: the feeling of beauty which accompanies our apprehension of nature is described by Kant as the symbol of the good, just as it is the principle of moral freedom which animates our experience of natural organization to produce a reflective Idea of divine natural purpose. Here, the productive imagination conforms to that creative, restructuring act which moves beyond ordinary (*alltäglich*), empirical nature to produce 'another nature out of the material actually given [*anderen Natur aus dem Stoffe, den ihr die wirkliche gibt*]'.[53] The supersensible element of this Aesthetic Idea is assumed, on the basis of Kant's transcendental idealism, to be a pure, rational form or principle, but might be understood in a more archetypal sense to correspond to a pure intuition of the Ideal of sensibility as a supersensible – or even subsensible – content of experience. Goethe's archetype or primal image (*Urbild*) of the formation (*Bildung*) of nature therefore extends the role of phantasy in the presentations of the pure intuition of Ideals from that of art into science, relocating the domain of aesthetics from the narrower focus on the disinterested pleasure in the beautiful or sublime that it had acquired in the late eighteenth century and back to that of perception in general, and specifically the perception of truth.

Goethe's insistence that 'we must necessarily think of science as art if we are to derive any kind of wholeness from it'[54] played a significant role not only in Benjamin's 'Epistemo-Critical Prologue' but also in Nietzsche's early philosophy, where in his notes for a planned dissertation on 'The Idea of the Organism in Kant' he draws on Goethe's artistic understanding of nature as the radical extension and transformation of the inadequate view of nature found Kant's third *Critique*. 'For Nietzsche', Miller argues, 'Goethe embodied the capacity to see nature simultaneously with the eye of the philosopher and with the eye of the artist … to see nature aesthetically' and this 'subjective aesthetic mandate' to proceed 'technically (from techne, or "art")' provides Nietzsche with one element of the central claim, made slightly later in *The Birth of Tragedy*, that science – understood in this context not simply as natural science but any systematic discipline of knowledge (*Wissenschaft*) – be examined 'from the perspective of art'.[55] *The Birth of Tragedy* in turn criticizes the 'optimistic dialectic' of Socratic science for driving 'music out of tragedy with the scourge of its syllogisms' and questions whether the 'ever-new configurations of genius' might lead to a 'music-practicing [*musiktreibenden*]' or 'artistic [*künstlerischen*] Socrates', to, that is, an artistic science.[56] In places, Nietzsche appears to idealize Goethe as such a genius: 'he was opposed to the sundering of reason, sensuality, feeling and will ... he *created* himself ... Such a spirit, *become free*, appears in the middle of the universe with a cheerful and confident fatalism ... I have christened it with the name of Dionysus'.[57]

Benjamin rehearses Nietzsche's criticism in his discussion of Plato's *Symposium*, where he ridicules the 'unmusical [*unmusisch*]' character of Socrates, while praising Plato for struggling to creatively express 'the young philosophy' through dramatic dialogue.[58] When, in the afterword to 'The Concept of Criticism in German Romanticism', he characterizes the Goethean 'quintessence of pure contents' as the plurality of those 'invisible – but evident – archetypes whose guardians the Greeks knew under the name of the Muses', his description of such archetypes as *das Musische* – the 'museworthy' or the 'artistic' – recalls this Nietzschean refrain.[59] In classical Greek mythology, each of the nine arts was guarded by a separate Muse under the sovereignty of Apollo, with their own pure contents or primal images to which the particular work aspires. To these invisible archetypes, particular works can only bear a 'resemblance' to higher or lesser degree to the extent that they permit what is in principle only intuitable in feeling to become perceptible. This perceptibility of the pure content of intuition, Benjamin concludes, is possible only 'after the fashion of a likeness' and so 'not in the nature of the world', where it is 'present' but 'overshadowed by what appears', but in art. In 'relation to the ideal', therefore 'the single work remains, as it were a torso' that 'can never vitally coalesce into the unity of the ideal itself' through the act of criticism; 'with this way of seeing', Benjamin adds, 'it is manifest that every single work in a certain way exists contingently over against the ideal of art'.

Benjamin makes similar use of Goethe's remarks on seeing science artistically as the epigraph to the 'Epistemo-Critical Prologue' of the *Trauerspiel* study. There, he compares the Goethean Ideal to the 'the Faustian Mothers' in order to insist on the aesthetic problem of the presentation of truth, which must be 'visualized in the encircling dance of represented Ideas [*vergegenwärtigt im Reigen der dargestel en Ideen*]'.[60] The realm of the Mothers, in the second part of *Faust*, exemplifies this Goethean view of the world as a restless – and, as explained in the next section, blind – dynamism: 'formation, transformation [*Gestaltung, Umgestaltung*], / Of eternal sense's eternal play [*Des ewigen Sinnes ewige Unterhaltung*]. / Encircled with images of all creatures [*Umschwebt von Bildern aller Creatur*], / They see you not, schemata are all they see [*Sie sehn dich nicht, denn Schemen sehn sie* nur]'.[61]

Teleological pessimism: ephemerality and multiplicity

Nietzsche's criticism of the 'optimistic dialectic' of Socratic science also relates to a second aspect he drew from Goethe's philosophy, one that is influential on Benjamin's critique of the historicist concept of progress and connects back to a recognition of the blind, purposeless strivings of nature in Arthur Schopenhauer's transformation of Kant's transcendental idealism. In rejecting Kant's explanation for the concept of natural purpose as one reflectively borrowed from our own understanding, entailing an agnosticism towards the possibility of a causal, mechanical explanation, Goethe instead sees the operation of an objectively dynamic force within the ceaseless transformations of nature, associated with what he terms a formative drive (*Bildungstrieb*). Goethe's essay on 'Sloths and Pachyderms', for example, imagines the 'colossal spirit' of a beached whale, whose inner tension concerning its contradictory existence, as it clumsily adapts to its new environment on land, is eventually expressed as a counter-spirit (*Ungeist*) in some of its descendants, who stretch out their limbs, grow claws and move away from the earth as they transform into sloths. This evolutionary development 'is not a product of plan or cosmic design' but nor is it 'a simple product of its environment': it is, rather, a 'spirit of negation' or a 'will-to-overcome' that Goethe imagines as ceaselessly driving the formations and transformation of life, without plan or purpose, into all its contingent and diverse forms.[62] Goethe's schematic outline therefore interposes 'power', 'force' and 'striving' as an interpenetration of matter and form in life.

Kant's *Critique of Pure Reason* is specially directed against the Leibnizian principle of sufficient reason, which states that everything existing, no matter when or where, exists by reason of something else. This principle is utilized, Schopenhauer argues, with the intention of 'theological flirting ... with the cosmological proof' when it is illegitimately applied not to causal changes in time related solely to becoming – what Kant defines as empirical contingency – but, in its disguised form as intelligible contingency, to prove the existence of the Absolute.[63] But Schopenhauer also seeks to correct Kant when he wrongly

> speaks of the thing in itself as the reason of the phenomenon, and also of a ground of the possibility of all phenomena, of an intelligible cause of phenomena, of an unknown ground of the possibility of the sensuous series in general, of a transcendental object as the ground of all phenomena and of the reason why our sensibility should have this rather than all other supreme conditions, and so on in several places.

This contradicts his own argument that 'the contingency of things is itself mere phenomenon, and can lead to no other than the empirical *regressus* which determines phenomena'.[64] This critical correction leads to Schopenhauer's reformulation of the thing-in-itself away from the idea of an intelligible cause of phenomena to that 'what we know directly and intimately and find within ourselves as the will', which is the 'sole truly real, primary, metaphysical thing in a world in which everything else is only phenomenon' and 'actually takes place throughout the whole of Nature, from the animal kingdom downwards', including 'not only the voluntary actions of animals, but the organic mechanism, nay even the shape and quality of their living body, the vegetation of plants and finally, even in inorganic Nature'.[65]

Schopenhauer's critique of the principle of sufficient reason also undermines 'the basis of all science', since this 'very assumption a priori that all things must have their reason … authorizes us everywhere to search for the why' and so binds together what would otherwise be a 'mere aggregate of disconnected' notions of causes, from which effects are deduced, and of conclusions, deemed necessary by reason, into the totality of a system.[66] Although we admire the 'indescribably and infinitely ingenious structure' of a 'highly complicated organism' such as even 'the commonest insect', our accompanying amazement at the 'wild prodigality' of such an organism being exposed 'daily and by thousands to destruction by accident, animal rapacity, and human wantonness' rests on this amphiboly of concepts, for we imagine nature's products to be wasteful only because we compare the work of nature to the intellectual effort of the intellect and the mastering of resistant material involved in the production of works of art.[67] Although the natural world may – like a work of art – be beautiful to look at, it would be terrible to endure: a 'scene of tormented and agonised beings, who only continue to exist by devouring each other, in which, therefore, every ravenous beast is the living grave of thousands of others, and its self-maintenance is a chain of painful deaths; and in which the capacity for feeling pain increases with knowledge, and therefore reaches its highest degree in man'.[68]

The suffering omnipresent in the world poses an insoluble theoretical problem for reason ('why there is not rather nothing than this world?'), since, morally, it ought not to exist:

> A seeing will would rather have soon made the calculation that the business did not cover the cost, for such a mighty effort and struggle with the straining of all the powers, under constant care, anxiety, and want, and with the inevitable destruction of every individual life, finds no compensation in the ephemeral existence itself [*ephemeren ... Daseyn selbst*], which is so obtained, and which passes into nothing in our hands.[69]

It is only the metaphysical foundation of a 'blind will to live, which as thing in itself cannot be made subject to the principle of sufficient reason, which is merely the form of the phenomenon, and through which alone every why is justified' that resolves this moral problem of the existence of the world. The ultimate contingency of existence becomes comprehensible to the intellect as time, Schopenhauer argues, specifically as ephemerality (*Vergänglichkeit*), which is 'the form by means of which that vanity of things appears'.[70]

For Nietzsche, Kant's critique of teleological judgement, which sought to determine the theoretical limits of the concept of purpose in science but its practical necessity as a regulative idea in morality, remained interlinked with the optimism of Enlightenment idealism that Schopenhauer's pessimism had rejected as anthropomorphic vanity. 'Teleology like optimism is an aesthetic product', Nietzsche suggests, interlinking the two as products of Enlightenment thought that not only viewed the organisms and the world itself as akin to a human work of art but, in Kant's critique of teleology, regarded this as a regulative and so fictitious necessity for moral action.[71] Nietzsche argues that by appealing to a supersensible purposiveness as a regulative moral Ideal, Kant succumbed to an anthropocentric view of life: in a notebook from around 1870, he quotes Goethe's comment that 'the human never grasps how anthropomorphic he [*sic*] is.[72] His response is not to necessarily reject this fiction – it is, after all, 'only as an aesthetic phenomenon that existence and the world are eternally justified', he argues in *The Birth of Tragedy* – but to fundamentally revaluate the production of art. If the Goethean view of nature provides 'our most truest experience of art',[73] then it is imperative for Nietzsche not only to look at science from the perspective of art, but just as fundamentally to reconsider art from this perspective of life.

Although Nietzsche concurs with Schopenhauer that 'life, the organism does not prove any higher intelligence: no continuous degree of intelligence at all' but only 'an indifferent will' and 'blindly effectuating forces', he is also critical of Schopenhauer for simply replacing Kant's intelligible thing as the cause of the appearance of phenomena with the singular and irrational metaphysical will, and so for replacing the purposiveness of Enlightenment thought (in the Leibnizian, theoretical, or Kantian, practical, versions of the optimistic belief in the best of all possible worlds) with a pessimistic but unified anti-purposiveness, one that culminates in Schopenhauer's speculation of this world as the worst of all possible worlds.[74] The second part of the notes for Nietzsche's dissertation utilizes Goethe's natural science, and especially his account of metamorphosis, 'to approach and modify Kant's position on teleology and the organisms, specifically Kant's attempt to trace, in Nietzsche's view illegitimately, the source of unity ultimately to the human supersensible self'.[75] 'Goethean metamorphosis, as Nietzsche understands it, improves on the Kantian technic of nature', Miller argues, 'in that it circumvents the issue of source by positing a constant transformation of everything into everything else.'[76]

Emphasizing the utter contingency of the present organization of the world, Nietzsche argues that 'a [*ein* = singular] reason', in the sense of sufficient reason, 'does not reveal itself in the "purposive" organisms', for 'even the highest reason (*Vernunft*) has been only sporadically effective' and the contingent form of the organism has 'evolved as one configuration out of infinite mechanically composed constellations or possibilities of constellations, among which countless others could have been capable of life'.[77] Nietzsche therefore holds open the possibility of multiple lesser 'reasons' underlying the apparent unity of the teleological. In his 1807 essay on metamorphosis in nature, Goethe presents this as a higher maxim of the organism:

No living thing [*Lebendige*] is unitary [*Einzelnes*] in nature; every such thing is a plurality [*Mehrheit*]. Even the organisms which appears to us as an individual [*Individuum*] exists as a collection [*Versammlung*] of independent living entities [*lebendigen selbständigen Wesen*] … These beings are parts originally already connected, parts that find and unite themselves. They split and search again, thus producing an infinite production in all ways and on all sides.[78]

This is also emphasized in Goethe's poem 'Epirrhema': 'Rejoice in true semblance [*Freuet euch des wahren Scheins,*] / In serious play: [*Euch des ernsten Spieles:*] / No living thing is One [*Kein Lebendiges ist ein Eins,*] / But always Many [*Immer ist's ein Vieles*].'[79] The ultimate impossibility of settling on any fixed structured form (*Gestalt*) for conceptualizing such a morphological nature is what, in Goethe's view, ultimately necessitates an aesthetics of science that views life from the perspective of art, and so prefers to speak of the archetypes (*Urbild*) and later *Urphanomen* of natural *Bildung* (formation/ cultivation) to indicate the mutability of production and the constellation of multiple possibilities.[80]

In his notes on Goethe, Nietzsche therefore observes that 'the eternally becoming [*Das ewig Werdende*] is life … our intellect is too obtuse to apprehend the perpetual metamorphosis: that which is cognizable to it, it calls form', although 'each individual has an infinitude of living individuals within itself'. The 'tree is something new at every moment', both temporally, in the sense that 'we are incapable of perceiving the most precise absolute movement' of its constant transformation, but also spatially because, in the Goethean sense, there is no individual but only an assemblage of multiplicities.[81] 'In truth', therefore, 'there can be no form', Nietzsche argues, 'because there is an infinite in every [imaginary] point' which therefore 'describes a line'. To view art from the perspective of life is therefore to recognize the multiplicity of forces at work in the arbitrary form and contingent unity of organized productions, as well as the possibility these might have taken multiple and diverse alternative forms, which indicates nothing about the perfection or completion of that which happens to exist.

Miller argues that the aesthetic theory that underpins Nietzsche's account of the birth of classical tragedy out of the Apollonian and Dionysian becomes explicable only in light of his 'concurrent interest in the critique of teleology and the organism in the philosophy of nature', and what in his planned dissertation on Kant and Goethe, with its 'strange analogy of natural life to tragedy', he describes as the precise question of 'what "life" is, whether it is just a mere principle of order and form (as with tragedy), or whether it is something entirely different'.[82] As already noted, *The Birth of Tragedy*'s call for a 'music-practicing [*musiktreibenden*]' or 'artistic [*künstlerischen*] Socrates' against the optimistic dialectic of science is echoed in Benjamin's characterization of the artistic or 'muse-worthy' character of Goethe's Ideal or archetype. As suggested in the preceding discussion of Nietzsche's 'Goethe', this involves not only an *aesthetics* of science, reflected in the 'Epistemo-Critical Prologue's emphasis on the philosophical problem of the representation of Ideas, but the virtuality of history that captures the contingent multiplicity of past and future possible iterations of the Idea.

A similar image is used in the essay on 'Goethe's *Elective Affinities*' to characterize artworks as figures (*Gestalten*) or constructions (*Gebilde*) in which 'the ideal of philosophy's problems appears': there can be no single philosophical question whose solution would encompasses the systematic unity or totality of philosophy, since any unity in the solution must give rise to a new question and so demand another solution that encompasses it.[83] The 'lawfulness grounded in the essence of the [philosophical] ideal' therefore entails that it can represent itself – as truth – 'solely in a multiplicity', which is possible only through its appearance in 'a manifold of works' of art.[84] Simmel was wrong to extract the erroneous belief that 'beauty is truth become visible' from Goethe's work, however, for it leads to the view that truth is essential and beauty mere semblance.[85] Beauty remains true to its essence only where it is semblance: in art and the appearances of nature. What art makes visible in its totality of multiple expressions, therefore, is not truth but rather truth's secret: the problem of philosophy.

Phenomena, as concrete elements of empirical reality, Benjamin claims in the 'Epistemo-Critical Prologue', lose their false unity when their elements are divided up by concepts (a destructive process of mortification of the world). In the reconfiguration of the concrete elements of empirical reality, sets of concepts enable the representation of the Idea as an actuality. The concept therefore has its roots in the extreme: those elements of the phenomenon which are elicited by the concept are most clearly evident at the extremes; in the representation of the Idea, the unique and the extreme stand alongside the general and the central. Ideas reconfigure such elements like points in constellations, Benjamin suggests, which permits the Idea to be outlined: 'Ideas are to objects as constellations are to stars ... Ideas are timeless constellations, and by virtue of the elements' being seen as points in such constellations, phenomena are subdivided and at the same time redeemed.[86]

In addition, Benjamin suggests that each Idea, as a pure essence, exists in complete isolation and independence from phenomena and from other Ideas, like suns that do not come into contact with each other but stand in a harmonious relationship of discontinuous finitude that constitutes the realm of truth. Because Ideas form an irreducible multiplicity (*bilden eine unreduzierbare Vielheit*), the philosophical description of the world of Ideas must treat every Idea as an original one (*einer ursprünglichen an*), contemplated as a 'counted – but actually named – multiplicity [*Als gezählte – eigentlich aber benannte – Vielheit*]'.[87] This analogy references not only the pre-established harmony between Leibnizian monads but also the harmony or music of the spheres from classical antiquity, which appears in Pythagoras, Plato and Aristotle. The great cosmological allegory at the conclusion of Plato's *Republic*, for example, describes the experience of a soldier killed in battle, who in the afterlife looks down from the heights of the cosmos upon its eight spheres with differently coloured whorls (corresponding to the orbits of the stars, the planets, the sun and the moon), each being rotated at different speeds and accompanied by a Siren who sings a single note, which combine into a harmonic chord.[88] These coloured whorls are held together by a rainbow-like girdle and through them runs the spindle of necessity, turned by the three Fates of the past, present and future.

Comparing these analogies opens up a confusing imagistic tension: Ideas are simultaneously the constellations that are revealed by the configurations of the stars and the isolated suns that possess a harmonic relationship to other suns. Does the sun, our closest star, therefore appear as a point in another constellation? Are Ideas the constellations (in which case, what are concepts in this analogy) or the suns and other stars that make them up (in which case, what are phenomena)? Although Graham Gilloch accuses Benjamin of merely mixing astronomical metaphors,[89] an understanding of Benjamin's practice introduces consideration of his own philosophical style of analogical reasoning and interruption as method, associated in the *Trauerspiel* book with the allegorical worldview of the Baroque (as well as twentieth-century Expressionism), in which anything can signify anything else in a constant and at times vertiginous slippage of signification that draws attention to the expression of convention itself; these images arrest our own logical process of conceptual reasoning, forcing us to attempt to visualize analogies, while often denying our ability to realize this.

A more productive possibility is to consider that the methodological employment of these two analogies can be understood as involving a transcritical shift in perspective, one that partly accounts for the impossibility of finding any solid ground to stand upon. Benjamin therefore switches from the familiar and earthbound view of the night sky, from which the light of our own sun must be absent in order for that of the other stars to appear, to that of a cosmological view of our sun at the centre of only one of innumerable 'world systems'. Ideas are both constellations in relation to phenomena (seen from the perspective in which the light of our sun is obscured and so looking up into the night sky at other galaxies) and suns in relation to other Ideas (seen from the perspective on the other side of the cosmos), because a star cannot be both a sun and a point in a constellation except to two such extreme viewpoints.

This discontinuity and multiplicity of truth – the realm of ideas – resists being possessed as knowledge by scientific consciousness, for which method is a guide to the acquisition of objects based on the intention inherent in the conceptual knowledge of objects as a unity of coherence produced by the intellect. Truth is, rather, the death of intention and the proper approach to Ideas is total immersion and absorption in an experience: achieved by remembering and renewing Adam's primal hearing (*Urvernehmen*) of the harmonic truth of names, the original hearing (*ursprüngliche Vernehmen*) of words, without cognitive meaning, in which Ideas are given. This fact also frustrated the earlier generation of Romantics, Benjamin argues, who replaced the linguistic essence of naming with a continuous infinitude of reflective consciousness.

The chapters that follow will examine how Goethe's concept of nature provided Benjamin with the foundation for reconstructing a Goethean classicism, whose emphasis on the Ideal or archetype, it will be argued, and his principle of the 'uncriticizability' of great works provided the latter with a way of thinking the necessary modification to the Early German Romantic Idea of art. If Weimar Classicism sought to re-establish the ancient culture of Greek antiquity, its origins lie in Goethe's trip to Italy from 1786 to 1788, where his understanding of the metamorphosis of nature was realized. But as David Lowe and Simon Sharp point out, his interest in Italian art during this trip is 'largely focused on the architecture of Palladio', who was not a classical architect but one 'struggling with … the classical orders of architecture – and trying to find an appropriate form for them in his own time' as a comparable 'metamorphosis of architecture'.[90] Nor was Goethe's use of blank verse (unrhymed iambic pentameter) characteristic of Weimar Classicism's attempt to 'approximate the prosody used in ancient Greek theatre' but a 'meta-technique for the dramatic expression that possessed the ability to accommodate the presentation of wide-ranging settings and complex character developments', deployed with 'world-literary and cosmopolitan intent, allowing it to accommodate classical Greek … Middle Eastern … Chinese … British … Italian … Spanish … and German, medieval French … and Swiss … settings'.[91] T. J. Reed has similarly emphasized the extent to which Weimar Classicism 'was never a stable and acknowledged literary mode', clearly distinguished from preceding romantic movements, but 'a process of struggle' arising at the same time as and intimately connected to an emerging generation of romantics.[92] As Theodor W. Adorno points out, drawing on Benjamin's critique of Goethe, the latter's classicism is emphatically distinct from all formalistic classicism, concerned instead with giving artistic form to the historical tension in the ideal of humanity through the experience of its antinomy, a stance that 'gives the text its unfading modern quality' more clearly than that of the Early Romantics.[93]

This explication of the implicit metaphysical structure of Goethe's corresponding Ideal reveals the contrasting features of his structure of the Absolute: as a sphere of pure content, a medium of destructive refraction and a plurality of discontinuous archetypes. Because finite, particular works can never be romanticized into the unity of an individual Absolute, they remain immanently incomplete and yet nonetheless incapable of higher consummation: like a classical torso, dismembered and corpse-like in relation to the whole and yet nonetheless ideal. In this context, the true task of criticism becomes not the consummation of the living work, but that destructive completion of the dying one. To be clear, the aim here is not to suggest that

Benjamin's philosophy is essentially 'Goethean' nor, indeed, that it is more 'Goethean' than it is 'Romantic'; rather, it seeks to reconstruct the 'Goethean' pole as an extreme generating a tension immanent within the romanticism of Benjamin's thought and work. In doing so, it aims to identify this 'Goethean' countermovement as the basis of a modernist – rather than neo-romantic – conception of criticism within Benjamin's thought.

4

Pure content: the ephemerality of colour

Howard Caygill convincingly demonstrates the extent to which Benjamin's early writings should be understood as an attempted recasting of Kant's critical concept of experience into a speculative one by replacing 'Kant's forms of intuition (space and time) with colour as a (transitive and shifting) medium of intuition'.[1] For Kant, 'space ... as condition of outer objects, necessarily belongs to their appearance or intuition' and so concerns 'only the pure form of intuition', an a priori anticipation that includes 'no sensation (nothing empirical) in itself'.[2] Colour, in contrast, is neither a necessary condition for the appearance of objects nor an objective quality of things, or intuited bodies, but a modification of the sense of sight and so 'mere alterations of our subject'. Colours are 'contingently added effects of the particular organization ... grounded on sensation', and so they are objects of empirical consciousness or perception, in which there is both an intuition of appearance and material of sensation.[3] The latter possesses not the extensive magnitude of space and time but an intensive magnitude, one that 'is not a successive synthesis, proceeding from parts to whole representation, but fills an instant' in relation to the degree of its influence on sense. As a result of this, colour is regarded as only an auxiliary of beauty in the *Critique of the Power of Judgement*, part of the sensible charm that enlivens a painting (and which, therefore, we may have a contingent empirical interest in) but not part of its beauty, for which the design (its formal presentation for judgement) is essential.

Like Kant, Benjamin dissociates the perception of colour from both the lawfulness of the categories of the understanding and the forms of space and time; colour for him is not, however, the merely material content of an empirical consciousness, reflecting the subjective modification produced by the effect of an intensive magnitude on the sense of sight. In Benjamin's early writings, the experience of colour is identified with a 'pure seeing', that is, a 'second realm of receptive sensation', possessing no creative capacity (*schöpferisches Vermögen*) and therefore a purely receptive one.

For this reason, colour is generated in what Benjamin describes as 'pure conception [*reinen Empfängnis*]', echoing the Catholic doctrine of the immaculate conception (*unbefleckten Empfängnis*) of Mary, who 'in the first instance of her conception … was preserved free from all stain [*labe*] of original sin'.[4] Benjamin elaborates on this notion in problematically gendered terms, identifying immaculate conception as 'the rapturous idea of purity'[5] for women: it is to become pregnant –etymologically to 'take' or to receive – in a way free from the sin that originates with Adam and Eve's eating from the tree of the knowledge and therefore, as the Catholic doctrine of the Assumption of Mary suggests, free also from death that enters the world through sin.

The notion of a pure conception associated with the experience of colour might therefore be understood as a strange kind of conception: a pregnancy with mental content that is morally innocent, free from the forms of knowledge associated with the necessary conditions of experience and possessed of a temporal infinitude untouched by death. This pure seeing is manifested most clearly in children, whose sense of sight – unlike that of adults, whose senses have become integrated – is disconnected from the spatial forms of 'substance' in the 'plastic' sense of touch and is therefore capable of perceiving a greater range of nuances.[6] The formless, 'diffused, spaceless infinitude [*zerstreute, raumlose Unendlichkeit*]' of an objective 'colour content' (*Farbigen Gehalt*) of objects, in marking and contouring their boundaries, 'constitutes an infinitely nuanced order'.

This order of colour is, however, marked by an extreme fluidity, as colour flits from one form (*Gestalt*) to the next, one in which it appears as the very medium – and not the mere effect – of temporal change. When Benjamin discusses the red produced by blushing, in his notes on 'Painting, or Signs and Marks', he therefore associates it with the temporal and impersonal medium of 'the expressionless signifying appearance of *des Vergehens*', implying the absolute mark of shame concerning a crime or moral sin (*das Vergehen*) while emphasizing its passing away (*vergehen*) in forgiveness[7]: 'it is the red of transience [*Vergängnis*]' that does not 'taint [*befleckt*] the skin, but is poured over … from outside' so they cannot be seen, thereby simultaneously expunging the disgrace.[8] For Benjamin, then, while 'becoming [*Werden*] announces itself in formation [*Gestalung*]', passing-away (*Vergehen*) – the mortuary decay of dissolution – does so in colouration (*Färbung*).[9] Formation –*Gestaltung* or, elsewhere, *Bildung* – and colouration are also the primal phenomena of Goethe's aesthetics of science, as represented in his *Metamorphosis of Plants* (1790) and *Theory of Colours* (1810) respectively.

As Caygill remarks, in such an intuition the infinity Kant restricted to the faculty of reason intrudes as a 'chromatic infinity' into the intuition of pure content distinct from Kant's spatio-temporal intuition.[10] Benjamin regards colouration as a pure content of perception, whose essence is one of transient ephemerality. This contingency of colour – which appears not, empirically, as the effect of change but the very medium of change itself – therefore provides a speculative experience of what Kant defined as an intelligible contingency: the non-spatial, infinite time of ephemerality itself. Benjamin understands the concept of experience contained in Goethe's tender empiricism in this way when he defines its object as 'pure contents ... in principle only intuitable', which announce themselves 'in the feelings as pure', and which are sensed as a 'necessity that the content ... become completely perceptible'.[11] Benjamin's essay on 'Goethe's *Elective Affinities*' develops this notion of pure content, in the context of art, in terms not of any simplistic opposition between content and form but a mutual relationship between material content (*Sachgehalt*) and truth content (*Wahrheitsgehalt*), which necessitates a philosophical intuition (*Anschauung*) of the imprint left by the truth content upon the matter of the material content.[12]

Such pure seeing is not restricted solely to children, however, but extended to the dream-world of adults and to the artistic experience of colour. The latter is exemplified for Benjamin in the colours of the German Renaissance painter Matthias Grünewald. Benjamin focuses on what he characterizes as the phantasy colours of Grünewald, who painted 'the halo of the angel on his altar in the colours of the rainbow, so that the soul as phantasy can stream through its holy shapes'.[13] It is significant that in his description of Grünewald's work from the following year, Benjamin adds that this spiritual effect associated with the chromatic infinity of colours is achieved through the polarity between radiance or light and the nocturnal or darkness: the saints' halos are said to emerge with such grandeur from the 'greenest black' because the 'radiant is true only where it is refracted in the nocturnal; only there is it great, only there is it expressionless'.[14] In his notes on phantasy, Benjamin uses a similar metaphor to describe the colours of phantasy: 'The light of ideas [*Ideen*] struggles with the darkness of the creative ground [*schöpferischen Grundes*] and in this struggle it creates phantasy's resounding play of colours [*erklingend Farbenspiele*]'.[15]

While Caygill emphasizes the significance of this paradigm of 'chromatic differentiation' for the development of Benjamin's speculative concept of experience, it is surprising that his account includes no reference to Goethe's own *Theory of Colours*.[16] For Benjamin's account situates itself within a spiritual and artistic, rather than scientific, tradition centred around the colour theory of Goethe: the model for this harmonically 'resounding play of colours' comes from Goethe's theological description of dawn in Goethe's poem 'Reunion [*Wiederfinden*]' in the Book of Suleika from the *West-Eastern Divan* (1819). The poem describes the moment when the world, which had lain as a possibility in the deepest ground (*tiefsten Grunde*) of God's heart, broke into actuality (*In die Wirklichkeiten brach*) and light parted the darkness. Creation remains 'rigid', 'mute … still and dreary [*öde*]', however – 'Without desire, without sound [*Ohne Sehnsucht, ohne Klang*]' – until God creates the dawn (*Morgenröte*) and from out of the turbid cloudiness (*Trüben*) of the world's atmosphere she draws forth a 'resounding play of colours'. Goethe's poetic description of creation here echoes his explanation for the sequence of colours that emerge at dawn, itself based on his earlier *Theory of Colours* (1810): as the light of the rising sun on the horizon or boundary of the Earth penetrates more of the atmosphere, whose transparent density acts as a turbid medium (*trübes Medium*), this refractive interplay of light and darkness give rise to the colours of dawn.

Esther Leslie has explored the importance of Goethe's theory of colour on Benjamin's thought. 'For over ten years colour – understood as an aspect of fantasy – played on [Benjamin's] mind', Leslie notes, and Benjamin had planned to write books on children's literature and colour and on phantasy for which 'he compiled a bibliography on the theme of colour', including works by Rudolf Steiner on Goethe's colour theory and Kandinsky's *Concerning the Spiritual in Art*.[17] In notes for these projects, Benjamin emphasizes how Goethe's remarks on the way the 'child looks at the soap bubble as a colourful toy, and the older child is fascinated by the brilliant colours which appear when he looks at a piece of cut glass' reveal 'the essence of children's games, games of pure contemplation in fantasy: soap bubbles, the damp colours of magic lanterns, indian ink and decal'.[18] Similarly, when Benjamin speaks of there being 'something spiritual in colour', he identifies this with the 'pure "sensuous-ethical effect"' of childlike experience of 'the blue semblance [*Schein*] … gleam [*Glanz*] … lightbeam [*Strahl*]' that also preoccupied Goethe in his theory of colour.

Caygill's elaboration of Benjamin's transformation of Kantian experience via a speculative account of colour will therefore be developed in the rest of this chapter in accord with Leslie's recognition of the significance of this Goethean philosophical and artistic tradition of colour theory. For Goethe, only a transdisciplinary aesthetics of science, rooted not in the scientific doctrine expounded by Newton but in artistic and spiritual teachings or theory (*Lehre*), could provide a full account of the experience of colour. Benjamin's notion of a pure sensibility or perception possessed by children, artists and dreamers is rooted in an understanding of the polarity of light and darkness that is found in the philosophy of Goethe, Schopenhauer and Nietzsche. The philosophical implications of this theory for Kant's concept of experience will be developed through a consideration of Eric Alliez's Deleuzian interpretation of Goethe's account of colour. Benjamin transposes such an account, it will then be argued, from the realm of nature to that of phantasy, such that the experience of colour is given its truest expression not in the colours of nature but in the modernist paintings of Grünewald, Philipp Otto Runge, Hans von Marées, Wassily Kandinsky and Paul Klee.

Goethe's colour theory: nature

Goethe began by conducting optical experiments in which light was refracted through a small hole into a darkened room, producing the effect of a colour spectrum on the opposing wall, which could be replicated using a refractive prism. The resulting 'round, white figure, transformed and elongated by the prism according to [the colour sequence Red, Yellow, Green, Blue, Violet] … calls to mind [Isaac] Newton's SPECTRUM SOLIS; and for a moment we believe we are witnessing the effects of a ray of light split up through a hole in the shutter'.[19] 'Newton felt himself obliged to conclude, from those phenomena of colour which occur under certain conditions of refraction', Goethe writes, 'that colourless light must be the result of a meeting of many coloured lights; he believed to be able to prove it'.[20] This predominant scientific account of colour, however, attempts to regulate nature by imprisoning the phenomenon of colour in the 'gloomy-empirical-mechanical-dogmatic torture chamber' of the dark room; in doing so it fails to capture the essential experience of colour.[21]

In contrast to Newton's method, Goethe insists that 'direct experience alone should lie at the foundation of all natural science' and that 'a theory has value only when it includes all experiences'.[22] The patient and attentive observer should not 'seek for something behind the phenomena', however, because 'everything in the realm of fact is already theory', so that the 'blue of the sky' already reveals 'the basic law of chromatics'.[23] Spurred on by an artistic experience of colour that differed greatly from Newton's description, what he found in his own further experimentation is that not only do the colours disappear when the aperture is widened, implying to him a necessary concentration of the light within its darkened border, but that a different spectrum of colours is produced when the border between light and darkness is inverted. If we invert Newton's prism experiment, Goethe writes, and 'look at the black band on the white paper … we see that darkness as well as light has been transformed into colour', but if we draw the same hasty supposition as Newton that 'we have also a ray of darkness which, like light, we have to split up into five or seven colours, we can easily see that we are on the way to great confusion'.[24]

In contrast to Newton's theory that white light is a composite of colours, which appear in the splitting apart of this unity and can be recombined once again to reproduce the effect of white light, Goethe offers a polar theory of colour which arises as the product of an interactive tension between light and darkness: the 'black as well as the white object appears entirely coloured through the coloured radiation of the border, and that we need not to look anywhere else for the cause of this phenomenon'.[25] Goethe's extension of this principle of polarity to other phenomena of nature, as an 'eternal formula of life [*die ewige Formel des Lebens*]', in his scientific writings represents a proto-Nietzschean understanding of nature as constituted primarily as the non-dialectical tension of forces.[26]

Goethe's initial experimentation therefore led him to believe that Newton's theory had disregarded the important and productive role of the prism itself as a turbid medium, and that it is not simply refraction that is required to produce colour, but the interaction and overlapping of the polarities of light and darkness which refraction produces. The primal experience of the blue of the sky can be said to express the truth of chromatics because 'the darkness of space creates this effect through the veiling' light of the sun. It is the Earth's atmosphere as 'a vehicle for moisture' which must be 'considered a turbid medium' in this instance, which refracts light through the darkness to produce our experience of the blue-coloured sky.[27] Similarly, a 'turbid glass held before a dark background and illuminated from the front will appear bluish. The less turbid the glass, the bluer it will look; the least turbid glass will seem violet'. This is also why mountains in the middle distance seem a darker blue than those in the far distance. Conversely, the same glass held before something bright will look yellow, just as the colourless light of the sun, 'seen through a medium but very slightly thickened, appears to us yellow'.[28] Here, then, 'yellow is a light which has been dampened by darkness, blue is a darkness weakened by the light'.

If the density of the medium is increased or if the light is refracted across a white–black boundary, such that there is an increased interaction with darkness, the yellow deepens into oranges and reds. Hence, Goethe believed, the 'sun seen through a thick yellow mist appears ruby-red' and that the 'sun is announced by a red light' in 'the red hues of the morning and evening' because it shines 'through a great mass of vapours' as it illuminates the atmosphere from an angle beneath the horizon. Goethe makes it clear that he considers this medium to be matter itself: 'In chromatics I oppose light and darkness to one another', he announces, adding that 'these would never have any connection if matter did not intervene', because 'whether matter is opaque, transparent, or even alive, the quality of light and dark will manifest in it, and colour in all its nuances will be created forthwith'.[29] Colour is not the splitting of the composite unity of white light, as Newton supposed, but a new entity which is produced in the refractive – we might say deforming – interaction of light and darkness in a material medium. Blue and yellow result from the primal interaction of light and darkness in a material medium: these produce green when they overlap or can be deepened into orange and violet when passed through a denser medium, which results in the compound colour of purple-magenta (*purpur*).

Éric Alliez's *The Brain-Eye* represents a profound engagement with Goethe's theory of colours, and its attempt to rehabilitate the latter for modernist aesthetics therefore provides an important starting point for a philosophical reconsideration of Goethe's ideas. In emphasizing, against the Newtonian model, not the refraction of light but chromogenesis as a 'contrasting affinity between light and shade', Alliez argues that Goethe approaches nature in terms of a 'pandynamism' and 'heterogenesis' of relational forces and visible forms.[30] With this Goethe elevates the sensible phenomenon of nature to the form of the Idea, Alliez claims, but seeks its lawfulness not, as Kant's transcendental idealism had done, outside of sensibility (governed by some higher form of ideality), but rather in a 'naturing' multiplicity that is, in Kant's transcendental sense, the condition for any possible creative experience.[31] Goethe's theory of colour constitutes a transcendental empiricism, Alliez suggests, of the kind that Deleuze, through his speculative transformation of Kant, developed.

In *Kant's Critical Philosophy*, Deleuze emphasizes how the judgement of taste demands a communicability that must involve no determinate concept but a felt accord between the imagination itself, in the freedom of reflective judgement, and the understanding itself, in its indeterminacy as a faculty of concepts.[32] The assumption of a common sense between aesthetic presentation and conceptual (logical) representation in the judgement of the beautiful must be accounted for through its own transcendental genesis,[33] Deleuze argues, as Kant had done in his account of the discord between the faculties that gives rise to the judgement of the sublime.[34] As with the earlier discussion of Benjamin's 'coming philosophy', Deleuze takes the correspondence between spatio-temporal-aesthetic and conceptual-logical determinations, which Kant had 'the most serious reasons' to separate and distinguish in order that there 'be something … irreducible to the order of the concept', to be the central problematic of post-Kantian philosophy. Although, in this context, he elsewhere briefly refers to the neo-Kantianism of Hermann Cohen as one way of overcoming the problem by taking the given as the product of an originative synthesis, Deleuze's own attempts take Nietzsche's genealogical philosophizing of forces in tension as one belonging 'to the history of Kantianism' to the extent it enables us to conceive of such encounters as 'truly genetic and productive' of subjectivity itself.[35]

Deleuze provides such a genesis by connecting the pleasure in the beautiful with the rational interest in nature's aptitude in organizing its content – colours and sounds – into forms whose symbolism overwhelms the understanding. The 'first sketch' of such an account can be found in the first *Critique*, where Kant examines the rational interest in the content – colours, sounds and 'fluid substances (the oldest state of matter)' – used by nature to produce objects capable of being reflected formally, which 'do not relate simply to the determinate concepts of the understanding' but 'overwhelm' it in the 'indirect presentation [of the Ideas of reason] ... called symbolism'.[36] As previously discussed, the *Critique of the Power of Judgement* relates such symbolism to genius, as the comparable faculty of Aesthetic Ideas, which produce an 'intuition of ... another [imaginative] nature whose phenomena would be true *spiritual events*'.[37] Deleuze's example in *Difference and Repetition* concerns the symbolic colour of the lily: 'Thus the white lily is not merely related to the [understanding's] concepts of colour and of flower, but also awakens the Idea of pure innocence, whose object is merely a (reflexive) analogue of the white in the lily flower.'[38] With this a 'material meta-aesthetic ... of contents, colours and sounds' is added to Kant's critical philosophy, an account of the astonishing experience of symbolism that bears witness to what Deleuze describes as a 'complex equilibrium' within the philosopher's aesthetics between 'mature classicism and nascent romanticism'.[39]

For Alliez, then, 'colour does not belong to the physical order of causes, but to the virtual iridescence of effects ... an event, an emergent property, the effect of an encounter', and Goethe's 'discovery of colour' enables us to 'constitute the profile and the animated depth of the visible' that thus 'blossom' as 'events ... in the eye'.[40] Deleuze identifies such 'spiritual events' in the symbolism of colour with the pure appearance characteristic of the distinctive ontology and temporality of 'pure events'. Stoic philosophy had distinguished between 'green' as the quality or predicate of a corporeal object in the present and the incorporeal event of 'greening' at an ideational 'surface which reddens and becomes green'.[41] The former is equated by Deleuze with a conceptual representation of colour but the latter with the aesthetic presentation of 'a paradoxical non-identity': 'To be green' is 'the analytic predicate of a constituted subject, the tree', whereas 'to green' 'indicates a singularity-event in the vicinity of which the tree is constituted'.[42] In the focus on colouration of the latter, there is, in other words, no ontological or temporal priority assigned to the form of the tree as logical subject *over* colour as a quality of appearance: 'To be green' involves the temporality of corporeal causality, composed of interlocking presents; 'to green' an incorporeal causality where the 'the present is nothing' because it is 'constantly decomposed into elongated pasts and futures'.[43]

This 'art of the surface' is comparable to the sense of humour, Deleuze suggests, where the nonsense produced through the shattering of phonetic elements is co-extensive with a 'pure sense', in which there is no longer anything specific to signify.[44] Slavoj Žižek attributes this experience of the incorporeal decomposition of events not to an individual as a distinct and substantial entity characterized by a 'wealth of positive features and properties' but a subject 'divided precisely in the Deleuzian sense of "dividual"'.[45] These 'true transcendental events ... presid[ing] over the genesis of individuals and persons' can consequently be linked back to the missing account of 'genetic productivity' Deleuze had sought for Kant's philosophy.[46] This apprehension of that 'in the sensible ... which can only be sensed'[47] – the 'phantom at the limit of a lengthened or unfolded experience' that Husserl had designated as a dimension of 'expression'[48] – is 'precisely the object of a superior empiricism [*empirisme supérieur*]'[49]: a transcendental empiricism of pure experience, of the kind that Goethe had sought in his own critique of sensibility, which regards the objective event of colouration as constituting a possible chromogenesis for what, in the 'Critique of Teleological Judgement', Kant had highlighted as the contingency of our subjectivity.

Goethe's philosophy emphasizes the 'far from *classical* significance' of colour, Alliez argues, in a way that nonetheless does not 'lead to the speculative "delirium" of an absolute subjectivism', nor the pathos of the 'romantic exaltation of the most profound internal depths'.[50] Nonetheless, the study of the ancients entailed, for Goethe, an objective tendency – to turn towards the real world and seek to express it – that therefore sets 'the Goethean cursor sliding in singular fashion in between classicism and romanticism'.[51] The result – a 'morphologically superior romanticism', a profoundly modified and disquietingly strange 'classicism' – reconfigures both the problems of modern philosophy, with its 'common philosophical notions of subject and object', and the conventional history of modern painting, which privileges a phenomenology of Impressionism that culminates in the exhaustion of abstraction.[52]

Benjamin's colour theory: phantasy

In his notes on phantasy, Benjamin claims that the 'unifying element' of dawn in Goethe's poetic description, as a turbid medium of interplay between lightness and darkness, is a suitable figure for the interplay 'between rise and fall' – the ephemeral temporality of coming into being and passing away in death, or vice versa in rebirth – that gives rise to a phantastical play of colours (*phantastischen Spiel der Farbe*), suspended between conception and cessation.[53] Goethe's scientific account of colour, dubious in his own day and influential a century later only in the mystical formulations of Rudolf Steiner, is therefore taken up by Benjamin in the transposed field of the 'spiritual' colours of phantasy, associated primarily with the sensibility of children, and, as we shall see, the phantasy colours of certain media of art. Benjamin connects the temporal experience of colour's play of appearance – in children's phantasizing, in adult's dreaming and in artistic creation – with a spiritual, religious dimension of the absolute, in line with his own attempt to transform Kant's system by connecting the intuitions of sensibility in the Aesthetic not with the scientific doctrine of the Logic but with *Lehre* as an ethical-historical medium.

In Benjamin's Socratic dialogue on colour, the character Margarethe elaborates phantasy as a 'second realm of receptive sensation to which no creative capacity corresponds [*zweite Reich der aufnehmenden Sinne steigen, denen kein schöpferisches Vermögen Entspricht*]' and in which colour allows the faculty of sense in pure reception to encounter what, in the preceding discussion of Deleuze's Goethean (transcendental) empiricism, was characterized as the incorporeal events of nature. For Benjamin, colour 'is the pure expression of phantasy [*der reine Ausdruck der Phantasie ist*]' because 'colour cannot appear in forms ... This is related to the formless appearance of phantasy'.[54] Phantasy is also the soul of the dreamworld, since the dream is pure reception of manifestation in the pure sense (*reines Aufnehmen der Erscheinung im reinen Sinn*). The creativity earlier associated with the childlike phantasy of colour is now said to have 'nothing to do with forms [*Gestaltung*] or formations' but 'manifestations [*Erscheingung*]' as 'de-formations [Entstaltung] of what has been formed'.

In contrast to the pure – empirically contentless – forms of reason, whose forms Benjamin associates with the canonical order or doctrine of law, the beauty of colour pertains to the formlessness of phantasy itself, which does not impose form in accordance with the 'canon' of pure reason outside itself but is a medium governed by its own law of deformation, in which colour, as pure content – as quality without substance – appears. Benjamin speaks elsewhere of the rainbow – the biblical sign of the new covenant between God and his creatures – as 'the purest manifestation of this colour that spiritualizes and animates nature throughout', one whose 'sacred realm' is transposed by religion 'into the clouds and its blessed realm into paradise'.[55]

As Sigrid Weigel comments, Benjamin here regards the rainbow – described as the *Urbild* or primal image of art – as 'the effect of a history in which heaven – formerly the seat of the Gods – is transformed into a formation of clouds', in which 'the afterglow of a perception, which was previously at home in religion, is active'.[56] This free play of phantasy induces, on the one hand, a feeling of delight which follows from the Paradisiacal purity of its birth, and, because its productivity 'creates no new nature' – and in this sense, it must be distinguished from Kant's productive imagination – it reveals, on the other hand, 'the world caught up in the process of unending dissolution', one that 'never leads to death, but immortalizes the doom it brings about in an unending series of transitions'.

Here, childlike phantasy is permitted to roam free, Benjamin suggests, unconstrained by the adult concern with memory and so without yearning grounded in regret. In a fragment on the colours of pure phantasy, Benjamin plots a version of the colour wheel resembling those of Goethe, Schopenhauer and Rung, including the opposition between light and shade (the term 'shade' appears at the bottom of the diagram, but there is no corresponding entry for 'light' at the top) and a horizontal opposition between blue and yellow – the basic effects of light's interaction with darkness in Goethe's theory – and associates these with the blue of Paradise (presumably in the monotheistic tradition of Judeo-Christianity) and the yellow of Elysium (corresponding to the polytheistic tradition of classical paganism); green appears as the mixture of blue and yellow produced when coloured edges overlap in a light spectrum, while opposed to this is red (Goethe's *purpur* or pure red perhaps), as what Goethe called 'the exaltation of Yellow and Blue, the synthesis, the vanishing of the bright light into the shadows' that appears when coloured edges overlap in a dark spectrum.

In his notes concerning the relation between phantasy and colour, the manufactured colours of works of visual art are differentiated from the pure colour of phantasy in that, while related to phantasy, the creation of visual art involves a spatial formation in accordance with the canon of forms related to the forms of nature.[57] Painted colours are categorized by Benjamin as 'marks' appearing on the spatial surface of the canvas, which are also said to achieve a synthesis of the imagination with the morally tinged yearning of humanity for Paradise, and so – unlike dreamlike experience of the pure colours of phantasy – also implicated in the temporal dimensions of the past (memory) and the future (anticipation). Here, the ephemerality of the experience of colour is spatialized (in-formed) and re-temporalized in the specific sense that it is invested with the subjective experience of time, such that the ephemeral is related to a past that remains (in memory) and a future that is anticipated (in yearning).

The structural movement from the physiological colours that appear in the eye to the physical and the chemical colours of nature and art in Goethe's treatise on colour similarly represent the different modes in which colour appears, ranging from the most 'fleeting' to the 'somewhat more enduring' and finally the 'permanent hues'.[58] Art involves both an 'awareness of and genius [*Genie*] for forgetting the de-formations of the future': the effect of all genuine art is, therefore, a yearning to be without yearning (to forget our memory of the future). Every painting, for example, is both receptive phantasy (*Phantasie*) and formative copy (*Abbild*).[59]

Such concentration of form might perhaps be associated more with the spatially unifying activities of the imagination (*Einbildung*) than the deforming dispersion and fluid ephemerality of phantasy (*Phantasie*) itself: fresco and panel painting, and later painting on canvas, are said by Benjamin to rely on the vertical projecting space of the wall and so appeal 'to the viewer's powers of imagination [*Einbildungskraft*]'. Indeed, in Kant's aesthetics it is the failure of the power of the imagination (*Einbildungskraft*) to apprehend the heights of such vertically orientated space that constitutes one important moment of the sublime; the experience of the infinite in the pure colours of phantasy must accordingly be distinguished from such a moment.

Expressionist colour (I): Grünewald and Marées

There are, nonetheless, instances of painting given in Benjamin's work that exemplify the possible manifestation of the colours of phantasy and therefore the representation of the contingency of pure content. Earlier artists that typify such use of colour for Benjamin – this discussion will focus on the paintings of Matthias Grünewald from the late sixteenth century and Hans von Marées from the late nineteenth century – are singled out, it will be argued, because of a relationship to the contemporary movement of German Expressionism and in particular Benjamin's interest in the paintings of Kandinsky, Klee and Macke. Expressionists artists and critics, such as Ernst Ludwig Kirchner, Otto Muller and Franz Marc and Paul Fechter, considered the spirit of Marées's work to be a significant forerunner of their own break from naturalism.[60]

Benjamin also considered the 'remarkable analogies' with the German baroque as the reason for a re-evaluation of its 'compelling force' that 'began with the emergence of expressionism'.[61] Although Grünewald's work predates the baroque, his contemporary Albrecht Dürer – on whose altarpieces Grünewald worked and to whom many of Grünewald's paintings were at one point attributed – plays a central figurative role in Benjamin's discussion of this period, his *Melencholia* anticipating the antinomic relationship between Christian faith and pagan fatalism that gives rise to the play of mourning.[62] Both periods are marked by an analogous 'state of disruption' in their 'spiritual constitution' and the presence of an 'unremitting artistic will', in which artists 'were attempting … to gain a mastery of that innermost formative power' characteristic of 'all periods of so-called decadence', and as a result of which 'a formed expression of real content can scarcely be extracted from the conflict of the forces which have been unleashed'. Here, it is in relation to the artistic content of a historical period rather than to the organic forms of nature that the productive genesis of forces in tension attempts articulation.

Benjamin's describes being 'seized' by Grünewald's *Christ on the Cross* during a visit to Basel in 1913, where he also experienced the 'greatest and most perfect impression' of Dürer's 'immensely deep' and 'highly expressive' *Melencolia I*. Later the same year, he made a special trip to Colmar to see Grünewald's Isenheim Altarpiece, of which a reproduction hung in his study, and was reportedly overwhelmed by the force of its expressionless (*Ausdruckslose*) quality.[63] As already noted, Benjamin considered the radiant to be most expressionless when it is refracted in the nocturnal, for here the expressionless signifying appearance of ephemerality manifests itself in the deformations of colour.

Benjamin's encounter with Grünewald's paintings echoes that of the French novelist and art critic Joris-Karl Huysmans, as fictionalized in the experiences of the artist Durtat in the novels *La-Bas* (1891) and *Trois Primitifs* (1904). Like Benjamin, Huysmans's Durtat emphasizes 'the unequalled chromaticism'[64] of Grünewald's paintings: the 'divine light' that plays about the ulcerated head of the crucified Christ in his Tauberbischofsheim Altarpiece; the 'Milky pus, which yet was somewhat reddish, something like the colour of grey Moselle'; 'the gripping toes, with the horny blue nail'; the 'ochre ground, ferruginous like the purple soil of Thuringia'; the cross against 'a dark blue night-sky'; the Virgin, 'wearing a hood the colour of mucous blood over a robe of wan blue'; and Saint John, 'his robe of a scarlet stuff cut … His mantle was a chamois yellow; the lining, caught up at the sleeves, showed a feverish yellow as of unripe lemons … his red and smoky eyes'.[65]

Similarly, *Trois Primitifs* concentrates on the 'most exalted mysticism' in the dramatic contrasts of light and dark, the dissonant 'simulacra of colour' and the raccourci distortions of Grünewald's Isenheim Altarpiece at Colmar.[66] Here, the yellowing flesh of Christ's dying body, pocked by grey-blue welts and stained on the forehead, ribs and feet with bright red blood, descends into the greenish-blue tones of his putrefying foot. These colours stand out against the inky blackness of the night sky, similarly punctuated by the bright red clothing of the mourners, with the last bluey-yellow light of the sun appearing as a strip of decaying colour against the horizon.

In the panel depicting the Incarnation, an orchestra is flanked by cherubic angels (and possibly one devil, feathered in greys, greens and blacks) whose remarkable faces glow with phosphorous – almost hallucinogenic – halos of yellowy-greens, yellowy-blues and orangey-reds, through which are scattered bubble-like patterns of light, resembling the latter photographic and cinematic effect of lens flares. Mary Rasmussen has suggested that the symbolism of objects (the tub and the chamber pot associated with water), activities (music) and colours (red-orange with a bluish fringe that echoes that of the sun risen behind Christ in the Resurrection panel) associated with this orchestra are intended to represent Venus, the morning star, and to convey 'the dawn of the new day emerging from the darkness of the old'.[67] The resurrected Christ also glows against the dark night sky, a radiant nimbus of yellow light deepening to orange, red and then rimmed by blue. When the inner wings of the piece are opened to reveal the statues inside, they show a scene of the temptation of St. Anthony by fantastical and grotesque demons. Here, then, the contrast of literal and metaphorical light and darkness gives rise to the most fantastical diversity of colours and creatures, both angels and demons, recalling the corporeal torture and mental anguish of earthly life and death, and its transcendence.

As previously noted, Benjamin plotted the temporality of the colours of pure phantasy as the appearance of the interaction of light and darkness made possibly by a deforming medium, whose play at dawn and dusk corresponds to the spiritual modes of becoming and passing away of the monotheistic traditions. Benjamin also identified the Elysium of classical paganism as a third mode of pure appearance identified with 'the reduced, extinguished, or muted' world of 'the grey Elysium we see in pictures' by the German painter Hans von Marées (1837–87). In his notes on children's books, Benjamin describes how the artist's vision is blocked by a grey 'wall of cloud on the horizon', in contrast to children for whom the 'wall opens up' to reveal 'brightly coloured walls' beyond. This cloud in which the artist rests is 'the grey Elysium of phantasy [*Phantasie*]'.[68] Elysium in the Greek classical tradition is a positive conception of afterlife, in contrast to Hades, identified by Hesiod with the Isles of the Blessed untouched by sorrow, by Homer with the Elsyian plain where life is easiest and by Virgil with a blissful meadow where happy souls rest in shady groves.

As with Grünewald, Benjamin emphasizes Marées as a unique or exceptional painter whose work resists the conventional categories of art history, combining a 'romanticism of subject matter based largely on the classical tradition of the academy and rapidly becoming fused with … realism' that heralded what the art historian Max Schmid would call a 'new period of fantastic art (*Phantasiekunst*)'.[69] André Domnrowski speaks of the 'untimely classicism' of Marées's Arcadian landscapes, especially his frescoes for the library of the Naples Aquarium (1873), in *The Judgment of Paris* (1880–1), *The Hesperides* (1884–7), *Courtship* (1885–7) and *The Three Horsemen* (1885–7), as a classicism that 'could only come along, after modernity has done its work' and one 'able to accommodate a more modern understanding of the nature of reality as contingent'.[70] Such classicism is primarily associated with Marées's movement, after his arrival in Italy in 1864 as part of what Pevsner called 'the Goethe tradition of Italian nostalgia', and his direct encounter with the work of the Italian Renaissance, from the 'bourgeois naturalism' of contemporary German painting towards a 'monumentality and nobility', resulting in techniques that are said to resemble early impressionism that sought not to capture 'a fleeting, momentary impression' but 'to arrive at order, form and style', in part through their striking use of colour.[71]

Fritz Novotny similarly describes Marées's work as 'a modern version of Winckelmann's "noble simplicity and tranquil grandeur"', characterizing it as 'a kind of Classicism [in which] a completely new role is assigned to colour'.[72] Marées's 'complicated tempera technique' permits 'a chromatic richness' in which 'colour is so powerfully used in the all-important endeavour to construct basic stereometric forms that it plays at least as great a part as the proportion and outlines, and indeed tends to obscure the latter'.[73] As a result of overpainting his 'canvases with layers of lacquer consisting of a mixture of tempera and oil', Marées's works appear 'pale and muddy … when viewed from some distance' but possess an 'interesting quality of iridescence on careful observation', an effect Julius Meier-Graefe found reminiscent of Japanese lacquer.[74] Dombroswki attributes this technique to Marées's 'never-ending reworking process', describing his paintings not as 'incomplete or unfinished, but *over*-finished'.[75]

This process may have been influenced by Marées's friend and patron Konrad Fiedler, who saw in the painter's work the expression of his own neo-Kantian aesthetics. In *On Judging Works of Visual Art* (1876), *Modern Naturalism and Artistic Truth* (1881) and *The Origin of Artistic Activity* (1887), Fiedler developed the principle that art, modelled on 'nature, life and reality – as emblems of the world's contingency', should replicate the processes of 'becoming' that *is* nature rather than the 'being' that *is like* nature. Art should be 'an eternal doing and undoing' or a 'play (*Spiel*) in constant transformation' with its 'own contingent reality', not the imitation of nature's outward appearances or visible forms.[76] This should be distinguished from the 'idealism of the Romantic school', which Fiedler rejected for 'having reduced beauty to a simple appearance, a transitory content to be dismissed in order to reach a higher truth'.[77] The artist's shaping visibility (*Sichtbarkeitsgestalung*) involves not only a 'pure seeing (*reines Sehen*)' or 'intuitive perception' connected to the reception of the sense but also an 'intuitive expression' connected to the 'expressive movement [*Ausdrucksbewegung*]' of the hand, capable of giving 'pure expression of an object's visibility [*Sichtbarkeit*]'.[78]

Benjamin connects Fiedler's aesthetic theory with the creative gestures that liberate the 'hazardous magical world of sheer phantasy', glimpsed only by the 'unusually perceptive', by applying them to materials: 'Fiedler is the first to have shown ... that the painter is not a man who sees more naturalistically, more poetically, or more ecstatically than other people' but the one 'who sees more accurately with his hand when his eyes fail him, who is able to transfer the receptive innervation of the eye muscles into the creative innervation of the hand'.[79] Fiedler claims that 'the artist develops his visual conception' to the point of 'visually comprehending appearances as such' and identifies this with Goethe's conception of the exact sensorial phantasy (*exakte sinnliche Phantasie*), 'a phantasy that is exact, without which art is essentially inconceivable'.[80]

Because, Fiedler argues, 'the territory of visible reality will always possess a residue of artistically unshaped reality', the 'labour (*Arbeit*) of art, will forever remain incomplete': 'From the very moment of their completion, step by step they [works of art] go forth to meet destruction.'[81] Marées's over-completion draws out a different aspect of this incompletion, however, emphasizing the origin of the work as a *fatal* – both mortal and opportune – moment: 'Always, at the right moment', he said, 'someone should take my pictures away from me.' The 'classical landscape' and 'classical body' are therefore captured by

Marées, Domnrowski suggests, in 'a state of development … revealing their incomplete construction' but also how the 'contamination of the temporal … in the classical inaugurates its annihilation'.[82] The 'alienating forces of modern experience have, in Marées's work, truly entered Arcadia and transformed it',[83] resulting in a modern classicism that captures this fraught contingency of a moment caught between construction and destruction. This can be seen in Marées's work as the moment his classical settings of Arcadia or the Garden of the Hesperides darken into Benjamin's 'grey Elysium', most notably in Marées's triptych *The Hesperides*, where the golden fruit guarded by the nymphs is enclosed within the dark foliage of the artist's overworked tempera, like orbs of glowing fire overwhelmed by the shadow, just as the visage of one of the men gathering the fruit recedes into the gloom itself.

Expressionist colour (II): Klee and Turner

Expressionist artists such as Kirchner and Ludwig Meidner found the archetype of their art in the visions of Dürer and Grünewald, just as critics such as Max Sauerlandt, Max Deri and Paul F. Schmidt have considered Grünewald as 'the strongest, the greatest and the most agitated of the Expressionists in European past'.[84] In seizing on the works of Grünewald and Marées, Benjamin therefore places them in conjunction with a particular kind of early-twentieth-century modernism. Martin Jay notes how Benjamin's early fascination with German Expressionism and especially that of *Der Blaue Reiter* group, above and beyond other Impressionist and post-Impressionist art movements, begins before the First World War, making it contemporaneous with his vivid encounter with the paintings of Grünewald in 1913.[85]

This fascination can be documented into the 1920s. In October 1917, he comments to Gershom Scholem that Paul Klee demonstrated 'the irreconcilability of great art and such "scholastic concepts" (*Schulbegriffen*) as cubism',[86] purchasing Klee's *Angelus Novus* a few years later; in 1920, he writes to Scholem that Wassily Kandinsky's *On the Spiritual in Art* 'fills me with the highest esteem for its author, just as his paintings elicit my admiration' and describes it as 'probably the only book on expressionism' that 'not … from the standpoint of philosophy, but from that of a doctrine of painting' is 'devoid of gibberish';[87] in 1921, he visits an exhibition by August Macke and writes, 'I can depend sight unseen, as it were, only on the paintings of Klee, Macke, and maybe Kandinsky'. For Jay, these painters and works 'held out for the young Benjamin the promise of a renewal of vision itself' rooted in the 'utopian potential' of colour.[88] One significant aspect of the understanding of colour in the works of *Der Blaue Reiter* group, based in Munich from 1911 to 1914, and even more so *Die Brücke* group, based in Dresden from 1905 to 1913, was their 'most far-reaching revival of interest in Goethe's principles' of colour, which enabled them to liberate 'colour from the traditional role of identifying objects' and with this to liberate 'a more profound emancipation of human experience'.[89]

Klee, who joined Kandinsky in *Der Blaue Reiter* group in 1912 and helped secure a position for Kandinsky at the Bauhaus a decade later, proclaimed, 'Colour has me. I no longer need reach out for it … Colour and I are one. I am a painter', and his pedagogical elaboration of his own colour theory from 1922 references Goethe, Philipp Otto Rung, Kandinsky and Delacroix.[90] In *The Thinking Eye*, Klee represents the cosmogenetic emergence of order out of primordial chaos by the 'grey point', a non-dimensional mathematical point that is 'neither white nor black or … white and black at the same time' and so stands 'at the fateful point between coming-into-being and passing-away'.[91] This dynamic interplay reflects 'Klee's expansive engagement with Goethe's morphology'.[92] Klee insists that the 'study of creation … emphasises the paths to form rather than the [finished] form [*Form*] itself', just as *Gestaltung* 'clearly contains the idea of an underlying mobility', indicating *Gestalt* as 'something more alive … a form with an undercurrent of living functions', which are 'purely spiritual', in the sense they cannot be perceived by 'the same senses as the familiar kind of matter', and indicates a 'power of creativity' grounded in 'a need for expression' comparable to Goethe's formative drive (*Bildungstrieb*).[93] As a result, Klee emphasizes the need for an education 'towards the functional', which visualizes 'the prehistory of the visible', as 'opposed to the impressional' and so teaches us to 'look down on formalism'.[94]

One apparent outcome of Klee's attention to Goethe's morphology and his resulting focus on the prehistory of underlying function rather than the present impression of formed structure is the novel distinction he formulates between the individual and 'dividual [*dividuell*]', previously acknowledged in the preceding discussion of Deleuze, Goethe and empiricism. This distinction is, Klee argues, 'decided by the criterion of indefinite extension or definite measure': an individual, because 'nothing is repeated, every unit is different from every other', cannot be indefinitely extended through addition nor arbitrarily divided through subtraction without altering the structural style and so changing it into a different individual.[95] To divide the individual would be to mutilate its organic unity. The dividual, in contrast, can be structurally repeated as a pattern or internally divided without ceasing to be the same. The conceptual distinction is a matter of perceptibility: 'In the higher unit [the individual] the limit of the perceptible is always reached … [in terms of] the perceptible whole' and 'thus the lower [unit] is always the dividual'; these units are, however, 'not absolute but mutually dependent' and 'when I broaden the conceptual field, I create a higher perceptible whole'.[96]

Klee gives as a visual example the structure of the fish, which 'seen as an individual, breaks down into head, body, tail and fins' but seen dividually either 'breaks down into scales and the structure of the fins' or, 'when it occurs in large numbers', builds up into the shoal, as well as a table of correspondences, such as between the individual tree and the dividual leaves, branches, twigs or the dividual forest.[97] Klee's distinction expresses a Goethean understanding of the multiplicity of forces and things aggregated in the contingent structure of organic individuals, a conception of nature that informed Nietzsche's own critique of romanticism and that Deleuze takes up as a sociopolitical category. Deleuze's 'Postscript on Societies of Control' suggests the former involves a linear and teleological progression between closed and complete spaces of enclosure, in which the individual is positioned and moulded within a relationship to the masses; the latter involves a networked system of variation and deformation between 'metastable states coexisting in one and the same modulation', in which dividuals are rapidly and continuously modulated as infinitely divisible elements.[98]

Klee's notes on painterly colours discuss the 'pure colour phenomenon' of the rainbow as 'a symbol of all use of colour'.[99] The rainbow, located in 'the atmosphere, the intermediate realm between earth and outer cosmos' (and, as Klee's diagram of the 'canon of colour' makes clear, located in the movement and countermovement between white light and black darkness), is able to communicate the 'pure colours … in an intermediate form and not in their transcendental form, which must be infinite.[100] As Goethe's colour theory had already suggested, pure red (*purpur*) is missing not only from Newton's scale but also from the colours of the rainbow, because 'in this phenomenon, as well as in the ordinary prismatic series, the yellow-red and blue-red cannot attain to a union'.[101] 'Completing' the limited and bounded spectrum by joining the 'two mysterious ends' of the rainbow 'together at infinity (endlessness)' produces Klee's 'cosmic' and 'spectral' colour circle, which enables the diametric and peripheral movement and countermovement between colours to be represented.[102]

Klee associates the diametric movement between opposing colours on the circle with the complementary colours discussed in Goethe's *Theory of Colours*, where 'colours diametrically opposed to each other … are those which reciprocally evoke each other in the eye', such that 'when the eye sees a colour it is immediately excited and it is its nature, spontaneously and of necessity, at once to produce another, which with the original colour, comprehends the whole chromatic scale'.[103] Located at the centre of Klee's cosmic colour circle, which as a result of his mapping of its dynamic interactions is transformed into a vortex-like 'canon of colour', is the grey point, which is the effect of both the peripheral and diametric movement and countermovement between colours. Klee's 'grey point' is both the origin and end of his dynamic chromaticism, a cosmic moment of coming into being and passing away of colour.

A comparable interplay of chromatic light and darkness and of temporal rising and falling, albeit one not referenced by Benjamin, occurs in the colours of J. M. W. Turner's paired paintings on the Deluge or the Hebrew flood from the Book of Genesis, whose 'most crucial underlying themes', writes Gerald Finley, 'concern the nature and relationship of light, darkness and colour and the biblical subject of fall and redemption'.[104] Finley has suggested that 'Goethe's reference to "the primordial phenomenon of light and darkness" may have contributed to the artist's decision to choose the deluge subject for his pictures from the first book of the Bible, Genesis, since darkness and light play such an important symbolic role in that book' and 'provide the appropriate tonalities for the sequential, narrative logic that orders their subject matter: the allegorical evening before and morning after the Flood'.[105] Exhibited together in 1843, the two oil paintings represent *Shade and Darkness – the Evening of the Deluge* and *Light and Colour (Goethe's Theory) – the Morning after the*

Deluge – Moses Writing the Book of Genesis. Both are centred around a vortex like whirl, of black cloud against a translucent sun in a blue sky in the first, and reds and yellows in the second.

Importantly, in his accompanying extracts for the exhibited paintings, both attributed to a non-existent poem entitled 'Fallacies of Hope', Turner associates the light conditions with the ephemerality of hope and its fallacious fancy. Jerrold Ziff has argued that the link between Turner's painted colours and his literary fragments can be discerned from an earlier and now lost watercolour exhibited by Turner in 1799, entitled 'Morning, from Dr. Langhorne's Visions of Fancy'. As with the paintings associated with the later oil paintings on light, shade and colour, Turner appends some poetic lines, in this instance taken from the poet John Langhorne's *The Visions of Fancy*:

Life's morning landscape gilt with orient light,

Where Hope and Joy,

and Fancy hold their reign,

The grove's green wave the blue stream sparkling bright,

The blythe hours dancing round Hyperion's wain.

In radiant colours youth's free hand pourtrays,

Then hold the flattering tablet to his eye,

Nor thinks how soon the vernal grove decays,

Nor sees the dark cloud gathering o'er the sky.

Mirror of life thy glories thus depart.[106]

References to the fallacies of fancy's visions of hope recur in a number of places in Langhorne's poems; significant here are the associations Turner draws between the interplay of light and shade that produces colour, between the receptive eye and the expressive hand of the youth that experiences this play of colours, as well as the temporal interplay between natural becoming and decay and between hope and despair in fancy that accompanies this experience.

The extract accompanying Turner's painting *Shade and Darkness* similarly describes the unheeded sign of woe – the red of dawn – put forth by 'the morn', how 'the dark'ning Deluge closed around' and then a moment that evening, captured in the painting, when the 'roused birds forsook their nightly shelters screaming' and the 'giant framework' of the ark floats as a 'last token' of the impending destruction. This sombre mood is evoked in the dominance of 'cooler colours, especially the striking accent of blue in the evening sky … in which areas of brooding black and purplish grey cloud ominously overhang a particularly dark landscape and are presented against a backdrop that includes … a portion of bright blue sky', one 'that identifies the ark situated in the middle distance'.[107] Turner's colours reflect a water-soaked nocturnal atmosphere – the arc of the dark storm cloud, which curves downwards into the deluge of rain, almost seems to rise from the swell of the flood itself – saturated by the light of the moon: Finley describes how 'a brilliant shaft of moonlight, an almost spiritual light, flashes down on the swelling flood waters'.[108]

Conversely, the dominance of warmer yellows and reds in Turner's *Light and Colour* signals the rising sun on the morning after the flood, again expressing, as the painting's title indicates, the influence of Goethe's colour theory. Finley has suggested that the 'shimmering, elusive, almost apocalyptic imagery' of the morning light, recalling the red dawn's unheeded signs of woe in *Shade and Darkness*, is 'not intended to be either cheerful or optimistic'.[109] The prismatic vortex that frames the scene of the Deluge in *Light and Colour*, which approximates the rotating effects of bubbles 'by means of brushwork that enhances the suggestion of a circular movement on its periphery', establishes the 'dynamic nature of colour … the coming into being, the changing and disappearing of colour' as the 'essential and dominant content' of the painting.

This reflects not only the polarity of light and darkness in Goethe's *Theory of Colours* but its concern with 'with material mediums, such as bubbles, that "have no colour themselves, and may be either transparent, semi-transparent yet transmitting light, or altogether opaque"'. It engenders, Finley argues, a 'mood of hopelessness' echoed in Turner's appended fragment from 'Fallacies of Hope', with its overtones of the Day of Judgement, which reflect on the very ephemerality of colour – as it appears on the surface of bubbles or is diffused and reflected through the water-logged atmosphere of the biblical morning – as anticipating and diffusing the sign of God's covenant with living creatures, the rainbow:

th' returning sun

Exhaled earth's humid bubbles, and emulous of light,

Reflected her lost forms, each in prismatic guise

Hope's harbinger, ephemeral as the summer fly

Which rises, flits, expands, and dies.

Turner's term 'summer fly' probably indicates a mayfly of the order Ephemeroptera, meaning short-lived and winged; the poet George Crabbe uses the same metaphor in his satirical poem 'The Newspaper', published fifty years before Turner's painting, to characterize the ephemerality of the daily newspapers as

Like insects waking to th'advancing spring;

Which take their rise from grubs obscene that lie

In shallow pools, or thence ascent the sky:

Such are these base ephemera, so born

To die before the next revolving morn.

This mood is perhaps carried over from its lowest ebb in Turner's infamous *Slavers throwing overboard the Dead and Dying – Typhoon coming on*, first exhibited in 1840 to coincide with a global anti-slavery convention in London, and accompanied by more lines from the 'Fallacies of Hope':

Yon angry setting sun and fierce-edged clouds

Declare the Typhoon's coming.

… throw overboard

The dead and dying – ne'er heed their chains

Hope, Hope, fallacious Hope!

Where is thy market now?

Like Grünewald's Isenheim Alterpiece, Turner anachronistically condenses several separate moments of the biblical narrative, including Noah's Covenant the morning after the deluge and Moses's writing the Book of Genesis, in which the story of the flood is told. The figure of Moses therefore reinforces the association with water and the ark: he is the one drawn out of the water, having been concealed in an ark to save him from drowning on the command of the Pharaoh, who draws the people of Israel through the waters of the Red Sea to the Promised Land and who records the divine creation and destruction of the world. He also appears raised above the flooded scene in the act of writing, emphasizing his role as lawmaker in recording the Ten Commandments on

Mount Sinai and establishing the covenant between YHWH and the Israelites, and so echoing Noah's covenant. At the centre of Turner's vortex is the 'brazen serpent' YHWH instructs Moses to raise in the wilderness to heal those bitten by the serpents sent to punish the Israelites and which for Turner anticipates the crucifixion and resurrection of Christ. David Jasper concurs with John Gage and Finley's evaluation, arguing that Turner's 'pessimistic, even cynical' placing of 'the biblical narratives of "salvation history"' within this chromatic frame dissolves 'the sequential movement of its history … taking all as a momentary vision, [which] grants no priority to no particular moment, and therefore denies the development of history as anything other than a blind succession of events'.[110]

The collapsing of teleological narratives in Turner's work condemns not only a Christian vision of historical progress but also its secular counterpart in science. For Jonathan Crary, the 'inescapable temporality' of Turner's chromatic vision, which prevents 'the immediate and unitary apprehension of an image', signals an 'irrevocable loss of a fixed source of light … and the collapse of the distance separating an observer from the site of optical experience' evincing 'the breakdown of the perceptual model of the camera obscura', which 'Kepler and Newton employed'.[111] This signals an artistic crisis not only of the Christian imagery in Turner's work but also of Newton's mechanistic worldview. In *Light and Colour*, however, the very ephemerality of the 'prismatic guise' of the earth's 'lost forms' is also 'hope's harbinger' and Finley more persuasively observes elsewhere that Turner's imagery of the ephemerality and contingency of the summer fly is simultaneously an 'allusion to the dynamic cycle of nature … that embraces individual and collective human life' and so 'a symbol of permanence in change'.[112]

As Benjamin suggests in his essay on Goethe's *Elective Affinities*, the most extreme and most radical kind of hope can only appear as that which is most ephemeral, contingent and expressionless: as a hope that 'had long faded away', in the glimmer of a star that momentarily passes over us unnoticed, the prismatic play of colour on the surface of a bubble or the flitting wings of the short-lived mayfly. W. J. T. Mitchell has argued that John Gage's attempt to extend Turner's bubbles of hope to a pessimistic reading of the fallacy of the covenant itself faces difficulties: the 'bubbles with human faces' that emerge from the receding flood in the bottom corner of the painting have a 'more complex role to play' because 'even in the transience and ephemerality, these "bubble heads" reaffirm a vision of permanence and stability … they "reflect" the "lost forms" of earth and light, if only for their moment of brief light'.[113] As with the bubble-like halos of Grünewald's celestial faces, Turner's human heads – 'images of the lost, disobedient souls who hoped the flood would never come' – are transformed in this imaginative interplay of redemptive light and apocalyptic darkness, subject to both colouration and perishableness. In both paintings, the figure – concentrated on the face itself as the receptacle of light and darkness – is subject to the deforming effects of colour, the human form caught on the point of corporeal annihilation or spiritual transfiguration.

Mitchell suggests that in Turner's late paintings his romantic imagination playfully subverts the religious iconography used, permitting him to stand at a precarious moment between the sacred and secular interpretation of historical change: between 'apocalyptic transformation, the institution of a new covenant' and a secular 'act of self-conscious originality'.[114] In matching his vortical experimentation with form with the biblical themes of destruction and renewal, Mitchell claims, Turner resolved the division between a classical, verbal and literary conception of painting and a modernist conception concerned with formal abstraction. Against such a perspective, however, John Gage emphasizes that Turner was opposed to formalism precisely because, as Goethe makes clear, colour as content, rather than form, involves a profoundly symbolic and linguistic meaning, undermining Mitchell's division between the classical and verbal versus modern and formal. The dynamic movement of Turner's colour content is used 'as a means of controlling the structures of his paintings', aligning his use of colour with a quasi-classical response to romanticism that complicates attempts to regard Turner as a progenitor of modernism understood in terms of formalism and abstraction.[115] Turner's modernism, in contrast to such a view, is evinced rather in the way his romantic conception of the world compelled him to seek a classical turn towards colour as the pure content of his paintings.

In emphasizing the 'expressionism' of the paintings discussed here, in which colour fleetingly emerges in a field of tension produced through the dynamic antinomy of the forces of light and darkness, in the phantastical realm of becoming and passing away, this chapter has sought to elaborate a dimension of Benjamin's work that Caygill briefly touches on in his own discussion of the colour of experience. As Caygill makes clear, Benjamin's dissertation on the concept of art criticism opposes two contrasting eschatologies of art: Early German Romantic criticism 'will in time ultimately overcome the contingency present in the work by revealing all of its possibilities and thus converting them into necessities', at the limit of which 'we *know* the work of art'; Goethean criticism 'does not progressively realise the work, but reduces it first to a torso or ruin and then, in the fullness of time, to nothing ... its formal possibilities reduced to pure contingencies', at the limit of which 'we can only *imagine*' the work of art.[116]

Benjamin's aim is not to dogmatically reduce artistic imagination and art criticism to one or the other but to reveal the depth of modern art in the oscillation between these perspectives. Schematically put, Benjamin aims to *experience* the contingencies. This touches, as Caygill's brief but richly suggestive afterword acknowledges, on the contingency of history itself. For Caygill, a 'better biblical precedent' for the 'bleak rigour of Benjamin's thought', where the eschatological 'intimations of last things' often lack the Messianic sense of completeness, 'is the appearance of the rainbow to Noah after the flood, marking the advent of a new covenant between Divinity, Nature and Humanity'.[117] The Angelus Novus who appears in Benjamin's late theses 'On the Concept of History', a text replete with Goethean resonances, is to be interpreted in this sense as bearing 'witness to ruination ... not in the expectation of redemption, but ... of a new covenant or law', one that does not arrive 'in a Messianic wave of power and light, but in the nuances of riotous colour'.[118] Just as the Angel is suspended between paradise and eschatology, so art may come to a standstill between its classical past and romantic future in the 'cessation of happening before the apocalyptic storm', or it may approach the paradisiacal duration beyond all memory and forgetting in the experience of the pure event that resides in the very movement of this tension, and so see beyond the storm to the paradisiacal rainbow of the truly modern.[119]

5

Pure expression: the critical
violence of language

The preceding chapter suggested how Benjamin drew on Goethe's tender empiricism of colour, understood via Deleuze as a transcendental empiricism, for a speculative recasting of Kant's transcendental idealism.[1] Goethe describes colour as part of the spiritual 'language of nature' and, in his notes on 'Socrates', Benjamin similarly associates the spiritual colours of Grünewald's paintings, discussed in the previous chapter, with the 'silence of a new language'.[2] The 'Metaphysics of Youth' identifies this language as closer to the spiritual silence of the *Genius* in prayer (using the Latin expression for the spirit within a person, thing or place) than the expressiveness of the artistic genius (*Genie*).[3] While Benjamin, like Goethe, emphasizes the symbolic and spiritual significance of colour, he is careful to characterize this in terms not of symbolic expression but the 'expressionless signifying appearance [*Ausdruckslos bedeutende Erscheinung*]' of the colours of phantasy.[4]

This chapter examines the implications of this Goethean experience of colour for literary criticism by detailing how Benjamin transposes the experience of colour into a philosophy or theology of language more broadly, such that colour as the pure (non-ideational) content of intuition is the correlate of a pure linguistic content that Benjamin associates, across his essays 'On Language as Such and the Language of Man' (1916), 'The Task of the Translator' (1924) and his thesis on the *Origin of German Trauerspiel* (submitted 1925, published 1928), with the Adamic *Ursprache* or 'pure noncommunicative language' of silence. It argues that Benjamin's account of expression is profoundly influenced by Goethe's own theory of interlinear translation and is modelled on the chromatic principles of Goethe's colour theory. As a consequence, the communicative expressiveness of human language is seen to involve an act of translation from this pure language, and so a movement between languages in which something is destroyed but through which a productive tension is generated such that something may also emerge. In this sense, human language – and most notably literary language, as the later discussions will explore – emerges in the antinomical relationship between silence and speech and may be characterized as the deeds and suffering of expression.

The task of literary translation, Benjamin proposes, is to regain pure language within its own language by turning the symbolizing power of linguistic expression itself into the very thing symbolized. Unlike Early German Romantic reflection, however, this does not raise language to a higher formal level but shatters the semblance of symbolic unity within the literary work. This critical violence repeats that of the expressionless moment, present in all literature, in which pure expression itself becomes expressed. The resulting torso of the symbol, identified in what follows with the allegorical, will be exemplified, first, in Benjamin's literary criticism of Goethe's *Elective Affinities*, which exposes the work's expressionless moment, and then through a comparable critique of the modernist aesthetics of the British poet T. E. Hulme, whose own Imagist poetry is similarly located in the antinomy between romanticism and classicism.

Translating the pure word

For 'Benjamin, unlike Kant, the fact of givenness is not tied to objectivity, nor, unlike Cohen, to the fact of the sciences, but to the fact of the linguistic nature of knowledge', writes Deuber-Mankowsky, and the 'totality, which makes thought possible and at the same time goes beyond the limits of knowledge, is understood by ... Benjamin as experience of the linguistic nature of all knowledge'.[5] 'On the Program of the Coming Philosophy' therefore situates the 'great transformation and correction which must be performed on the concept of experience' for Kant in the context of a 'relating knowledge to language'. This refers to Johann Georg Hamann's metacritique of Kant and specifically Hamann's theological idea of creation through the divine Word as the transcendental condition of possibility for knowledge. From this linguistic essence of things follows the semiotic idea that all experience involves an act of expression: we 'cannot imagine anything', either animate or inanimate nature, 'that does not communicate its mental nature in its expression', Benjamin writes, such that the 'language of this lamp, for example, communicates not the lamp ... but the language-lamp, the lamp in communication, the lamp in expression'.[6]

The original Word of God in things is understood as the 'germ of the cognizing name' that demands to be expressed in human language and the task of human expression as an act of naming through which language in its absolute wholeness communicates itself to God.[7] Naming is therefore 'the language of language (if the genitive refers to the relationship not of a means but of a medium)': a critical medium which extends between signifier and signified. The 'Epistemo-Critical Prologue' to the *Trauerspiel* book confirms the philosophical importance of this Adamic practice of naming for Benjamin's philosophy of language, describing it as primal history (*Urgeschicte*) of signifying.[8] Its description of Adam's primal language as a primal-interrogation (*urvernehmen*) rhymes the primordial (*ur-*) act of giving names (*Namen*) to each creature with an emphasis on an intimate perception of nature (*vernehmen* – to hear, to learn; *Wahrnehmung* – perception) and the use of a critical violence or interruptive judgement (*Vernehmen* – a court hearing or interrogation, etymologically linked to *nehmen*, meaning to take) that liberates the truth.[9]

But the Word that is the 'nucleus of pure language' is 'tied to linguistic elements and their changes' and so, in this ephemerality, 'seeks to represent, indeed produce, itself in the evolving of languages themselves' by being symbolized.[10] Detached from the flux of the various ways of meaning in different languages, it 'persists in linguistic creations only in its symbolizing capacity', where 'it is weighed with a heavy, alien meaning'. To name is therefore to liberate the pure linguistic element within the concepts of knowledge: to find a transitional language capable of denoting not universals but the ephemerality of particulars, detached from concepts and bound up with signifying words.[11] Benjamin therefore links expressive signification with the principle of translation as a process of continual change and transformation, in the first instance from the object-language of language as such – the experience of the lamp in expression – into the subject-language of humans.

The idea of language as a 'continuum of transformations' evokes the Early German Romantic concept of translation as 'a medial, continuous transposition of the work from one language into another', one that, for Novalis, exemplifies the 'perfecting, positive criticism' as understood by German Romanticism.[12] But Benjamin insists in 'The Task of the Translator' that while genuine translation enacts a transformation of the nameless into the name, this act of completion subsequently means the translation itself proves to be untranslatable.[13] Because translations themselves remain untranslatable, however, the act of translation does not set into play the infinite intensification of Romantic reflection, but provides a multiplicity of partial completions each of which, at the point it touches the original, provides the tangent of its path to infinity.

This multiplicity involves not, therefore, the decomposition of an original, historical unity but a productive tension which liberates the purity of language. This appearance corresponds to that 'limited, harmonic discontinuum of pure contents' associated with the Goethean Ideal in 'The Concept of Criticism', a harmony expressed by the relationship of elements on the colour sphere or, in relation to naming, the natural music produced by harmony of the cosmic spheres. Here, then, the early account of chromatic interplay is developed into a Goethean theory of translation that enables the modification and transformation of the Romantic concept of criticism.

In 'The Task of the Translator', Benjamin directly cites Goethe's 'Notes on Translation' for his *West-Easterly Divan* – which, along with Rudolf Pannwitz's *The Crisis of European Culture*, is declared to be 'the best comment on the theory of translation' – to extend the notion, deployed in the earlier essay on language, that a linguistic realm extends between the poles of the original language and the language of the translator which is not one of 'abstract areas of identity and similarity' but 'media of varying densities'.[14] The task of the translator is 'to realise in his own language that pure language which is exiled among alien tongues' by turning 'the symbolizing into the symbolized itself, to regain pure language fully formed from the linguistic flux'.[15]

Here, the continuous transformation of language – the process of formation and deformation itself – becomes the object of expression, and an image which is able to fix and isolate this movement is sought. Translation therefore seeks to redeem the pure language in the name, and each translation offers a 'completion' which is angled towards the realm in which the meaning of pure language is ultimately fulfilled. The kinship between human languages 'cannot be defined adequately by an identity of origin' but only as a transcendental identity between the totalities of their meaning as a whole, which is 'achievable not by any single language but only by the totality of their intentions supplementing one another'.[16]

Translation occurs as a linguistic element passes through this dense media – equivalent to the conception of turbidity as the matter in which the deforming tensions of light and darkness interact – and because of this language becomes a 'continuum of transformations', in which the play of words is equivalent to the play of colours: the deeds and sufferings of expression. What the genuine translation achieves is to allow the language of the translator, in the words of Pannwitz cited by Benjamin, to be 'powerfully affected by the foreign tongue'.[17] The intention is not to turn Greek into German, but to permit something new to emerge by phantastically deforming German into Greek.

Furthermore, Goethe's theory describes the highest kind of translation as that which makes 'a translation identical to the original, not in such a way that the former replaces the other [*anstatt des anderen*], but rather occupies the place of the other [*an der Stelle des anderen*]'.[18] For Goethe, 'the translator who follows his original closely more or less abandons the originality of his nation, and thus a *tertium quid* comes into being for which the masses slowly have to develop a taste'. This difference between replacing the other and occupying the same place as the other implies an interaction between coexisting languages that produces a temporary change. Goethe describes the 'third thing' which is produced between the two languages in the same terms as Benjamin as an 'interlinearity'. This provides a model for the kind of non-synthesis in which existing polarities do not disappear with the emergence of the new, but which continue to exist in a productive, overlapping tension upon which the created thing always remains dependent. The 'identity' of the third thing is an appearance which is instable, contingent and utterly dependent upon the antinomical relationship out of which it emerges.

While Goethe's own language emphasizes the strange temporality of translation, it is the optical terminology of Benjamin's writing which brings out the chromatic model inherent in this theory of linguistic production. A 'real translation is transparent', Benjamin says, 'it does not cover the original, does not block its light, but allows the pure language, as though reinforced by its own medium, to shine upon the original all them more fully'.[19] Like colour, it is the tension between the original language and the new language which permits the purity to appear as a result of the material turbidity of the medium. The optical imagery utilized here suggests that the productivity of naming in the medium of language is, as Caygill suggests, modelled in part on a Goethean metaphysics of chromatic differentiation.

The implications of this theory for a broader account of artistic expression and a corresponding notion of literary criticism will now be examined in relation to Benjamin's commentary on Goethe's *Elective Affinities*, which identifies the pure word with the critical violence of the expressionless. The shock of this violence, Benjamin suggests, induces a turbidity within the mode of expression that permits representation itself to become experienceable and so turns the signifying or symbolizing medium of linguistic expression into the signified or symbolized itself: in the expressionless, expression becomes expressed, and so the language of creation is revealed anew. The task of criticism, it will be argued, is to reduplicate the critical – differentiating – violence of the expressionless.

In his essay on Goethe's *Elective Affinities*, Benjamin suggests that artistic creation 'enchants chaos momentarily into the world' through the harmonic semblance of beautiful form (*Form*): that semblance of or bordering on life that a work possesses by virtue of its linguistic expressiveness. That 'in which the indissoluble and necessary bonding of truth content to material content appears', Benjamin adds, is the organic unity of 'the symbolic [*Symbolisch*]'.[20] Modern philology, however, with its inadequate conception of criticism, commits the error of seeking to understand the content (*Gehalt*) of a work solely as an expression of the lived experience (*Erleben*) of the author, rather than by precise insight into the expressive subject matter (*Sache*) of the work itself.[21]

As the discussion of symbolism in the *Trauerspiel* book explains, classical art is preoccupied with a profane concept of the symbol, which Georg Friedrich Creuzer associated with the 'plastic', as exemplified in Greek sculpture. It takes its cue from the organic totality of the semi-divine hero of classical art and is connected to the apotheosis of existence in the individual who is perfect: the heroic incarnation of the classical synthesis of the true, the beautiful and the good. The tension between the finite and the infinite is therefore resolved in this classical solution by humans as semi-divinities.

Romanticism's attempt to secure knowledge of the Absolute led it to conceive of the symbol as the manifestation or appearance of an Idea or essence in the work of art and to place the symbolic individual found in classical myth within the Christian context of redemptive but infinite progress towards redemption: the beautiful is supposed to merge with the divine in an unbroken whole.[22] As Benjamin makes clear in the footnote appended to the description of the infinity of this aesthetic concept of the symbol, this emphasis upon the symbolic results from a tradition which has its roots (even if it does not appear in such a form) in the Early German Romantic understanding of the medium of reflection and finds its false apotheosis in that 'false, errant totality – the absolute totality' which is condemned in the essay on Goethe's *Elective Affinities* as the 'Nazarene essence' of the novel's conclusion.

The allegorical is largely understood as the negative counterpart to this aestheticized and profane notion of the symbol: for Goethe's aesthetic theory, albeit not in his artistic practice, allegory merely designates the relation between a concept and a phenomenon, so that 'the concept continues to remain circumscribed and completely available and expressible within the image'; Schopenhauer similarly disapproves of artistic allegory as 'the expression of a concept' rather than 'the expression of an Idea' and Yeats assumed that 'allegory is a conventional relationship between an illustrative image and its abstract meaning'.[23]

What is essential to art, however, and what distinguishes art from the semblance of nature, is the expressionless (*Ausdruckslose*).[24] This corresponds to a critical violence (*kritische Gewalt*) within the work that interrupts the harmony, petrifies the semblance of 'living beauty' and prevents the latter from mingling with what is essential in it.[25] Importantly, Benjamin identifies the expressionless with the 'pure word [*reine Wort*]' that Hölderlin defined as the caesura, a 'counter-rhythmic rupture [*gegenrhythmische Unterbrechung*]' that permits 'representation itself' to appear (*Vorstellung selber erscheint*). The violence of that which is expressionless is characterized by Benjamin as a 'great emotion of shattering' within that which is given expression as semblance.[26] This violent shock causes the semblance of beauty to grow 'more and more turbid [*trübt*]', like a fluid that forms crystals when subject to a sudden blow.

Just as translation, in its Goethean sense, was understood to involve a transformation of meaning as it passes through the turbid medium of languages, so this increased turbidity of the semblance as a result of the expressionless violence produces a refraction or deformation of expression. If the immanent translatability of a linguistic creation corresponds to the Romantic conception of criticizability as an essential incompleteness, such translation is completed in an expressionless Goethean moment of untranslatability: a moment of expressionless violence in which the pure language of emotion is revealed by turning the symbolizing into the symbolized itself.

The expressionless therefore completes (*vollendet*) the work *as* a work by ensuring the separation of the material content and truth content bonded in the living unity of the symbolic. It does so by 'shattering it into a thing of shards, into a fragment of the true world', such that in symbolizing the symbolized, the symbolic becomes translated into 'the torso of a symbol [*Torso eines Symbols*]'.[27] The task of literary criticism is therefore to make the conditions of possibility of the experience of the artwork – the expressionless – into an object of knowledge. It does this by reduplicating the critical violence of the expressionless: not by the Romantic 'awakening of consciousness' of the artwork through criticism but rather by 'the colonization of knowledge within the dead [*Ansiedlung des Wissens, in ihnen, den abgestorbenen*], through a process of mortification'.[28]

Benjamin's conception of critical violence is grounded in a pure language of the divine and exemplified in his essay on Goethe's *Elective Affinities* from 1924/5. This conception can be usefully compared to the critical concept of violence (*Gewalt*) that is transcendentally deduced in Benjamin's 'Critique of Violence', published a few years earlier. The latter examines the concept of violence within the political and theological contexts of law and justice, in which coercion and law frequently comingle, and attempts to defend the position that only the individual has the ethical right to use force.[29]

Benjamin's example of language, specifically the conference or parlay (*Unterredung*), as a policy of pure means operating outside the instrumentality of coercive violence has led Jürgen Habermas to discern a theory of linguistic communication within Benjamin's concept of criticism, more amenable to his own theory of communicative action.[30] For Benjamin, however, the individual right to violence is grounded on the deduction of a pure violence, justified by a concept of divine violence associated not – as Habermas intends – with social evolution but with an intensive messianic temporality, with the pure and law-destroying power of justice and with the French political theorist George Sorel's defence of the revolutionary myth of the proletarian general strike (against all social democratic visions of progress) as the expression of a will to act.[31]

For this reason, Benjamin tends to identify such pure violence not so much with the linguistic communication of humans but with the educative power (*erzieherische Gewalt*) that is manifested in the expiating moment of divine judgement. As with the shattering of false semblance associated with the critical violence of the expressionless, through which pure language is redeemed, so this critical conception of violence is at once destructive, annihilating the semblance of law that the state uses to monopolize coercive force, and redemptive, possessing an invisible power to expiate from guilt for the sake of the living.[32]

The educative aspect of such violence can be further connected to Benjamin's claim that the order of education 'completely coincides with the religious order of tradition', to the extent that instruction involves 'education by means of *Lehre*': a medium of interplay between generations that involves not the identical replication of fixed content but transmission as a process of translation, through the transformation of a multiplicity of learners into the ones who teach by communicating the tradition in their own way.[33] Such reflections attest once more to the inherently transdisciplinary nature of the concept of criticism associated with such pure violence in Benjamin's thought, shifting as it does in his writings from the political domain of law, to that of theological justice, from the order of education to that of religion, and from revolutionary violence to the violence of literary criticism.

Expressionist language (I): Goethe's *Elective Affinities*

Benjamin conceives his essay on Goethe's novel *Elective Affinities* as an 'exemplary piece' of such criticism. It was intended as the 'legally binding condemnation and execution' of Friedrich Gundolf, a member of the circle around the poet Stefan George and whose 1916 biographical study of Goethe exemplified the contemporary philological practice of mere 'commentary', that Benjamin's concept of criticism set out to oppose.[34] But in paralleling

Schlegel's own 'romanticizing' of Goethe in his critical essay 'On Goethe's *Meister*', Benjamin's dissertation on 'Goethe's *Elective Affinities*' may also be regarded as providing a counterpart and countermovement to the infinite intensification of living expression in Romantic criticism, exemplifying the violent mortification that seeks to separate what is living and what is dead in the work.

The philological criticism of commentators such as Gundolf seize upon the 'abundance of premonitory and parallel features' in Goethe's *Elective Affinities* as 'the most obvious expression of the novel's character'. Yet because Goethe strove to conceal the novel's purely constructive techniques, the material content that determined the novel's material had remained concealed. This technique resembles the literary form of the parable or allegory (*Gleichnis*), resting on an order of similitude (*gleichheit*) and correspondences (*Entsprechende, Korrespondenzen*) that represent Goethe's recovery of the artistic principle of the 'tendency toward the typical [*Typus*]'.[35] What Georg Simmel identified as this 'recited' (*Vorgetragen*) style of *Elective Affinities* – the 'absence of formal-artistic realism', the 'emphasis and exaggeration of type and contour' and the 'formulaic quality' – lends the story a 'plastic, perhaps stereoscopic' pictorial quality, pushing the reader's sympathy away from the centre of the action and characters with all 'the hallmarks of the classic form of the novella'.[36]

Benjamin associates this artistic technique with Nietzsche's rediscovery – whispered by the daemon (*Dämon*) of *The Gay Science* – of the Stoic wisdom concerning the eternal recurrence of the same (*ewige Wiederkunft alles Gleichen*).[37] The real material content of the novel, Benjamin suggests, resides in the 'mythical chaos of symbols' as a 'symbolism of death [*Todessymbolik*]': a daemonic (*Dämonischen*) 'sign of fate' whose mythical conception of reconciliation in sacrifice attests to the 'obviously pagan tendencies' in Goethe's expression.[38] This sacrificial logic is evident in the critical glorification of Ottilie's death, premised on the reduction of her life to a passive, silent semblance of spiritual innocence, understood as the necessary 'renunciation of all things earthly'. The heathen demand for immortality attested to in such sacrifice – the incapacity to die – stems from a daemonic indistinguishability within signification: the inability to separate signs from their objects, the true from the false, the innocent from the guilty, the living from the dead.[39]

Just as Benjamin's critique of violence had taken issue with a mythic conception of law-making violence, so the essay 'Fate and Character' takes issue with this mythic conception of fate for conflating a recurring experience with character, understood in a vague sense as the cause of this fate. This involves a disengagement from Nietzsche's Heraclitean aphorism, in *Beyond Good and Evil*, that 'if a man has character, he has an experience [*Erlebnis*] that constantly recurs'.[40] This understanding of character regards it as a mere network of threads, composed of broad character traits that are connected by finer strands to external events of fate and tightened by knowledge into a dense fabric, from which the cloth of character is cut.[41]

Benjamin proposes instead that an adequate conception of character needs to be delimited more clearly from the concept of fate. To do so, he introduces the distinction between cultic myth and theological justice: fate must be detached from its association with religious punishment, Benjamin insists, since this conception refers to misfortune only as divine punishment of the guilty, without any historical index of good fortune or happiness and the liberation from guilt. In Benjamin's fragment on capitalism as religion, this understanding of fate pertains to the mythical domain of the absolute cult, whose modern apotheosis is a capitalism that knows only duties and punishment and nothing of redemption and bliss. Benjamin identifies such fate with the law as 'a residue of the demonic stage of human existence'.[42]

Goethe's ethical revolt against the mythic, his 'struggle to free himself from its clutches', beginning with his marriage in 1806, is attested to as a 'purer promise' in the truth content of his work from *Elective Affinities* onwards and 'unfolded ever more powerfully in his later work': the 'historicizing of his life' in *Truth and Poetry*, the *West-Easterly Divan* and the second part of *Faust* 'became the three great documents of such masked penance'.[43] This promise is not to be identified, however, with the false, Nazarene conclusion of the novel, which oversteps the symbolic limits of aesthetic reconciliation when the poet guarantees the lovers joint resurrection: 'And thus the lovers lie side by side. Peace hovers about their abode, smiling angelic figures (with whom too they have affinity) look down upon them from the vault above, and what a happy moment it will be when one day they awaken together.'[44]

Rochelle Tobias demonstrates how Benjamin's critique of this Nazarene promise is grounded in conflation of the finite contingency of the aesthetic realm with the reconciliation hoped for in the ethical judgement that pertains only to the transcendence of God.[45] Such reconciliation is 'entirely supermundane and hardly an object for concrete depiction in a novel', finding its 'worldly reflection' only in the moment of conciliation (*Aussöhnung*) of one's fellow humanity and in the moment of expressionless violence when 'every expression simultaneously comes to a standstill' and the mystery of the work juts 'out of the domain of language proper to it into a higher one unattainable for it'.[46]

Tobias suggests that Benjamin's critique of Goethe's Nazarene conclusion also draws on the critical limits delineated in Hermann Cohen's discussion, in *Religion of Reason Out of the Sources of Judaism*, of Yom Kippur, the Judaic Day of Atonement or Reconciliation (*Versöhnungstag*).[47] True reconciliation, as a reconciliation with God comparable to Cohen's understanding of the Day of Atonement, is one in which each individual stands, unmediated by priest or sacrificial offering, in a direct relation with God. In 'The Meaning of Time in the Moral Universe', Benjamin opposes what he calls the heathen conception of the Last Judgement as the date 'when all postponements are ended and all retribution is allowed to free rein', by bringing it closer to this Judaic understanding of judgement in the Day of Atonement or Reconciliation: the 'immeasurable significance of the Last Judgement' is not the idea of judgement and retribution but its suspension of judgement through forgiveness.[48]

Benjamin's objection to this conclusion therefore 'represents a more general critique of the … glorification of the artist as a creator in the image of God and the elevation of the work of art to reality in its own right', and so any commingling of the artistic and religious – finite and transcendent – realms.[49] This Nazarene conclusion repeats the errors of what Gasché characterizes as the mystical faults of Romantic criticism: 'Criticizability … is thus tied up with what impedes criticism, and that against which criticism ought to prevail: transition, continuity, reconciliation between what can be brought together only at the price of paradox, false interpretation, or in other words, a complete surrender of the critical notion of the Absolute to the profane' and so the 'radical loss of transcendence' *as* transcendence.[50] For Benjamin, this 'transcending gesture of critique', the possibility or hope for reconciliation, can only depend upon another kind of redemptive justification before which 'critique must be suspended', just as the divine violence of judgement remains invisible and cannot itself be judged.[51]

As the deformations within German baroque *Trauerspiel* reveal their 'content [*Gehalt*] and true object' not as mythic fate but historical life, so the deforming tensions generated by the inclusion of the parable of 'The Marvellous Young Neighbours' within the already parable-like form of the central novel inverts not only 'the novel's plot but also, and more important … the [mythical] logic underlying it'.[52] This parable concerns two young lovers whose leap into a river symbolizes a moment of decision in which each, 'wholly alone', isolate themselves from their families and community in order to find individual reconciliation with God, and in this way find conciliation with others.[53] The clarity of the decision to act, rather than passively endure as a gesture of innocence, places each individual beyond both freedom and fate, corresponding with the true expression of natural innocence: the simplicity of 'character' as the unity of spiritual life.[54]

Benjamin explains the theological, rather than aesthetic, difference between symbol and allegory not in terms of a difference in *what* they express (the infinite Idea or the finite concept) but the temporality of *how* they express it: in the symbol 'we have momentary totality' and 'in the allegory 'progression in a series of moments'. If the object of allegorical intention is the 'creaturely world of things, the dead, or at best the half-living', its strongest impulse is nonetheless to rescue the ephemerality of things for eternity.[55] Only from this theological perspective is a more critical understanding of allegory – not as 'a playful illustrative technique, but a form of expression' – possible.

Formally, the allegorical is both *convention* – because, like writing, there is an arbitrary and constructed relationship between the sign and its meaning – and *expression* – because, like the divine Word, it is created; it is not, according to the aesthetic misunderstanding, the 'convention of expression', however, but rather the 'expression of convention'.[56] In the same way that interlinear translation, by calling attention to itself, turns the diachronic transformation of signifying language into the object signified (the symbolizing of the symbolized), the temporality of allegory transforms the empirical contingency of its object (the ephemerality of natural passing) into a messianic hope for the logical contingency of such contingency (the radical contingency of the contingent). Ephemerality is displayed as the allegory of (symbolic) resurrection:

> Allegory thereby loses everything that was most peculiar to it: the secret, privileged knowledge, the arbitrary rule in the realm of dead objects, the supposed infinity of a world without hope. All this vanishes in this one about turn, in which the immersion of allegory has to clear away the final phantasmagoria of the objective and … rediscovers itself, not playfully in the earthly world of things, but seriously under the ideas of heaven.[57]

Although unrepresentable, such reconciliation finds its 'worldly reflection' in the conciliation (*Aussöhnung*) of one's fellow humanity, which intrudes into the novel in a moment of critical violence in which 'every expression simultaneously comes to a standstill, in order to give free reign to an expressionless power', permitting the mystery of the work to jut 'out of the domain of language proper to it into a higher one unattainable for it'.[58] As with Grünewald's chromatic composition, the 'lawful character' of the novel's parable of 'The Marvellous Young Neighbours' is able to 'stand out in bold relief' against the darkness of this fatalistic framework, like 'a brilliant light … shining into the dusk-filled Hades of the novel' or an image that brings the bright daylight of the exterior into the dark interior of a cathedral.[59]

Such conciliation is reflected, outside of this parable, in the main novel itself only 'as a first weak premonition, as the almost hopeless shimmer of dawn', just as the semblance of reconciliation 'once again dawns sweetest before its vanishing'.[60] As 'at twilight, as the sun is extinguished, rises the evening star which outlasts the night' and whose 'glimmer … is imparted by Venus', so the 'most fleeting hope' for reconciliation, to awaken together in a blessed world, receives its glimmer from the artistic semblance of conciliation.[61] The 'hope that Goethe had to conceive for the lovers' had 'once appeared to him' in the 'symbol of the star' as the expressionless caesura of the work: 'Hope passed, like a star falling from heaven, away over their heads [*Die Hoffnung fuhr wie ein Stern, der vom Himmel fällt, über, ihre Häupter weg*]'.

The counter-rhythmic rupture or signifying violence of this sentence operates on a number of levels. First, Eduard is expecting the prearranged sound of cannons or the appearance of rockets in the sky to signify Charlotte's acceptance of the Major's proposal, which would liberate him to marry

Ottilie, but instead we are given the unexpected symbol of the falling star (a substitution of signs). Second, this 'star' cannot be seen by the lovers not only because it passes over their heads but because it only exists as a symbol, introduced by the author for the reader alone (a substitution of interpretants). This is, third, connected to the strange inversion of the interpretant's expected relationship between the sign and the object, such that it is *hope* that passes across the sky above their heads *like a falling star* and not the *star* that passes across the sky *like hope*. As such the star is doubly symbolic: as that which symbolizes hope (*hope, like a falling star*) and, because it is not even present to the lovers in the fictional world of the novel, that which is symbolized by hope (*hope passes over their heads*). Fourth, the insertion of the simile, *like a star, falling from the sky*, between the hope that is immediately connected to its action of 'passing' (through the unusual proximity of the noun and verb in German) and the preposition 'over' and, through the punctuation, to the final adverb 'away', intimates both the ephemeral temporality of *a hope that passed away, over their heads*, and a spatial metaphor of incomprehension: *a hope that passed, way over their heads*. Finally, these inversions in the order of signification draw attention to the act of semiosis itself and so permit signification itself to be signified.

The abyss that opens between the emergence of hope and its passing is that of the symbolism of the star with the interrupting movement or gesture of the falling star. The symbol of the star can therefore be said to interrupt the symbol of hope. More specifically, since the star is both the image of movement which symbolizes hope, and that which is symbolized by the concept of hope (which here functions as an imageless image: it is 'hope' itself that passes over their heads), the symbol of the star can be said to interrupt its own symbolizing.

Here the act of critical violence that Benjamin identifies with the expressionless becomes apparent and its literary effect becomes explicable: the symbol of the star, in interrupting its own symbolizing, itself becomes the 'torso of the symbol' that simultaneously prevents the work from attaining a false semblance of unity. Unlike the intensification of Romantic reflection, when this semblance itself becomes the object of a higher-level semblance, a refractive dissonance is opened up. In focusing its efforts on representing this caesura, genuine criticism in turn deepens the refractive violence, performing a destructive or mortuary act of self-annihilation upon the work, in order to expiate it from the fatal moment of guilt. Art, at the very limit of its mimetic capacity, draws attention to its construction and in doing so finds the resources to encapsulate truth's secret.

As a consequence, the work itself becomes a torso of a symbol of Goethe's life, preventing the mythological act of closure around the figure of the heroic genius, and the unity of Goethe's life is prevented from becoming a historical sign of the Age of Goethe itself (neither the triumph of the Enlightenment nor the counter-Enlightenment, neither the age of romanticism nor of Weimar Classicism). With the expressionlessness of this pure word – the sentiment of hope – Goethe succeeds in approaching the Adamic act of naming. Just as the task of the translator is to liberate the pure language imprisoned within the work by enabling such language to represent itself by turning its symbolizing capacity into that which is symbolized, here the symbolizing capacity of language becomes symbolized through a critical violence.

In doing so, the artistic and historical necessity apparent in the work is opened up once more to its own critical moment of contingency, a moment that pertains to both the origin of the work and of the criticism to which it is related. For where else is the rising and falling, the becoming and passing away of hope located, if not in the abyssal depths of what Kant and Cohen defined as intelligible contingency: the ephemerality of natural perishing – the glimmer only discernible in the twilight – becomes in Benjamin's reading the ground of the most radical metaphysical hope for reconciliation, the pure light of the new morning. As Benjamin comments, 'It could not be said any more clearly that the last hope is never such to him who cherishes it but is the last only to those for whom it is cherished.'[62] The most paradoxical but therefore richest and most extreme hope, in other words, never belongs to the one who can still hope (whose position is therefore not hopeless) but only to those incapable of hoping, the hopeless ones: the dead.

In Benjamin's essay on Goethe's *Elective Affinities*, a theological concept of reconciliation is discovered in the work's expressionless moment, in which mere aesthetic symbolization – the unity of life and work itself – reaches its limit and in doing so comes to symbolize its own process of symbolization as the torso of the symbol. This Goethean modification of the Romantic fragment preserves and deepens the central antinomy of 'The Concept of

Criticism' between the Goethean torso and the Romantic fragment. 'Goethe's work', Caygill therefore argues, 'challenges the assumption that the symbolic is the only relationship conceivable between truth and material contents': as a 'torso of a symbol' or 'the symbolic relationship subject to time', the work is 'torn between the claims of finite and infinite experience', expressing the philosophical 'secret' of 'the inexpressible presence of death in life which is *marked* by beauty'.[63]

This recovery of a concept of allegorical experience from the history of seventeenth-century *Trauerspiel* in terms amenable for that of twentieth-century modernity justifies the theoretical formulations in the 'Epistemo-Critical Prologue', which are directed at a transdisciplinary overcoming of the methodological one-sidedness of the existing disciplines of the philosophy of literature and the history of literature. Influenced by Heinrich Wölfflin, Alois Riegl and Hans Sedlmayr, Benjamin claims that the emergence of the academic discipline of 'literary studies' in the eighteenth century remained isolated from the older theological and philosophical traditions of history, rendering it amenable to the positivist approach of the natural sciences, while also accounting for its misunderstanding of the symbol and allegory discussed earlier.[64]

As a result of this integration, a dual epistemology tended to emerge: a regulative metaphysics of historical progress (produced through the 'values' of Kant's transcendental idealism and coded, via the Enlightenment, into contemporary conceptions of modernity) and an empirically realist attention to the correctness of past historical 'facts' whose meaning is construed as something singular, constituted and completed. Benjamin's philosophically informed theory of literary criticism is directed against both aspects of this inadequate conception of history. This transdisciplinary aspect of Benjamin's thesis may partially account for the difficulties in its reception at the University of Frankfurt, where the thesis was rejected by the departments of both philosophy and literature.

Benjamin advocates that literary history begins from 'a dignified, serious and ambitious conception of history (pragmatic history, in short) of which the methodological distinctions between written and oral sources' – a distinction central to the tradition of biblical hermeneutics, for example – 'forms an integral part'.[65] This would be guided by the kind of 'pedagogical task' – equivalent to that which continues to inform the *Arcade Project*'s aim to 'educate the image-making medium within us'[66] – envisaged by the historian Georg Gottfried Gervinus in the nineteenth century, whose literary-historical pragmatism is singled out by Benjamin as an exception to this impoverishment. Although Gervinus's 'brilliant but methodologically naïve works' were unable to clarify the 'true relationship between literature and history – let alone ... between history and literary history', he was the first to explicitly raise this relationship as a problem.[67] Gervinus condemned the 'usual, spiritless *Faktensammler*, who merely puts things together like a chronicler', on the grounds that all 'the forces of mankind concentrate on action' and the 'active life ... is the focus of all history'.[68] According to what Gervinus called his 'literary-historical pragmatism', the task of the true historian is to guide and instruct, through the construction of historical examples that compel to action.

Any 'effective physiognomic definition' of the uniqueness of the particular work therefore requires, Benjamin suggests, the decomposition of 'the rigid partitions between the disciplines that typified the concept of the sciences in the nineteenth century'.[69] This structural antithesis between the philosophy and history of art reflects that between natural philosophy and natural history in Goethe's own morphological writings, and Benjamin's efforts should be understood as the foundation of a modern comparative criticism in line with Goethe's own morphological comparative anatomy. Philosophical history, as the science of the origin, involves a contemplation of the 'original phenomenon [*Ursprungsphänomen*]' through the inner history of the 'life of the works and forms'.[70] This historical concept of *Ursprung* must be distinguished from the merely genetic process by which the existent comes into being, and so cannot be revealed in the naked and manifest existence of the factual, since its revelation must be capable of doing justice to the essence of truth as a secret: as that which is hidden out of necessity and would be destroyed by any attempt to expose it immediately in its nakedness, but also from any timeless and 'purely logical category'. The importance attached to the Goethean 'Ideal' as a literary Absolute in the afterword to the essay on German Romanticism is developed in the Prologue in the context of Goethe's scientific theory of the *Urphänomen*, and it is in relation to this that Benjamin develops his own concept of *Ursprungsphänomen*.

This 'natural history' of works surveys not only the actual phenomena of a given period but also their subsequent development in the understanding of later epochs, including apparent excesses of development (*Entwicklung*), and so as something subject to a process of becoming and passing away (*Werden und Vergehen Entspringendes*), and therefore only ever partial and incomplete (*Unvollendetes, Unabgeschlossenes*).[71] The Idea does not abstract something common or construct a unity out of a sequence of historical formulations but absorbs them to become a totality as something redeemed: it establishes the becoming of phenomena in its monadological being or essence. Criticism attempts to reassemble virtually the fore- and after-history (*Vor- und Nachgeschichte*) of the phenomena into a historical constellation, which reveals the configuration of the idea in the remotest extremes. This virtual exploration of the whole possible inner range of extremes represents the mapping of its contingency.

The precedents for this formulation are first described in 'The Concept of Criticism' as that 'determination of the form in which an idea will constantly confront the historical world, until it is revealed fulfilled, in the totality of its history', and beyond this Schlegel's Goethean claim that the particular history of Greek art is the natural history of art in general and therefore a primal history of art.[72] The redeeming, messianic function – in the sense recovered from Early German Romanticism discussed in Chapter 2 – of criticism, in relation to the historical Absolute, is therefore charged with the task of grasping the whole within the archetypal particular, in the sense recovered from Goethe: the whole of history in the archetypal epoch, the whole of the epoch in the archetypal life, the whole life in the archetypal work and the whole work in the caesura of the expressionless.

This is to be understood in terms of a historical relation between the 'what-has-been' and the 'now of recognisability [*das Jetzt der Erkennbarkeit*]', which 'bears to the highest degree the imprint of the perilous critical moment on which all reading is founded'.[73] Benjamin defines this as an 'historical index', which determines how they 'attain to recognisability only at a particular time'. The mediated expressiveness of this 'now' is anticipated in an earlier fragment from 1920–1, where the truth which 'belongs in one sense or another to the perfected state of the world' is also said to reside 'in the "now of recognizability"', described as a 'medium' or a 'nexus between existing things and also with the perfected state of the world'.[74] Benjamin is clear, however, that things can enter in such a nexus only in a disjointed and broken state as what he there calls 'symbolic concepts' or 'primal phenomenon'. Nonetheless, the truth of the perfected state of the world identified with messianic fulfilment is manifested only as something 'erratic, disconnected, utterly unknowable'. What he there calls the logical time of this medium of historical recognition is therefore articulated according to this refractive dialectic of incompletion and completion: a historical conjuncture that registers the immanent possibility of its own disappearance, forgetting and passing; the aporetic presence of fulfilment which is gestured towards in the shattered symbol. To the extent that a transdisciplinary literary criticism must be informed by philosophical history, Benjamin's philosophical history bears the traces of a literary, indeed linguistically expressionist, conception of history.

Expressionist language (II): T. E. Hulme's Imagist poetry

Benjamin's suggestion of an underlying affinity between the allegorical worldview of the seventeenth-century Baroque and that of early-twentieth-century literary Expressionism, mediated in the preceding discussion by his criticism of Goethe's *Elective Affinities*, can now provide the transcritical perspective for a genealogy of modernism in the work of a British poet unknown to Benjamin: the founder of the Imagist movement, T. E. Hulme. Hulme, described as 'one of the most important conduits for modern thought in the pre-1914 phase of a barely emergent British modernism',[75] developed a theory of modern literature that bears a number of striking theoretical affinities with those of nascent German Expressionism as well as Benjamin's theories of baroque allegorical expression. Significantly, the genesis of these ideas concerning modernism, which are themselves staged in public cafes, salons and journals of England, Canada, Brussels, France and Germany,[76] can be traced through Hulme's transcritical oscillations between romanticism and classicism.

Hulme describes the ideas proposed in his 'Modern Art and Its Philosophy' as 'formulated quite independently' from, but nonetheless 'practically an abstract' of, the views of Wilhelm Worringer, whose *Abstraction and Empathy* produced a considerable impact on the nascent Expressionism of Klee and *Der Blaue Reiter* group, discussed in the previous chapter, as well as that of *Die Brücke*. Hulme had first encountered Worringer's ideas, as well as those of Alois Riegl, in an article by the writer Paul Ernst, whose neo-classical rejection of naturalism in the early 1900s helped clear a way for Expressionist experimentation that was to come.[77] Hulme had also become briefly immersed in the Expressionist scene during his stay in Berlin in 1912 and 1913, although he is ambiguous about the poetry itself. Describing the performances and poetry of Kurt Hiller, Ernst Blass, Elsa Lasker Schuler, Georg Heym and others, Hulme emphasizes their linguistic experimentation with 'short sentences ... sometimes so terse and elliptical as to produce a blunt and jerky effect ... sometimes so abrupt that the prose ... almost resembles Futurist verse.'[78]

Worringer, influenced by the aesthetics of Kant, Schopenhauer and Riegl, had proposed an antithesis in the history of art between a largely Western subjectivism, centred on a will to empathy and the naturalistic imitation of the beauty of the organic, and an objectivism, centred on a will to abstraction and the non-naturalistic beauty of the life-denying inorganic, manifested in that 'vast complex of works of art that pass beyond the narrow framework of Graeco-Roman and modern Occidental art', such as Egyptian, Byzantine, Asian art and the European art of Late Antiquity.[79] The psychological conditions of the urge to abstraction reside in a 'spiritual dread of space', related to an 'instinct for the relativity of all that is ... the entangled inter-relationship and flux of the phenomena of the outer world', that lead to an urge to 'wrest the object of the external world out of its natural context, out of the unending flux of being, to purify it of all its dependence upon life, i.e. of everything about it that was arbitrary, to render it necessary and irrefragable, to approximate it to its absolute value.'[80]

Hulme compares the shift in perspective made possible by Worringer's work to a Copernican revolution: Worringer's introduction of the alternative perspective of abstraction, largely occluded from Western art since the Renaissance, enables Western critics to appreciate Egyptian, Indian, Byzantine, Polynesian and African work not as archaeology or ethnology but as art and, because of this, forces them to see the unity of European art as 'a coherent body of work resting on certain presuppositions, of which we become conscious for the first time when we see them denied by other periods of art.'[81]

Influenced by Worringer, 'Modern Art and Its Philosophy' claims that the post-Impressionism of Gauguin, the late Cézanne, Jacob Epstein and Wyndham Lewis demonstrate a similar attempt to find a new mode of expression in order to 'make of impressionism', concerned precisely with capturing temporal flux of phenomena, 'something solid and durable like old art'.[82]

In his 'Lecture on Modern Poetry' from 1908, Hulme had already associated the desire of painters such as Whistler to 'fix an impression rather than narrate a story' with a modern trend away from the construction of absolute truth and towards the 'maximum of individual and personal expression … and communication of momentary phrases in the poet's mind'.[83] This is said to necessitate a poetic emancipation from 'the moulds which language and ordinary perception force on him and … to see things as they really are', including the particularity of one's own emotional response to things, and so utilizes language to express more than ordinary perception and 'the lowest common denominator of the emotions'.[84] Hulme's concern, in the essays quoted, with a superior expression of the impression reflects a constellation of what Mary Ann Gillies characterizes as the opposing forces of Henri Bergson's romantic intuitionism and Worringer's classical abstraction 'at work within Hulme's construction of the image'.[85]

Hulme, Joseph Frank argues, was one of the first to realize the implications of Worringer's ideas for modern European literature.[86] In his earlier writing, Hulme emphasizes Maurice Denis's description of the post-Impressionists as 'classical in the sense that they were trying to impose the same order on the mere flux of new material provided by the impressionists movement',[87] anticipating T. S. Eliot's defense of Joyce's *Ulysses* as 'manipulating a continuous parallel between contemporaneity and antiquity … [as a] way of controlling, of ordering, of giving a shape and a significance to the immense panorama of futility and anarchy which is contemporary history' and thereby making the 'modern world possible for art'.[88] For Hulme, this 'new attitude' in 'comparison with the flat and insipid optimism of the belief in progress … may be in a certain sense inhuman, pessimistic'.[89]

But Hulme's interest in Expressionism provides the theoretical conduit for a deeper underlying pessimism that, as Miriam Hansen points out, describes an underlying allegorical worldview resonating with the conservative revolutionary one of Benjamin's own thought.[90] This is evident in the 'fragmentary and emblematic tendencies of his antisymbolic turn' in poetry, which emphasizes the building up of a solid vision through 'a deliberate choosing and working-up of analogies',[91] the way the 'shocking, the sudden and the exhausting succession of images' emphasizes the 'accident and contingent' and 'ephemeral, artificial character of poetic vision'.[92] This melancholic sensibility is reflected in the fragmented, discontinuous form of his theoretical writing and its mode of thinking too: the use of startling analogies – reality is cinders, appearance organizes the world like a lady's ball-dress, language is a gossamer web or counters on a chess-board – and allegorical figures (Aphra as the planned allegorical hero of cinder theory), its expressive use of landscape-thinking to fix and communicate internal ideas, emotions and states spatially (Oxford Street in London at 2 a.m., the Rue de la limite in Brussels, a young girl dancing, descending in a tube lift, the last bus) and Hulme's 'propensity for direct action and his frank espousal of sensual immediacy'.[93]

The inhumanism and pessimism of Hulme's allegorical worldview is evident in *Cinders*, sketched during his travels working as a labourer in Canada in 1906–7 and posthumously published in 1922/4. At its core, *Cinders* concerns the 'peculiar quality of feeling' Hulme experienced contemplating 'the flat spaces and wide horizons of the virgin prairie of western Canada', where he was struck by the sense of 'man's cosmic insignificance': a realization of the incomprehensibility of the landscape 'on any single theory' that led to the urge to philosophize a 'cinder theory' and to formulate an imagistic poetry capable of expressing such a feeling.[94] It is Hulme's travels that provided his 'education in cinders', he writes, for only when we see 'these different manifestations of the cinders' can we 'work the extended clay'.[95] Similarly, Hulme's experience of learning other languages and teaching English as a foreign language taught him to adopt the transcritical perspective of 'adapt[ing the] same method to English' in reading, copying out and learning phrases in order to have all possibilities at the tips of his fingers.[96]

If Hulme had been inspired to philosophy and poetry by the wastelands of Canada, the feeling of humanity's cosmic insignificance is deeply reflected in the fragmentary form and bleak vision of *Cinders*: Hulme writes of how 'a melancholy spirit, the mind like a great desert lifeless, and the sound of march music in the street, passes like a wave over that desert, unifies it, but then goes'.[97] Edward Comentale has identified Hulme's profound sense of sadness and loss as 'a way of relating to the world' that reveals the self in relation to its environment, producing a basis for sensual as well as ethical judgement of value, one that has been aligned with the significant influence of a Nietzschean anti-humanism underlying his worldview.[98] Significantly, in this context and in relation to those aspects of Nietzsche's thought influenced by a Goethean conception of nature discussed in the preceding chapters, Hulme's cinder theory views the 'unity of Nature' as 'an extremely artificial and fragile bridge', 'the world ... a plurality' with no fundamental unity, common purpose or comprehensive organizational scheme and whose absolute reality 'consists in the nature of an ... ash-pit of cinders': an imperfect, unheroic, unhappy, bad, chaotic, cold, sick, disgusting, bored, primeval and indescribable infinitude of contingent plurality into which all life decomposes (Hulme frequently employs negative analogies tied to the waste products of organic matter: ash, mud, grit, dust, faeces and drains).[99]

'Only in the fact of consciousness is there a unity in the world', and this comprises of artificially constructing an organized and ordered 'gossamer world of symbolic communication' that is 'woven between the real things'.[100] The values of the good, the true and the beautiful are therefore only pragmatic constructions of this finite, simple and ordered arrangement, 'artificially built up in and out of [the cinders], like oases in the desert, or as cheerful houses in the storm', but cannot be taken as themselves real. With regard to knowledge, there are no ultimate principles but 'an infinite of analogues, which help us along, and gives us a feeling of power over the chaos when we perceive them ... here is the land pre-eminently of shadows, fancies and analogies'.[101] With regard to beauty, Hulme insists that 'beauty does not exist by itself in nature, waiting to be copied' by the artist, but that it exists in nature only as 'organised pieces of cinders' and so it is art that creates beauty.[102] 'A judicious choice of illusions' is therefore 'the only means of happiness, e.g. the exhilaration of regarding life as a procession or a war'.[103]

The cosmic insignificance felt in Hulme's fundamental experience of the Canadian prairies is connected to Worringer's 'spiritual dread of space' because this aesthetic experience of nature, so intransigent to philosophical conceptualization or poetic expression, evades the conventional categories of modern European aesthetics evinced in Kant.[104] Hulme's experience perhaps comes closest to Kant's account of the 'insipid sadness' the Genevan scientist

Horace-Bénédict de Saussure felt in the Savoy mountains, which Kant associates with an 'interesting sadness ... inspired by a wasteland [*Einöde*] to which people would gladly transfer themselves so as to hear or find out no more about the world, which shows that such wastelands cannot, after all, be quite so inhospitable as to offer no more to human beings than a most troublesome abode'.[105] Kant distinguishes such misanthropy from the unsociability that results from a mania (*Wahnwitz*) of the imagination (*Einbildunskraft*) that, when 'unrestrained' by a 'deep-seated and brooding passion', attempts to positively exhibit the rational idea of freedom as a freedom from human society. The 'fantastical wish [*phantastische Wunsch*]' to sacrifice all social joys and live in isolation or as a small family in the wastelands of nature is, rather, connected to a disposition 'philanthropic enough as regards benevolence', and so unwilling to hate human society, 'but as the result of long and sad experience ... has veered far away from a liking for people'. This melancholic indifference to humanity is, perhaps, closer to Hulme's cindery aesthetics.[106]

There is, then, a rare and deep pessimism to Hulme's experience of nature's indifference to humanity, one that Elizabeth Kuhn associates with a dehumanized, impersonal sadness 'detached from an ... otherwise coherent subject' and that Miriam Hansen sees as degrading all poetic values, like all human values, as utterly accidental and contingent and yet therefore no less meaningless than any other activity and so curiously 'endowed with a transformative potential that promises "a different future"'.[107] Benjamin had likewise drawn attention to the semiotic temporality of the allegorical imagination by pointing out how the aesthetic experience of nature's eternal passing-away is connected to the punctual symbolic violence of eschatological redemption. The very contingency of the ephemeral, which induces such melancholic reflection, becomes the construction site for a – no less contingent – cosmic redemption.

In his earlier writings Hulme identifies the poetry produced by members of the Secession Club, including F. S. Flint and Ezra Pound, in terms of a classical reaction against a belated romanticism. He associates the latter with a belief in the infinite and unlimited possibilities of individual people, which corresponds to the implicit humanism of a 'spilt religion', because it 'mess[es] up, falsif[ies] and blur[s] the clear outlines of human experience' by extending transcendent concepts such as God and Heaven outside of their right and proper sphere and into that of the profane and finite world.[108] This, it should be recalled, is the same charge Benjamin levelled at German Romanticism and the Romantic theory of criticism. 'Classicism', in contrast, is a belief that the human is an 'extraordinarily … limited … finite and fixed creature', one that should not be equated with the secular worldview of materialism but of the religious attitude, which maintains the proper boundary between the profane world of creatures and the divine. Later Hulme will attempt to clearly separate the ontological discontinuity between the inorganic, organic and moral realms, whose blurring culminates in the political values of humanism and the aesthetic values of romanticism. This 'bad metaphysics' is exemplified for Hulme in the aesthetics of Ruskin, Coleridge and the German Romantics and their privileging of the solemnity of the imagination; Hulme's own aesthetic theory therefore sets out from an opposing principle of allegorical fancy.

For Coleridge, fancy, in contrast to the imagination and akin to the concepts of the understanding, does not create something new through synthesis but 'has no other counters to play with, but fixities and definites … like memory [it] receives all its materials ready made from the law of association' and brings together 'images dissimilar in the main by some one point or more of likeness'.[109] Just as the 'analytic, abstracting activity' of the understanding 'gives us the world of distinct entities … as "a heap of little things"' rather than 'a living divinely given unity', so fancy, Alan Gregory argues, permits human subjectivity to access itself only as a finite and objectified subject.[110] Fancy is therefore comparable to 'the Gorgon Head, which looked death into every thing'.[111] For this reason, Coleridge 'aligns *phantasia* or fancy with allegory' and argues that 'because allegory transforms persons into personifications and abstractions, it is antithetical to the transcendental imagination, which he allies with the symbol as the figure in which the particular and the universal are held to be "translucent" to each other'.[112]

In a series of challenging inversions of this viewpoint, Hulme's 'Romanticism and Classicism' describes modern verse as sculptural (a spatial, plastic image associated with the classicism of antiquity) rather than musical (a temporal, acoustic image associated with the modern poetry of romanticism) but compares symbolic metaphors ('the hill was clad with trees') to reflexes of mere 'convention' and privileges fresh allegorical images as more 'direct' and 'vital'. Classicism in verse is associated with the fixed, limited, finite, sincere, reserved and occasionally witty fancy of the literature of Horace, Shakespeare, Pope and Racine and with post-Impressionist art.

The invocation of fancy, in contrast to the imagination, indicates the aim of 'accurate, precise and definite description', which depends on 'the particular faculty of mind to see things as they really are, and apart from the conventional ways in which you have been trained to see them' (a pure perception that Hulme equates with the detached interest of Platonic contemplation and in accordance with the Kantian definition of aesthetic judgement) and 'the concentrated state of mind, the grip over oneself which is necessary in the actual expression of what one sees' (pure expression). This expression must hit upon a visual concrete or imagistic language using fresh and new but exact and precise epithets, metaphors and analogies to 'arrest' the reader and make them see.

Hulme's example, taken from the final two lines of Shakespeare's funeral dirge in *Cymbeline*, epitomizes the cindery worldview he recognized in classicism. Guiderius, unknowingly burying his own sister Imogen, sings:

Fear no more the heat o'th' sun,

Nor the furious winter's rages;

Thou thy worldly task hast done,

Home art gone and ta'en thy wages.

Golden lads and girls all must

As chimney-sweepers come to dust.

Hulme emphasizes the wit of the analogy, which punningly links the prosaic soot cleared by the young and poor chimney sweep with the biblical dust to which all bodies, even 'golden ones', must return. As Tom Sutcliffe so poetically puts it, the image also 'trembles between the botanical and the human', in its analogical association with the eventually dispersed heads of flowers.[113] Hulme also picks out the colloquial bathos of the word 'lads', which mirrors the earthly finitude emphasized in the analogy.

It is important to recognize that Hulme's description of classical verse as 'small', 'earthly and definite ... dry and hard' – as opposed to large, flying, vague, damp and flaccid romanticism – has been rightly associated, given his own insistence on bodily instincts, as sexualized and masculine, although his emphasis on dryness also resonates with the cinderiness of burnt embers and arid wastelands and, in association with hardness, even implies an ideal of renunciation ('the concentrated state of mind, the grip over oneself which is necessary').[114] It is also influenced by the proto-fascistic political theories of Maurras, Lasserre and *L'Action Francaise* that Hulme had become fascinated with in 1911.[115] Hulme's adoption of such a political ideal seems partly related to its pragmatic usefulness: as Hulme writes in 'Romanticism and Classicism' and in his introduction to Sorel's *Reflections on Violence*, also influential on Benjamin's notion of critical violence, it is primarily the liberal political ideology of progress and bourgeois social democracy that he opposes, along with a theological abhorrence towards the blurring of the profane and the transcendent demonstrated in humanism and romanticism.

If Hulme conceives history as a movement between these conflicting attitudes, he is also clear that the classical revival he anticipates 'will be different [from the classical] because it has passed through a romantic period' and so may not even be recognizable as classical'.[116] This post-romantic or modern classicism that Hulme associates with modern art is situated in the tension 'between these two' positions: it differs from 'the old classical view which is supposed to define it as lying in conformity with certain standard fixed forms' and from the 'romantic view which drags in the infinite'.[117] But as commentators have frequently pointed out, Hulme's thought is never fixed or stable but frequently and pragmatically oscillates between positions or between tensions within positions in order to delineate lines of attack as cultural guerilla warfare.

Even within the essay, Hulme's romantic Bergsonism returns in his appeal to Coleridge's concept of the 'vital' as an organic wholeness or synthesis that escapes the intellect but is grasped by the intuition of intensive multiplicities, a position that repeats the embrace of impressionism of his earlier 'Lecture on Modern Poetry' and that he later opposes (in his 'Modern Art and its Philosophy', where geometrical art is opposed to vital and organic art). Yet Hulme will later repudiate his classicism in his commitment to Worringer's account of abstraction. All of this indicates the centrality of romanticism to Hulme's own thought and the complexity of his embrace of the classical, not as a disposition but rather the pole of a necessary movement: a tension manifested in the modernism of Hulme's poetry.

Broadly speaking, there are several kinds of allegorical poems in Hulme's work. While poems such as 'Autumn', 'Above the Dock', 'The Man in the Crow's Nest', 'Susan Ann and Immortality', 'A Sudden Secret', 'Town Sky-line', 'As a Fowl' and 'The Sunset' are the products of fancy in the classical sense of using fresh, sometimes witty analogies to fix and express impressions, others such as 'A Tall Woman', 'A Sudden Secret', 'In the City Square', 'At Night!', 'Madman' and 'Autumn (II)' are more directly allegorical in the sense of seeking to personify abstract feelings and concepts such as love, sex, night and death.

Perhaps the most interesting of Hulme's poems are those, like 'A City Sunset', 'The Embankment', and 'Conversion', that are situated in a tense relationship to both romanticism and classicism, often linguistically dramatizing the oscillation between them within the course of the poem itself. An example of this shift can be discerned immanently within Hulme's 'A City Sunset' from 1908. The more traditional, incantatory use of metre and rhyme is exemplified in the opening three lines: 'Alluring, Earth seducing, with high conceits / is the sunset that reigns / at the end of westward streets.'[118] Here, the first three phrases (including the technical caesura between 'seducing' and 'with high conceits') each grow progressively longer in the number of syllables like the beating of an introductory fanfare, while the repetition of earthy vowels produces an intensity that is lifted towards the end of the line, with the silence of the caesura and alliteration of softer sounds reflecting the sublimation of earthly concerns with the romantic flight into the sky, as the gaze lifts in the second and third lines to the 'sunset that reigns [over] … westward streets'.

Both diction (alluring, conceits, reigns, jocund) and imagery (Cytherea, Lady Castlemaine) are self-consciously pretentious, forced by the adoption of the rhyme scheme: 'conceits/streets' and 'flaring sky/passer by'. Hulme's use of the verb 'reigns' also threatens to be an abstract linguistic 'counter': although the sun 'rules over' the city like a Queen with her 'high conceits', there is a danger the metaphor is passed over in thought without being visually imagined, not merely because it is familiar but also spatially and temporally imprecise, making it difficult to visualize the setting of the sun in these terms. The regal metaphor jars with and directly contradicts the, characteristically misogynistic, sexualized imagery of the mistress and the whore, who tempts the male gaze with her smooth flesh and trailing robes (Lady Castlemaine is not the Queen who reigns but the King's mistress who seduces).

Yet this apparently unstable decline within the imagery of the sunset – from ruler with monarchical power to mistress or maid ('heaven's jocund maid') with sexual power – reflects not merely the movement of the sun itself, which produces the poetic object that tempts the romantic poet, but dramatizes the subjective fall of poetic language within Hulme's verse. The romantic qualities of the first half of the poem, evident despite its irregular structure, give way to something more, even if not resolutely, classical in the second half, beginning with 'A frolic of crimson' that crystallizes the allegorical image of the setting sun as a 'maid', who in her linger vanity, trails her 'red robe / along the fretted city roofs'.

The metaphor 'fretted' is more successful here, capturing the rooftops in a process of being slowly worn down – physically and psychologically – by this movement of the light itself and so mirroring the anxiety of the 'homeward going crowds', troubled by this sudden and unexpected vision and either indifferent or provoked into resistance to its poetic allure. The anthropomorphized sunset in this and other poems represents the transitory, illusory and wistfully partial organization of cinders, 'seducing the poet into one of those moments of apparent insight that he both loves but knows will disappoint or merely distract', and so a promise of redemption to be embraced only with caution.[119] The oscillation between romanticism and classicism is particularly effective here precisely because the movement is embodied within the poem itself, leaving traces of the tensions and struggles within its own construction, signifying the conventions that appear as poetic temptations and dramatizing the resistance to these seductions.

There is a similar effect in Hulme's temptation to 'poetize' through moments of syntactic reversal in the opening lines of 'The Embankment' ('Once, in a finesse of fiddles found I ecstasy') and 'Conversion' (Light-hearted I walked into the valley wood'), which is never fully relinquished but comes to increasingly stand out against the content of the poems. Consequently, the decorative flurry of alliteration in 'The Embankment', which functions like the incantatory fanfare discussed at the beginning of 'The City Sunset', is a fitting introduction for the poet's ecstasy in the 'flash of gold heels' (or the 'sudden flaring sky'). But these give way to the spectator's distress and the plea to 'make small / The old star-eaten blanket of the sky, / That I may fold it round me'.[120]

The poet's 'ecstasy', evoked through the syntactical reversal, is not abandoned in the third line ('Now see I / That warmth's the very stuff of poesy') but dissolved in the smaller act of phonetic inversion, ensured by the caesura and line break: rather than reverting to the conventional syntax (Now I see), which would half-rhyme with the 'ecstasy', Hulme maintains the syntactic reversal in order to invert, or at least avoid, the potential rhyme. The poem calls attention to this with the unnecessary line break and enjambment, deferring the half-rhyme itself to the fourth line (ecstasy/poesy). Even as the alliteration fades away, the rhyme structure forestalled in the first half of the poem sporadically breaks out across the second half, with the rhyming of the third line's 'I' with 'sky', 'That I' and 'comfort lie' and the end and beginning of the final two lines and the fourth line's 'poesy' with 'round me' midway through the final line.

The desire to poetize the bodily warmth of a blanket, rather than the metallic flash of gold on the hard pavement or the shimmer of stars in the cold night sky, is matched by the shift within the poem from hard dissonance to comforting rhyme and a shift in perspective, from the downward gaze to the heels on the pavement of the past to the upward gaze from the same pavement to the sky in the present, produced by the punning literalization of the clichéd metaphor of the 'blanket of stars'. Even here, the desire to 'make small' the 'stuff of poesy' and bring the stars down to the earth is ultimately tinged with a cold sadness rather than comfortable warmth: the blanket of the sky is old and the light of the stars suggests it is decayed and riddled with holes – 'star-eaten' rather than 'moth-eaten'.

More dramatically, the 'scented cloth' of beauty cast over the poet in the valley wood of 'Conversion' is transformed into a stifling and suffocating net that leads to the poet's doom, the punishment for 'peeping' on this forbidden scene: 'Now pass I to the final river / Ignominiously, in a sack, without sound, / As any peeping Turk to the Bosphorus.' The irony of this poetic 'conversion' is that, despite the poem's lack of rhyming scheme or structure metre, the poet, described as 'pass[ing] … to the final river / … in a sack, without sound', still survives to give voice to their humiliating seduction.[121]

The downcast gaze of the melancholic in 'Susan Ann and Immortality' visualizes the earth as if a green sky, across which chestnut leaves seem to blow like brown clouds. If, momentarily, the earth itself seems to open itself up to a deeper vista, Hulme seems to resist this through a sudden reversal of anticipated meaning in the substituted homonym ('And brown clouds past', where we would be anticipating 'passed', switching the spatial movement for a temporal one) and inversion of imagery ('Til the earth was sky, / Sky that was green, / And brown clouds past, / Like chestnut leaves arching the ground').[122] Accepting the 'green sky' that is produced through the parallax between the real green earth and the imagined blue sky, we are thrown by the literal reference to 'brown clouds … Like chestnut leaves', where we are expecting the opposite. As with 'Embankment' and 'Conversion', Hulme dramatizes a dynamic movement between perspectives (present and past, high and low, literal and metaphorical, romantic and classical) that sometimes leads to a tenuous and temporary synthesis, one whose foregrounded process of construction reveals it to be artificial, but verges on the edge of a perspectival switch once more.

This movement of struggle is absent from the more classical moment of realized allegory in Hulme's other poems. Like the desire to 'make small … the stuff of poesy', 'Autumn' deals with the prosaic details of 'A touch of cold' (both a colloquial turn of phrase and the fanciful exactness, but not symbolic depth, of allegorical analogy: coldness is felt at the surface of the skin), the silent gesture of acknowledgement ('I did not stop to speak, but nodded') and the metaphorical reduction of the moon and stars into the 'red-faced farmer' and white-faced 'town children' (the latter are not raised to the heights of poetic grandeur through symbolism, nor is there any more symbolic depth to the simile than the expression of colour).[123] Similarly, in the 'quiet' of 'Above the Dock' the distant inspiration of the moon is brought closer as a forgotten 'child's balloon' that hangs, 'tangled in the tall mast's'.[124] Other analogies, such as that in 'The Man in the Crow's Nest', where the sound of the wind in the ship's rigging is 'like [the whistling of] a village boy / That trembling past the churchyard goes' are momentarily striking and witty but do not combine into the imaginative synthesis of a more profound image.[125]

If these poems are the 'fixing of an impression', in Hulme's definition, it is less the impressionistic snapshot of a frozen moment than the constructive process of repairing or mending, in which the impression at risk of crumbling away is held together by clamps or props or clad in scaffolding, which are semiotically assembled and dissembled before us. The impression is not, in this way, expressed as a lived moment but ephemeralized as a constructed artifice or convention. It is the labour of abstraction, to use Hulme's later term from Worringer, that is expressed in many of these poems and that stands in the background of those that appear as classically finished modernist verse.

6

Pure history: the untimeliness of technology

At the beginning of the 1920s Benjamin became immersed in what was planned as a large-scale study of political thought, of which only a few fragments and the 'Critique of Violence' remain. As Uwe Steiner notes, Benjamin's political thought during this period should be placed in, and ultimately differentiated from, 'the context of the Nietzsche-reception in the milieu of early Expressionism'.[1] One central source of such Expressionism in Benjamin's writing at this time was the literary and philosophical work of Salomo Friedländer, whose publications were influential in the literary Expressionism associated with the avant-garde journals *Der Sturm* and *Die Aktion* and on the Berlin Dadaist Raoul Hausmann and Hannah Höch.[2] Friedländer's major philosophical work, *Creative Indifference* (1918), was highly esteemed by Benjamin, and Steiner rightly draws attention to the 'immediate bond of affiliation' between this work and Benjamin's concept of the political, as well as to the significance of Friedländer's 1920 review of Ernst Bloch's *Spirit of Utopia*, especially in the centrality attached to the concept of the profane.[3]

Friedländer insists that 'the most general characteristic of any possible phenomenon is the distinction, that is, difference, which can go to extremes'.[4] This accords with the 'methodological extremism' of Benjamin's own epistemo-critical conception of truth in the book on *Trauerspiel*, indicating – as Brendan Moran's discussion of the influence of Friedländer on Benjamin demonstrates – a more immediate source of Benjamin's method than that of Carl Schmitt.[5] 'While Kant opened the path to insight into the conditions of the possibility of all experience', Steiner writes, 'Friedländer went one step further' in contending that 'thought and volition must be conceptualized by an indifference prior to all polarity and all partition into subject and object, a point that serves as a creative principle from which the I and the world first emerge'.[6] In terms that anticipate Karatani's transcritical development of Kant, as discussed in the first chapter of this book, Alice Lagaay has characterized this 'pure mediality [*reine Medialität*]' as a point of indifference, as the '"in between", the gap … or zone of indifferentiation … from which all polarity stems' referred to by Friedländer in places as '"the nought of world" or as the "absolute"'.[7] The resulting principle of creative will effectively reads Kant's transcendental idealism through the Nietzschean lens of Friedländer's earlier philosophy, much as Deleuze's transcendental empiricism, with its attempt to insert Nietzsche's genealogical philosophizing of forces into the history of Kantianism, regards experience itself as productive of subjectivity. The preceding chapters have argued for a Goethean undercurrent to such an empiricism, and Thomas O. Haakenson has similarly noted the centrality of Goethe's natural philosophy to Friedländer's work, a centrality that helps explain Benjamin's receptivity to *Creative Indifference*. In 'Modern Victory of Goethe's Theory of Colours', for example, Friedländer concurs with Goethe that 'colours differentiate themselves not through the Newtonian tendency toward the ordering of waves but, on the contrary, only through a cyclical index of tensions … Polarity is a constitutive phenomenon'.[8] Friedländer's 'unique relationship to Goethe's work', Haakenson argues, expanded the latter's polar understanding of colour into a more general philosophy of experience.[9]

As suggested in the previous chapters, Benjamin's own concept of experience is informed in a comparable way by a Goethean understanding of a productive polarity of tensions. Writing of the *historical* experience of the Soviet Union in the late 1920s, for example, Benjamin emphasizes the utter contingency of the political situation, claiming that 'in schematic form, Moscow… reveals the full range of possibilities: above all, the possibility of the revolution's utter failure and of its success', and noting that it is 'impossible to predict what the upshot of all this will be … Perhaps a true socialist community, perhaps something entirely different'.[10] His article for the German journal *Die Kreatur* therefore sought to represent this experience by depicting the moment of historical contingency through an image of Moscow.

Whereas Kant had sought to grasp the French Revolution as a historical sign of an Idea of inexorable moral progress, Benjamin presents the contingency of Russian Revolution through an everyday image of the city and its people. To do so he must seize and comprehend the 'very new and disorientating language that loudly echoes through the acoustic mask of an entirely transformed environment'.[11] This creatural language must be allowed to 'speak for itself', Benjamin explains in the letter to Martin Buber, for it cannot be theoretically articulated. The article would therefore be 'a picture of the city of Moscow as it is at this very moment. In this picture "all factuality is already theory" and therefore it refrains from any deductive abstraction, any prognostication, and, within certain bounds, even any judgement'. This formulation takes up Goethe's description of a tender empiricism which seeks a higher standpoint through the construction of the *Urphänomen*.

In Convolute N of the *Arcades Project* this identity between the Goethean methodology of tender empiricism and the judgement of historical criticism is explicit: the 'origin [*Ursprung*] of the forms and mutations of the Paris arcades from their beginning to their decline' are to be located in 'economic facts', but these economic facts are not to be grasped 'from the standpoint of causality … and that means considered as causes'.[12] These forces are instead to be constructed in terms of the 'primal phenomenon [*Urphänomen*]' of history 'insofar as in their own individual development – "unfolding" might be a better term – they give rise to the whole series of the arcade's concrete historical forms, just as the leaf unfolds from itself all the riches of the empirical world of plants'. Benjamin therefore sought to grasp the ascent and decline of the Paris arcades as a 'primal history' of modernity itself, according to a Goethean conception of the arcade's concrete historical forms as primal phenomena (*Urphänomen*) which render perceptible their immanent economic forces. Benjamin later claims that this view of history begins with Goethe and understands his own concept of the original phenomenon (*Ursprungsphänomen*) as a transposition of the truth of the primal phenomenon (*Urphänomen*) 'from the pagan context of nature … into the Jewish context of history'.[13]

Goethe's untimeliness: Nietzsche, Koselleck and Benjamin

Nietzsche makes a comparable suggestion, but without reference to the Judaic conception of justice, in a comment from his notebooks from around 1872, within a series of notes related to themes taken up in the *Untimely Meditations* begun in 1873: 'The meaning of *history*: a metamorphosis of plants'.[14] As the editor of the *Unpublished Writings* notes, Nietzsche similarly proposes 'transferring Goethe's biological model to the realm of history'.[15] In this context, Diane Morgan has argued that Goethe's methodological approach to nature, as discussed in the previous chapters, shifts from the question of 'why' or 'to what purpose?' to that of 'how' or the interrelatedness between living forms. Similarly, in an 1831 letter to Zelter, Morgan points out, 'Goethe explains that his interest in Niebuhr's history books on the Romans and their agricultural laws lies not ... in the "what" ... but in the "how" ... the historian himself and *how* he operates ... Here Goethe displays a free relation to the past and a wish to find methods to live productively by.'[16]

Goethe's pragmatic conception of life against the objectivity of scientific knowledge figures in Nietzsche's own reflections on 'The Advantage and Disadvantage of History for Life' in his *Untimely Meditations*. There, Nietzsche protests against the 'historical education of modern people' that has in part sprung from Hegelian philosophy and proceeds instead from Goethe's words that we must 'hate everything that merely instructs ... without augmenting or directly invigorating ... activity' and so judges the worth or worthlessness of history not on the basis of a science of history but, as with Benjamin's admiration for Gervinus, on the pragmatic value it serves for living and acting.[17] For Goethe, the one who acts is always without a conscience and so, Nietzsche argues, unhistorical, in that he is 'always without knowledge', for 'he forgets most things so as to do one thing'.[18]

Reinhard Koselleck's concern with 'the way Goethe experienced, lived, and conceptualized "history"' is focused on the latter's untimeliness in contrast to a contemporary preoccupation with theories of world history that emerge during this period.[19] Koselleck argues that, since the emergence of the Enlightenment, history has become 'codified ... teleologically' as 'an agent of higher necessity that could redeem the different hope and desires' of whatever social or political narrative was at stake: 'the present day as a necessarily transitional phase on the way to a better future'.[20] If Goethe's mistrust of 'the voice of the majority' appears as 'conservative, anti-revolutionary, anti-patriotic', Koselleck argues, his 'language produced a surplus value that cannot be exhausted by any one exegesis' and so produced an untimeliness that 'evaded all such reductive operations'.[21] In contrast to the traditional view, Koselleck sees this activity of 'self-historicization' or 'self-formation [*Bildung*]', captured in Goethe's 'seemingly paradoxical formulation of "self-conditions [*Sichbedingen*]"', not as 'any kind of hidden or withheld inwardness' but as the integration of the conditions of the historical world into his life and its externalization in literary form.[22]

The 'attempt to co-opt [Goethe] in the name of "history"', Koselleck writes, is prevented by 'what we might *ex post* call Goethe's epistemology', which, as we have seen, was 'guided by pairs of opposing concepts and categories' that always stood in a relation of exchange to each other.[23] He neither fully rejects nor fully embraces the 'idea of relative religious progress leading to spiritualization', stressing instead the opposed concept of regression and the 'simultaneity' of the sedimented experiences of the ever-present pre-givens (*Vorgaben*) of classical polytheism and pantheism, alongside the monotheism that continued to inform, in an aestheticized way, romanticism.[24] 'Through their formal structure', Koselleck argues, 'all such oppositional pairs make a metahistorical claim, for they precede concrete particular histories, while at the same time being inextricably linked back to human nature'. Consequently, Goethe 'never addressed questions of [historical] method in an isolated way' but embedded them alongside the 'anthropological paradigms' of historical experience, juxtaposing the authority of past facts and the meaningful experiences of the present, and born of the 'foundational hermeneutical experience' that 'because new situations raise new questions', 'every recorded, written, and spoken word changes its meaning with time and needs'.[25]

If historical knowledge is attained by moving 'from sensuality through intuition to perception, from perception via the imagination to judgment and conviction', Goethe also recognized, Koselleck argues, 'that all knowledge was subject to perspectival refractions' – individual and generational – and that 'every gain accomplished by recollection thrives on forgetting: the same event sounds different in the evening than it did in the morning'.[26] 'Goethe's history of events remained open to the future', Koselleck elaborates, 'but its multi-layered conditions repeated themselves, overturned each other, again and again, without ever becoming timeless as a result. They bear witness to a different rhythm than what the events themselves can manifest'.[27] If, in this way, Goethe 'seeks to identify history's conditions of possibility', his concern with understanding 'the incommensurable of world history' entails that a 'purely chronological representation of true history remains impossible'.[28]

Goethe's structuralism utilizes multiple oppositional concepts in order to capture 'the combinational plurality of each historical situation' and 'describe ever-new constellations' of possible histories. For Morgan, the flipside of this Goethean untimeliness similarly involves an 'openness to radical change' and 'an affirmative, even empowering, intensification of what it might be to be a human being in this world' that is associated with the cosmopolitical, defined as 'the attempt to think the political in relation to the cosmos in a situation in which both the political and the cosmos have become plural rather than singular unified entities'.[29]

Nietzsche's transposition of Goethean empiricism from the realm of nature to that of history is distinct from that of Benjamin, however, to the extent it lacks the latter's Judaic reference to messianic redemption. Celebrating the fall of the Paris Commune of 1871, for example, Nietzsche declared himself against all such 'Franco-Jewish levelling' and 'the greedy instincts of the present [*Jetztzeit*]' and was particularly agitated by reports circulating in the European press that the retreating Communards had torched the Louvre.[30] The anti-egalitarian view of culture put forward in 'The Greek State' is formulated against the backdrop of these events:

> Slavery belongs to the essence of a culture … The misery of men living a life of toil has to be increased to make the production of the world of art possible for a small number of Olympian men … Therefore, we may compare the magnificent culture to a victor dripping with blood, who, in his triumphal procession, drags the vanquished along, chained to his carriage as slaves.[31]

For Nietzsche, Goethe is the great exemplar of Olympian individualism – the only European who experienced the egalitarianism of the French Revolution with nausea and the precursor of what, in his later writings, he will define as the *Übermensch*: 'A strong highly-cultured human being … What he aspired to was totality … he disciplined himself to a whole, he created himself'.[32] Similarly, justice is to be desired not 'as cold, ineffectual knowledge, but as a regulating and punishing judge … truth as the Last Judgment … the unconditional … pure will to justice'.[33] Because 'the doctrines of sovereign becoming, of the fluidity of all concepts, types and species, of the lack of any cardinal distinction between man and animal' are 'true but deadly', they require the suprahistorical and eternalizing power of art and religion.[34]

Benjamin, in contrast, retained Nietzsche's critical suspicion towards modern bourgeois culture and its ideological values, but his concept of history is oriented towards a Judaic remembrance of the oppressed and a Marxist overcoming of the oppressive material conditions of existing cultural production and reproduction. In opposition to any Zarathustran politics of the *Übermensch*, which Benjamin reads as 'the most radical and most magnificent realization of the religious essence of capitalism', he constructs his own 'definition of politics' as 'the satisfaction of unenhanced humanness'.[35]

In the famous lines from the late theses 'On the Concept of History', Benjamin does not object to or criticize Nietzsche's conception of slavery as essential to culture, as claimed in 'The Greek State', but draws the opposite political conclusion from it:

> Whoever has emerged victorious participates to this day in the triumphal procession in which the present rulers step over those who are lying prostrate. According to traditional practice, the spoils are carried along in the procession. They are called cultural treasures, and a historical materialist … cannot contemplate [them] without horror. They owe their existence not only to the efforts of the great minds and talents who have created them, but also to the anonymous toil of their contemporaries. There is no document of civilization which is not at the same time a document of barbarism.[36]

This approach provides Benjamin with a catastrophic vision of history redeemable by a recuperation of the very revolutionary *Jetztzeit* that Nietzsche identified with the 'Franco-Jewish levelling' of the Communards: the placing of Goethe's pagan conception of nature into a Judaic concept of history.

Although Koselleck does not mention Benjamin's biography of Goethe, written for the Great Soviet Encyclopaedia but published in a shortened version in *Die literarische Welt* in 1928, a similar construction appears there. Writing in his *Moscow Diary* about a meeting with a representative of the Encyclopaedia, Benjamin recalls how the orthodox materialist depiction sought by the editors recommended a 'biographical portrait against a sociological background'.[37] Contrary to this, Benjamin argues that 'an artist's existence and even his purely temporal oeuvre can offer no object whatsoever for materialist analysis' if 'abstract[ed] from its posterity' and its 'historical after-effects'. In tracing the after-history of reception and scholarship, Benjamin notes how

Goethe declined to 'enjoy anything like the success that his genius merited' in his own time and that his later prestige only grew with the rise of German imperialism. Goethe therefore gave 'the contents [*Gehalte*] that fulfilled him the form which has enabled them to resist their dissolution at the hands of the bourgeoisie – a resistance made possible because they remained without effect and not because they could be deformed or trivialized'.[38]

Benjamin insists that 'Goethe could understand the past, history, only to the extent to which he could integrate it into his life'.[39] Benjamin characterizes such a life as that of the cultural representative and eventually great critic of the ascent of the German bourgeoisie. Hence, while Goethe 'founded a great literature among' the bourgeoisie, 'he did so with face averted' and his 'whole work abounds in reservations about them'.[40] While Goethe was unable to express this reaction other than 'from within the framework of an idealized feudal state', 'the bourgeoisie has never been able to make more than a limited use of his genius, to say nothing of how far they have understood his intentions'.[41] Benjamin describes *Elective Affinities* as 'giving a critical view' of the European nobility's 'mode of life', tracing the disintegration of the family within the aristocracy as 'a feudal society … restored to its primordial state' by the 'magical forces of fate'.[42]

Such a perspective reiterates a position on the greatness or historical significance of writers presented to the Austrian playwright Bernhard Reich and recalled in Benjamin's *Moscow Diary*. Reflecting on 'the specific structure of "greatness"', Benjamin argues that whereas average authors are measured by their success, 'great' writers are those whose effect is historical, but who, conversely, had no effect on history through their literary powers.[43] The paradoxically 'historical' character of this effect is described in the essay on Fuchs, where the 'effect that the work of art has on us today' is said to depend 'on an encounter not just with the work of art alone but with the history which has allowed the work to come down to our own age'.[44] As a consequence, 'historical "understanding" is to be grasped, in principle, as an afterlife of that which is understood; and what has been recognized in the analysis of the "afterlife of works," in the analysis of "fame," is therefore to be considered as the foundation of history in general'.[45]

In a note on criticism from 1930, Benjamin writes that his account of 'the theory of the survival of works' is 'closely linked both to the fact that works cannot be judged, and to the strategically judging stance of criticism', adding that 'the whole critique of materialist literary criticism turns on the argument that it lacks a "magical", non-judging side – that it always (or almost always) gets to the bottom of the mystery'.[46] Against such criticism, Benjamin attempts to develop the non-judging element, retaining the expressionless mystery of the work's truth content by refusing to reduce it to an expression of its historical genesis. If we take seriously his claim, made in the essay 'Eduard Fuchs, Collector and Historian', that 'the beginnings of any consideration of history worthy of being called dialectical' – dialectical in a way that, as previously suggested, differs significantly from that of Hegel – reside in a 'characteristically veiled' comment made by Goethe ('Everything that has had a great effect can really no longer be judged'), we can recognize this as a reference to what Benjamin calls the aporetic element of semblance operating in the beautiful in relation to history.[47]

Benjamin's recovery of a transdisciplinary concept of criticism from within Kant's philosophy is connected, the first chapter argued, to a crisis of literature and an accompanying crisis of judgement that was initiated by the growth of journalistic criticism within the public sphere, associated by Nietzsche with the problems of an ephemeral politicality and a levelling of distinctions. For Benjamin, that which judgement refers to in the work 'cannot be found in the work [itself]', he argues, and therefore cannot itself be judged. Instead, it 'gleans what earlier generations admired in it'.[48] To be 'moved' by this semblance, in the judgement of beauty, for example, 'means *ad plures ire* [to join the many], as the Romans called dying'. The contingency of the work means this allusion is not simply a metaphor of the public or the masses for Benjamin, because this conception of the historical experience of the object includes with it a reflection upon the survival of the creation not only beyond that of its creator, but also beyond that of every particular reception of the work. At the same time, it is this reception that transforms and thereby destroys the very object being judged. This registers the impossibility of any judgement of the historical object in itself and the necessity for criticism to grasp the work's contingency according to an image of its essence as a historical index.

Benjamin's concern to rescue the contingency of the particular as contingent therefore leads him to integrate the concept of the torso associated with a Goethean theory of art – the impossible moment of negativity associated with the uncritizability of the work – *into* the Early German Romantic concept of criticizability. To the extent that Benjamin's concept of criticism is based upon the impossibility of any experience of the work as complete within a historical actuality, it retains this Goethean emphasis upon the problematic judgement of the object and the necessity of its semblance character.

Expressionist technology (I): Klages, Marx and the Soviet avant-garde

If, for Nietzsche, the meaning of historical untimeliness is encapsulated in Goethe's concept of nature, this is because 'Goethe understood the position of the human being in nature, and that of surrounding nature itself, to be more mysterious, enigmatic, and demonic than his contemporaries did'.[49] Benjamin also accuses Goethe of sharing this 'idea of the daemonic', which he had named 'after the example of the ancients and others who had perceived something similar'.[50] Goethe exhibits such a worldview when in his essay on Winckelmann, described as a 'thoroughly born pagan [*gründlich gebornen Heiden*]', he writes: 'One must persevere ... where destiny more than choice places ... to hold fast, relate everything to it; ... to do everything, renounce everything, and enduring everything.'[51] This accords with the 'common feature of all pagan vision ... the primacy of cult [*Kultus*] over teachings [*Lehre*]', Benjamin claims, for which the reconciliation with mythic powers cannot be obtained except through the constancy of sacrifice.[52]

As discussed in the previous chapter in relation to Benjamin's notion of critical violence, this leads to the Nietzschean conflation of character with a constantly recurring experience (*Erlenbis*), daemonically conceived as fate. The characteristic structure of myth is that of isolation from one's own bodily sensuality and the wider community, experienced as an impotence which appears as fate. Fate, for Benjamin, is the nexus of a natural guilt among the living into which humans fall 'when they turn their attention away from the human', their ethics to a supernatural life (*übernatürlichen Lebens*) and as a consequence succumb to the biopolitical power of 'natural life' that is in league with 'mere life [*bloßen Lebens*]'.[53] The 'divine [*Göttlichen*]', however 'does not ground life without truth, nor does it ground the rite [*Ritus*] without theology [*Theologie*]'.[54]

Goethe's mythical ambiguity between 'nature' and *Urphänomen* as 'true nature' leads to a 'formless panarchy of natural life' associated with the daemonic.[55] For Benjamin, the truth of nature 'must be rigorously distinguished from that [visible] nature on a conceptual level', which suggests the 'paradoxical resolution' that 'true, intuitable, *Urphänomenal* nature would become visible after the fashion of a likeness, not in the nature of the world but only in art, whereas in the nature of the world it would indeed be present but hidden (that is, overshadowed by what appears)'.[56] The intuition of primal images must therefore be located within the theory of art, such that archetypes are understood as residing 'in that sphere of art where art is not creation but nature'.[57]

Under the influence of Winckelmann's classicism, Goethe's aesthetics consequently offers 'reference to the criterion of certain prototypes [*Vorbild*]', specifically the 'sublime naturalism' of Greek plastic art (encapsulated, Benjamin says, in the anecdote concerning the sparrows alighting on the grapes painted by a Greek master, which Goethe mentions in 'On Truth and Verisimilitude in Art') but fails to provide any 'philosophical clarification of the problem of form' itself.[58] As a result, Goethe neglected the philosophical problem of the absolute form of art, investigated by romanticism, because he is unable to distinguish this from the presentational form of particulars works. In identifying the archetype (*Urbild*) with a genetically original, perfect and complete prototype (*Vorbild*), Goethe renounces thought by effectively denying the possibility of any positive moment in the judgement of particulars (which are always incomplete and imperfect in relation to the preexisting ideal) and therefore leaving the problem of absolute form unresolved. His understanding of form, as a result, is based upon the historically determined form of Greek plastic art, rather than any historical consideration of artistic form, which is generalized into a theory of 'style' that privileges 'representation of a typifying sort'.[59]

While in his early writings Benjamin criticizes Goethe for ambiguously conflating nature and art, in a 1928 review of Karl Blossfeldt's *Primal Forms [Urformen] of Art: Photographic Plant-Images*, he describes Blossfeldt's photographs of magnified plant organs as visions in which 'a geyser of new image-worlds hisses up at points in our existence where we would least have thought them imaginable'.[60] Blossfeldt's photographs therefore accord with that archetypal realm of art which, in his earlier criticism of Goethe, he described as 'sphere of art where art is not creation but nature'.[61] His 'Short History of Photography' the following year explicitly presents August Sanders's collection of social photography in *The Face of Our Time* as a tender empiricism, referencing Goethe's transdisciplinary description of his scientific approach as that of comparative anatomy: 'So it was quite in order for an observer like Döblin to have hit on precisely the scientific aspects of this work, commenting, "Just as there is comparative anatomy … so this photographer is doing comparative photography." '[62]

In a discussion of the *Critique of the Power of Judgement*, Howard Caygill argues that because of the 'historical limitations to his concept of technology', Kant recoiled from attributing any biological function to technology, which he 'still considered externally, as something that has motive but not formative power'.[63] As a consequence, Caygill claims, Kant was unable to fully think through the equivocation he discerned in the organistic character of living things and retreated from this insight to 'an extremely limited conception of the technic of nature as a regulative idea', leaving 'the source of organization or life inscrutable'. Yet Kant's reflections upon the causal reciprocity involved in natural purpose 'clearly points to a prosthetic negotiation between the inside and the outside of an organism', Caygill suggests, which threatened to turn the living thing into the 'ambiguous site of experience, both internal and external to mind and body'.

If Goethe's morphological writings share the historical limitations of Kant's concept of technology, his struggle to overcome the Kantian theory of experience leads him to conceptually anticipate the optical capacity of technology. In his scientific writings, Goethe assigns all sorts of visionary insights to the unaided human eye in scientific observation – insights which only find their true achievement in technology – while denying the most basic advantages of existing technology: 'The most disastrous aspect of modern physics: that experiments have been, as it were, segregated from the human factor and that nature is to be recognized only by the evidence of artificial' and 'microscopes and telescopes really only serve to the unaided human senses'.[64] As Benjamin became increasingly preoccupied and familiar with the use of technologically reproduced images in avant-garde art practices, he came to recognize and reassess this implicit feature of Goethe's work, and to reformulate his earlier rejection of Goethe's aesthetics of science.

This technological visualization puts into practice, as a 'second nature', the construction of primal phenomena that underwrites the tender empiricism of Goethe's scientific writing on biology, optics and colour, but which Goethe refuses in his confused conflation of the 'empirical nature' given to our sensual experiences and 'truth' immanent within it. Benjamin now offers a more nuanced description of such pure contents, insisting such forms are not merely 'originary forms of art' in the sense of mere models, but 'originary forms of nature … at work as originary forms in all that was created'.[65] Here, then, it is the technological form of photographs that 'reveal an entire, unsuspected horde of analogies and forms in the existence of plants', as 'inner image-imperatives [*Bildnotwendigkeiten*], which have the last word in all phases and stages of things conceived as metamorphoses'. In contrast to New Objectivity (*Neue Sachlichkeit*) in art, Benjamin insists, photography therefore represents a 'truly new objectivity', which is anticipated by the 'fraternal great spirits – sun-soaked eyes, like those of Goethe and Herder'.[66] He adds that 'this touches on the one of the deepest, most unfathomable forms of the creative, on the variant that was always, above all others, the form of genius, of the creative collective, and of nature … the fruitful, dialectical opposite of invention: the *Natura non facit saltus* of the ancients'.[67]

Here, then, the possible experience of a merely intuited 'true nature' is not restricted to the realm of art but granted to technology as a sphere capable of mediating the relationship between humanity and nature. In the final version of 'The Work of Art in the Age of Its Technological Reproducibility', dating from the last years of the 1930s, Benjamin characterizes this realm as 'another nature which speaks to the camera as compared to the eye', no longer informed by human consciousness but by the unconscious.[68] But even in the 'Outline of the Psychophysical Problem' from 1922–3, the claim that it is 'technology in which the unity of life is formed' suggests that while the realm of *Urphänomen* should not be directly conflated with the visible nature of phenomenon, it is nonetheless in the whole realm of 'second nature' and not merely that designated as art that the truth of nature may become perceptible for us.[69] It is by virtue of this material division and reorganization of the organic first nature through technology, Benjamin argues in the 'Outline of the Psychophysical Problem', that 'humanity is able partly to draw nature, the nonliving, plant, and animal, into this life of the body of mankind'.

The importance of the technological within Benjamin's understanding of history needs to be contextualized not just in relation to its contrast with the natural and not just solely in relation to its impact upon art but in relation to the biopolitical – and more specifically what Caygill draws out, in his discussion of prosthetics, as the biomechanical – and even further to what, in the earlier discussion of the influence of Goethe's philosophy of nature upon his conception of history, was termed the cosmopolitical. The tour of German inflation represented in *One-Way Street*'s 'Imperial Panorama' proclaims that 'mass instincts have become confused and estranged from life', producing a 'perversion of vital instincts', while the concluding visit 'To the Planetarium' singles out the 'dangerous error of modern humanity' as the devaluation of our communal cosmic experience (*kosmische Erfahrung*) – achieved by the ancients through ecstatic trance (*Rausch*) in which we are assured 'what is nearest to us and what is remotest from us' – to individual, poetic enthusiasm (*Schwärmerei*).[70] *Schwärmerei*, it should be recalled, is denounced by Kant as the delusional fanaticism of those who claim to be in supernatural communion with a higher nature and it is against such a metaphysical drive of reason itself to overstep its own bounds that Kant's critical philosophy is directed.[71]

As a result of this devaluation of communal cosmic experience, a 'new and unprecedented marriage with the cosmic powers' erupts in an uncontrollably destructive manner, 'on a planetary scale, that is, in the spirit of technology [*Geiste der Technik*]'. Simmel's anticipation of the slave revolt of technology, rather than of the proletariat, in *The Philosophy of Money*, is influential in Benjamin's description here. Simmel argues that 'if we consider the totality of life', the cost of the technological control of nature is a 'dispensing of spirituality as the central point of life', whose paradoxical implications are that 'the machine, which was supposed to relieve man from his slave labour in relation to nature, has itself forced him to become a slave to it … we serve it in so far as we dominate it'.[72] For Simmel, this implies that the 'significance and intellectual potential of modern life' has not been transferred from the individual to the masses, as erroneously thought, but rather from the subject to the object: the ' "revolt of the slaves" that threatens to dethrone the autocracy and the normative independence of strong individuals is not the revolt of the masses, but the revolt of objects'.

Benjamin rightly emphasizes the connections between Simmel's account of technology and spirit and the intellectual group around the poet Stefan George, which included Ludwig Klages whose concepts of cosmic experience, ecstatic trance, erotics of nearness and distance, and planetary destruction by the spirit (*Geist*) of technology were also influential on Benjamin's work.[73] For Klages, 'technology is without the slightest capacity to enrich life', capable only of contributing to what he, in another context, calls a 'poverty of experience' that can only be counteracted when the poet's genius of language transports the soul 'with almost demonic magic [*dämonischer Zauberkraft*] … into a whirl of more-than-human [*mehr als menschlichen*] experience'.[74] In *Spirit as Adversary of the Soul*, Klages insists on the thesis that

> has guided all our enquiries for the past three decades or so: that body [*Leib*] and soul [*Seele*] are inseparably connected poles of the unity of life into which spirit [*Geist*] inserts itself from the outside like a wedge, in an effort to set them apart from each other, that is, to de-soul the body [*den Leib zu entseelen*] and disembody the soul [*die Seele zu entleiben*], and so finally to smother any life which it can attain.[75]

According to Klages, the capacity for rhythmic movement is grounded in a drive (*Trieb*) to expression identified with a creative or formative force (*Gestaltungskraft*) inherent to all living organisms and connected both to basic motility (the body's capacity for self-motion) and to formativeness (the capacity for shaping of forms). Klages connects this instinctive drive with a theory of primal images (*Urbilden*), derived from the natural philosophy of Goethe: with the 'concept of primal phenomenon [*Urphänomen*]', Klages writes, Goethe's 'worldly sensuality' pursued 'not to primal things [*Ur-sachen*]' but 'primal images [*Ur-Bildern*]'.[76] These vital images are present even in the most basic germ cell, Klages claims, since 'in the fertilized cell there acts, as moulding power, the image of the growing body', such that 'the process of growth and ripening (which is certainly profoundly unconscious) take[s] place by virtue of the power of images'.[77]

In the natural state of organisms (such as a healthy human child), there is equilibrium between the capacity for and urge towards expression, that is, between bodily motion and the processes he names the image-creating capacity of life. This equilibrium is still occasionally experienced in those moments of profound rapture or intoxication of *Rausch*: the rush of cosmic ecstasy, in which the separation of the subject and object is dissolved and the fixed coordinates of 'here/there' and 'now/then' are replaced by a 'perpetual present with a boundlessly mobile now-point' and a 'boundlessly mobile "here"'.[78] In dreams and intoxication it is 'the Eros of the distance, which releases us from the tangible world of things, and transports us to the ungraspable actuality of images [*betastende Wirklichkeit der Bilder*]!'[79] Such experiences accord with Klages's 'pagan' conception of time, which 'in complete opposition to logical consciousness, which – feeling its way along the straight line of time – considers each past thing to be destroyed, but in the present sees only repetitions of it, the Pelasgians – bound up with the circle of time – live, know, and teach the eternal return of the origin [*ewige Wiederbringung des Ursprungs*]'.[80]

This capacity for expression becomes impoverished, however, to the extent that only the willed impulse to bodily motion remains, no longer associated with the expression of *Rhythmus* (rhythm) of natural reflexes (such as breathing and heartbeat, but also the rhythmic movement of tides and planets), but instead governed by a mechanized and rationalized *Takt* (beat) of industrial modernity. If, under such conditions, the lack of capacity for spontaneous expression is accompanied by a powerful desire after expression, a conflict would arise which would be unendurable in the long run, and especially would prove destructive of the self-esteem of the person in question, were it not that the troubled organism found a substitute in an impulse (of progressively increasing independence) towards representation of states of feeling.[81]

There 'is no more insipid and shabby antithesis', objects Benjamin in the *Arcades Project*, 'than that which reactionary thinkers like Klages try to set up between the symbol-space of nature and that of technology'.[82] Yet although Benjamin's own 'version of the "doctrine of the ancients" differs point by point from Klages', Irving Wohlfarth argues, 'it is from Klages's that it differs' and in turning 'Klages on his head', Benjamin ends up producing 'a kind of left-wing Klages'.[83] 'To the Planetarium' therefore distinguishes a different and expressive conception of technology through analogy with the pedagogical gaze that Benjamin had used to criticize the Late Romanticism of von Savigny's concept of history. The purpose of the father's gaze is not that 'mastery of children' violently proclaimed by cane-wielders, Benjamin argues, but the 'the indispensable ordering of the relationship between generations and therefore mastery (if we are to use this term) of that relationship and not of children'.[84] By analogy, the purpose of technology is not the mastery of nature but the mastery of the relationship between nature and humanity, and therefore the ordering or organization of that relationship.

In a discussion of technology in the second version of 'The Work of Art in the Age of Its Mechanical Reproducibility' from the mid-1930s (passages which are expunged from the last version of the essay), Benjamin articulates these differing conceptions of an expressive versus an instrumental and repressive concept of technology according to a contrast between 'second' and 'first' technology. When art and technology exist in fusion with ritual, the resulting 'first technology' is orientated towards the maximum possible use of the human: an ideological vision which culminates in 'the irreparable lapse or sacrificial death, which holds good for eternity'.[85] Simultaneous with this exploitation of the human, first technology also seeks to 'master nature'. Against this daemonic and mythical conception of instrumentality, Benjamin distinguishes a 'second technology' which arises at 'the point where by an unconscious ruse, human beings first began to distance themselves from nature'. In contrast to the concept of instrumentality involved in first technology, this second technology reduces the use of the human and the mastery of nature to a minimum, aiming instead at 'an interplay between nature and humanity'.

The introduction of a collective-bodily *Geist* permits Benjamin to differentiate between a first (annihilatory, negative, acosmic) and second (formative, positive, cosmic) technology. A footnote to the second version of the 'Work of Art' essay suggests that a new collective body of humankind has 'its organs in the new technology', just as *One-Way Street* proclaims that currently in 'technology, a physis is being organised through which mankind's contact with the cosmos takes a new and different form', characterized as an 'immense wooing of the cosmos … on a planetary scale'.[86]

This prosthetic and cosmopolitical conception of a second technology that reorganizes the relationship between humanity and nature – and therefore between human beings – takes on the character that Marx anticipates for industry in the early *Economic and Philosophical Manuscripts*: 'Industry is the real historical relationship of nature, and hence of natural science, to man', because where 'natural science has intervened and transformed human life all the more practically through industry' it has 'prepared the conditions for human emancipation, however much its immediate effect was to complete the process of dehumanization'.[87] Here then, what Marx calls the merely 'fantastic illusion' of a 'momentary union' between a theoretically abstract philosophy and an instrumentally practical natural science is achieved for real, transforming them both in this aesthetico-technological fusion, an organization of technology Marx defined as communism. As Wohlfarth argues, it is the 'Marxian dialectic between the forces and relations of production' that for Benjamin opens a 'one-way street out of Klages's *système sans issue*'.[88]

It is this context of a second nature given expression in art and technology that Benjamin reclaims for Goethe's *Urphänomen*, as the basis from which to develop his own original phenomenon of history. Crucial to Benjamin's insights concerning the 'social fact of art-as-photography' is his experience of a technological transformation of aesthetics towards an understanding of production as collective creation and reception. Benjamin himself draws on this 'new optics' for his description of historical life in socialist Russia in the 1927 essay on 'Moscow', envisaged as already noted through its conjunction with Goethe's tender empiricism.[89] What Benjamin perceives in the cultural and technological concretions of Russian life are not empirical facts, he insists, but the concrete convergence of the real and the true: *Urphänomen*.

The First Working Group of Constructivists, established in March 1921 by Aleksei Gan, Alexander Rodchenko, Varvara Stepanova, Karl Ioganson, Vladimir Stenberg, Georgii Stenberg and Konstantin Medunetsky, 'set out to "involve its members in the revolutionary inventive work of the Constructivists, who … have decided to realise the communist expression of material structures"', while Aleksei Gan's subsequent manifesto on *Constructivism* opposed bourgeois artistic composition as the representation of reality by insisting on construction as an 'organisation of life' through the integration and arrangement of material, real elements.[90] Rodchenko says of his constructivist practice of photomontage:

> In order to teach man to look in new ways it is necessary to photograph ordinary, familiar objects from totally unexpected viewpoints and in unexpected positions, and to photograph new objects from various vantage

points so as to give a complete impression of the object. We are taught to look in a routine, inculcated manner. We must discover the visible world. We must revolutionize our visual thinking. We must remove the cataract from our eyes.[91]

Christine Lodder describes the resulting work as one which exploits 'the objective descriptive content of the photograph to give reality to impossible but allegorical images, conveying coherent ideas'.[92]

While the influence of avant-garde practices of montage in Benjamin's writing from *One-Way Street* onwards is well recognized, less attention has been paid to the associated biomechanical theory of expressive movement upon which such principles are based. What Benjamin discovered, in the radically transformed social context of post-revolutionary Russia, was a technologically affirmative and non-individualist updating of *Lebensphilosophie* debates about bodily rhythm that Benjamin was already familiar with and fascinated by. Sergei Eisenstein's 'A Dialectic Approach to Film Form' approaches cinema in terms that broadly correspond to the first two principles of Friedrich Engel's *Dialectics of Nature*: the interpenetration of opposites in conflict, or rhythmic tensions, and the quantitative change in energy that results in qualitative transformation, or dynamic expression.[93] But his reference to Marx and Engels is preceded by an epigraph from Goethe's *Conversations with Eckermann*: 'In nature we never see anything isolated, but everything in connection with something else which is before it, beside it, under it, and over it.'

Eisenstein's practice of cinematic montage, as described in 'The Montage of Film Attractions', is developed from his earlier theory of 'The Montage of Attractions' in the theatre, which combines 'free montage with arbitrarily chosen independent effects (attractions)', defined as the calculated use of 'any element of it that subjects the audience to emotional or psychological influence ... to produce specific emotional shocks'. Eisenstein and Sergei Tretyakov claimed in their essay 'Expressive Movement' that their biomechanical theatre training was rooted in a theory of expressive movement that divided all gestures into 'subconscious, instinctive, the pure biological' reflexes (such as the internal bodily movements associated with breathing, digestion, the heartbeat and the involuntary muscular responses to bodily stimulus, such as the grasping and startle reflexes found in infants), and 'the conscious, controlled, co-ordinated, and restrained' movements. When reflexes and conscious movement come into conflict, false 'tensions' may be produced that can cause muscle fatigue, cramps and temporary paralysis, as well as the possibility that 'the voluntary impulse and nervous expenditure turn inward, so to speak, disorganizing the reflexive apparatus'. Biomechanical training is intended to overcome such psychophysical tensions through 'releasing' exercises, which provide the basis of the biomechanical 'postures' used in actor training, directed 'toward elimination of false tensions'.

The notion of filmic conflict later formulated in terms of an Engelsian-Marxian dialectic not only resonates with 'the vitalist models of rhythm so important for the early 20th century's understanding of the body' but, as Robert Leach points out, 'the direct physical base upon which Tretyakov and Eisenstein built their system of Expressive Movement' was that of Rudolf Bode, which Bode claimed were explicit developments of 'the line of thought found in Klages's work'.[94] In a 1936 letter to Klages, prompted by the publication of a revised and retitled edition of Klages's *Expressive Movement and Formative Power*, Eisenstein states that 'film brings a great deal to the problem of expression' and that Klages's 'works have always [been] of the greatest interest in this connection (already 13 years have gone by since I read your Expressive Movement)'.[95] In 'The Montage of Film Attractions', Eisenstein values Klages's 'statements that only the affect can serve as the cause of organic motor manifestation and not the volitional impulse whose fate it usually is to act merely as a brake on and a betrayer of intentions', and, as his diaries from 1928 show, he planned to dedicate his future theoretical work to – among others – Klages, Bode and Meyerhold. Eisenstein also criticized Klages for treating expressive movements in an insufficiently dialectical manner and his montage of film attractions may be said to be a materialist revisioning of this account of the Klagesian-Goethean image, in line with Benjamin's own political thought.

The work of the Soviet avant-garde effectively renders Goethe's philosophy of science true, only now not as an aesthetics of science but as the technological practice of art. If, as Benjamin suggests, Epic Theatre's 'discovery and construction of the gestic is nothing but a retranslation of the methods of montage – so crucial in radio and film – from a technological process to a human one', we might equally add that the construction of montage in cinema was itself conceived as the translation of expressive gestures of bodily language from the media of the human body to that of technology.[96] In the section 'Prayerwheel' in *One-Way Street*, Benjamin connects the formative movement of the will to the vitality of images: 'Only the represented image [*vorgestellte Bild*] vitally nourishes the will. Conversely, the mere word can at most ignite it, but then, shrivelled up, it smoulders. No undamaged will without exact imagistic representation [*genaue bildliche Vorstellung*]. No representation without innervation [*Keine Vorstellung ohne Innervation*].'[97] Benjamin's Schopenhauerian reference to the relation between will and representation, which extends to the invocation of the Buddhist practice of breathing in accordance with the holy symbol as a model for the bodily activation of images, recalls Goethe's exact sensorial imagination (*exakte sinnliche phantasie*) but the title 'Prayer Wheel' emphasizes the spinning wheel used as a technological aid for such bodily visualization.

Expressionist technology (II): cinematic modernism in Goethe's *Faust*

An understanding of how such a technological *phantasie* expresses itself in Goethe's thought requires further consideration of how the literary visualization or making present (*Vergegenwärtigung*) of history encompasses a prehistory of (technological) visualization. In this respect, it is significant that Benjamin claims it is not in the contemplative ease of Bergson's *durée* that the near-impossible task confronting the poet of modernity, who must rescue the historical moment from out of the sedimented depths of time, becomes apparent. Bergson's attempt to 'grasp "true" experience' as an intuition of the uninterrupted stream of becoming, in the actualization of the *durée* in pure memory, overcomes the modern obsession with time only in a way that aestheticizes lived experience (*Erlebnis*), eliminating a theological consideration of death and with it the historical and prehistorical orders.[98]

The allegorical understanding of the moment of completion as death also operates in Benjamin's 1935 review of Johann Jakob Bachofen, where Benjamin speaks of how 'death in no way suggests a violent destruction' for antiquity but, as 'something greater than life or less than life', implies 'the key to all knowledge, reconciling antithetical principles in a dialectical movement'.[99]

Death is therefore the 'prudent mediator between nature and history', he remarks, rehearsing the baroque understanding of significance introduced in the discussion of German mourning-plays: 'what has become historical through death reverts ultimately to the domain of nature; and what has been made natural by death reverts ultimately to history'. Yet it is the 'alienating, blinding experience of the age of large-scale industrialism' that prevents the contents of our individual past (*Erlebnis*) combining in 'commemoration' (*Eingedenken*) with material from a collective tradition – Benjamin's understanding of the ethical-historical terrain of *Lehre* discussed in relation to Kant – to form an 'experience' (*Erfahrung*).[100]

In contrast to the Bergsonian *durée*, Benjamin praises 'Valéry's … Goethean insight' for recognizing the '*here* [*das* hier]', which 'Bergson sees in reach before his eyes', as that 'in which the inadequate becomes an event [*in dem das Unzulängliche Ereignis wird*]'.[101] Benjamin's reference is to the final refrain of the Chorus Mysticus in Goethe's second part of *Faust*: 'All that is ephemeral [*Vergangliche*] / Is only an allegory [*Gleichnis*]; / The inadequate [*Unzulangliche*] / Here becomes an Event [*Hier wird's Ereignis*]'.[102] This Goethean insight identifies the 'here' in which the inadequate becomes a pure event or pure appearance, in the sense that Deleuze's *Logic of Sensation* equated with Stoic colouration (the tree 'greens'), precisely as that of the allegory of eternal passing away. For Deleuze, as already discussed, this is variously associated with the Stoic conception of the phantasm, 'a pure event … [that belongs] to an ideational surface over which it is produced as an effect', with the 'superior empiricism' that Alliez identifies with Goethe's philosophy of nature, with the fanciful wit of the sense of humour, but also with Paul Valéry's 'profound idea: that which is most deep is the skin'.[103] To reverse this formulation of Valéry's profound idea, in line with the Goethean insight presented earlier, is to say that the surface of phenomena – the event – is constituted by sedimentations of temporal depth almost impossible to grasp.

The refrain of the Chorus Mysticus exemplifies the Baroque melancholy of Goethe's mature gaze. Faust's incessant striving – premised on the impossibility of any moment blissful enough to satiate desire – is subverted into an experience saturated with decomposition and death in the conclusion of the play, a completion only possible in Faust's death. The irony of Faust's final anticipation of the highest moment, to which he would dare to say 'Stay a while! You are so lovely!', lies in the morbidity of its context: as István Mészáros notes, Faust's mistaken enthusiasm for the noise of his own gravediggers is an ironic wish fulfilment, the 'actual realization of the great Faustian dream',[104] and his grand plan for a kingdom reclaimed from the sea is unknowingly premised on the sacrifice of countless unnamed human lives, the murder of Philemon, Baucis and their guest, and the subsequent blinding and ultimate death of Faust by Care (*Sorge*).

Faust's pact with the devil is premised on the possibility of a moment blissful enough to satiate worldly striving. If Mephistopheles should ever show him a moment (*Augenblicke*) to which he would say,

> But stay! – you are so beautiful [*Verweile doch! Du bist so schön*]
>
> then you may lay your fetters on me,
>
> then I will gladly perish [*zugrunde gehn*]!
>
> … the clock may stop, its hands fall still,
>
> And time for me is finished![105]

In what has been called a 'melancholy version of the Faustian *Verweile doch* [But stay!]'[106] in thesis IX of Benjamin's 'On the Concept of History', it is the Angel of History who 'would like to stay [*verweilen*]', but not because the moment is so beautiful but because he is transfixed by the unfolding catastrophe.[107]

The resemblance to Faust's pact is further emphasized if we compare the Angelus Novus of the theses with the Talmudic angels, referred to in Benjamin's 1922 announcement for a journal entitled *Angelus Novus*, who are created 'anew every instant [*neue jeden Augenblick*] … in order to perish into the void [*in Nichts zu vergehen*], once they have sung their hymn in the presence of God'.[108] The open mouth of Klee's Angelus Novus suggests that the Angel of History is about to break into a song of lament, perhaps hope, for the world before perishing. As Mephistopheles declares: 'All that exists deserves to perish [*Alle ist werth, dass es zu Grunde geht*].'

Conversely, what drives (*treibt*) the angel onwards is not a voluntary striving, for, as Irving Wolfharth comments, 'he is torn away only by the force of destruction itself'.[109] The force of destruction – the storm that blows from Paradise – therefore drowns out the Angel's hymn, but also prevents the ephemeral angel's vanishing just long enough for him to become perceptible.

One way to read this paradisiacal storm is as an allegory of the messianically destructive potential of Benjamin's concept of now-time (*Jetztzeit*).

Thesis IX represents the snapshot or freeze-frame of an ephemeral moment, in which history is being blown apart. It is only the angel's momentary struggle that reveals the force of now-time to us, who are caught in the process of destruction, but because of this recognition a new conception of history, one that like the ephemerality and contingency of the angels is created anew every instant in countless number, becomes apparent. This Paradisiacal storm is what we optimistically misidentify as 'progress'. Conversely, the critical violence of 'catastrophe' is revealed to possess an eschatological force.

Indeed, thesis X goes on to present the theses themselves as meditations designed to strengthen our resolve to turn away from the world and its strivings (*der Welt und ihrem Treiben*): to liberate the 'political Worldchild [*Weltkind*]' from our spurious faith in progress.[110] The term '*Weltkind*' first appears in Goethe's autobiographical poem 'Dinner at Coblenz', as a description of the poet caught between the Spirit and the Fire of the religious and the Enlightenment prophets (*mit Geistund Feuerschritten, / Prophete rechts, Prophete links / das Weltkind in der Mitten*), and similarly returns in the Classical Walpurgis Night of Faust to denounce those pious hypocrites who consort with the devil at the witch's altar. Michael Löwy quickly excavates Benjamin's 'somewhat odd expression' from its Goethean context and associates it with Benjamin's own French translation, *les enfants du siècle*, which he glosses as Benjamin's own generation.[111] Benjamin's translation, which presumably borrows from Musset's autobiographical *La confession d'un enfant du siècle*, juxtaposes the experiences of his own generation as the children of twentieth-century Berlin – 'A Berlin Childhood around 1900' – with the generation of bohemians and the utopian socialists born at the beginning of the nineteenth century in Paris and explored in the *Arcades Project*.

But in identifying the subject of the theses with a specific epoch, Löwy neglects the connection between this historical *Weltkind* and Benjamin's 'revolutionary' method in the *Arcades Project*: for '*every* epoch has a side turned towards dreams, the child's side', Benjamin insists, and here the economic conditions of life find collective expression.[112] If it falls to the child to 'recognize the new' and to assimilate these images for humanity by bringing them into symbolic space, then this collective, revolutionary task falls to the Worldchild. According to this 'pragmatic conception of history', the historian – including the literary historian – must turn away from or suspend the politics of the present and make a leap into the past, similar to that of the revolutionary, in order to liberate the forces unleashed by the suffering and oppression of previous generations.[113]

This leap should take place not in the current *political* arena where the ruling class gives the commands, in accordance with a politics of progress, but in the 'open sky (*freien Himmel*) of history', in which 'what has been', by dint of a 'secret index [*heimlichen Index*]' that refers to redemption, 'strives [*strebt*] to turn … towards that sun which is rising'.[114] In accordance with the insight into the redemptive interior of the allegorical, the storm that prevents completion is also Paradisiacal time itself. Benjamin's use of the term '*Himmel*' recalls that dramatized eternity which enfolds the narrative of Goethe's drama (the Prologue in Heaven, the heavenly ascension of Margaret at the end of the first part of *Faust* ('Lost! Saved!') and the deus ex machina which concludes the second part) and provides the transcendental frame for that other – divine – catastrophe that threatens to engulf each moment. If each moment is found to bear the imprint of this incompleteness, each might therefore hold this redemptive hope.

Benjamin's allusion to the political *Weltkind* functions partly to denounce the shared progressivism of both idealist and historical materialist conceptions of history (the prophecies of the Right and Left). Cohen's idealism had proclaimed that 'all that is ephemeral … perishes [*alles Vergängliche … geht unter*] … in the self-consciousness of eternity'.[115] Marx and Engels also liked to quote Mephistopheles's assertion, as 'the spirit that always negates', from *Faust* that 'all that exists deserves to perish [*alle ist werth, dass es zu Grunde geht*]', and typically associated this with the dialectics of Hegel (rather than Goethe).[116] Hence, for Marx and Engels, under the ceaseless dynamics of modern bourgeois society itself, 'all … that is stationary evaporates [*alles … Stehende verdampft*]'.[117] That the standard and more poetic English translation of this phrase in Samuel Moore's 1888 translation, 'All that is solid melts into air', is inspired by a line from Shakespeare's *Tempest* ('These our actors … were all spirits and / Are melted into air') reinforces the literary associations between Goethe's and Marx's lines here, since Goethe's *Faust* was written as a response to the meditations on appearance and reality, art and nature, found in Shakespeare's play.[118]

But the Goethean inversion of this spirit or daemon of negation proclaims, 'All that is ephemeral … becomes an event' or a contingent occasion for redemption. Unlike Faust, the Angel of History would like to stay, but he would 'have little luck' if he 'remains in living time [*lebendige Zeit*]'.[119] This living time is that which Marx also speaks of as the 'transitoriness [*die Vergänglichkeit*] of things, their temporality, as their formation by living time [*Formung durch die lebendige Zeit*]'.[120] Historical materialism must therefore recover a concept of the now not as endless transition but the radical contingency of the empirically contingent itself. Benjamin calls this messianic conception of time one that regards the present not as a transition but as 'the sign of a messianic arrest of happening' which allows 'a moment of humanity'.[121]

The 'Theological-Political Fragment' emphasizes the significance of the profane order for such messianic cessation, a profane order whose worldly restitution of the original condition involves an 'eternally transient [*ewig vergehenden*] worldly existence' whose rhythm is that of happiness.[122] One of the 'essential teachings of the philosophy of history', reconceived on the basis of an ethical-historical *Lehre*, is that this profane order is a decisive category for the messianic because although the direction in which its actions point runs 'counter to the messianic direction' of redemption, it promotes the latter in the same way that a 'force, by virtue of the path it is moving along, can augment another force on the opposite path'.[123] Consequently, 'nature is messianic by reason of its eternal and total passing away'. Here, the opposing forces of Faust's worldly striving for happiness and messianic redemption, of transience and immortality, are brought into the same kind of productive tension repeatedly seen in Benjamin's thought, such that from the intensification of a worldly restitution of the original condition emerges the messianic perishing of perishing itself. The Faustian 'stay' is transfixed by this movement and countermovement.

The messianic model of nature which awaits no Judgement Day, as an eternal passing away, therefore intersects with the theological idea of forgiveness. To forgive is to pass beyond all judgement of good and evil: not to forget, but to place beyond all remembering and forgetting. Max Horkheimer's comment that past injustice must be completed for the 'slain are really slain' makes it evident that to construct virtuality as some alternate history in which the dead have not died is to abandon not only the problematic continuity between past and present but even a philosophical relationship of discontinuity so important for Benjamin.[124] Nonetheless, historical remembrance can, as Benjamin remarks, 'make the complete (suffering) into something incomplete'. The cosmopolitical 'task of world politics' for the historical *Weltkind* is to 'strive for such a passing away' but not because everything that exists deserves to perish but to make such ephemerality into an event.[125] This transcritical violence is founded, Benjamin claims, on a method of nihilism. Löwy's description of this as 'essentially a wager, in the Pascalian sense, on the possibility of a struggle for emancipation' should, in this context, be reconceived – in a sense in which the central terms have been inverted – not as a Pascalian wager but rather as a Faustian pact with the Angel of History.[126]

For Valéry, in contrast to Bergson, the poetic task of modernity is concerned with the problem of classicism itself. In a 1931 review of *The Problem of the Classical and Antiquity*, Benjamin argues that 'reflection on the practice of art in the classical epoch of the Greeks is [in the work reviewed] free from any reference to a historical becoming, to a historical index of its own existence', and that for this Valéry's materialist perspective on the principle of artistic construction in classicism offers the deepest insights.[127] This is evident in the way Valéry frames the modern problem of poetry in the work of Charles Baudelaire as a classicism in the midst of a romanticism, in so much as the ordered and rational conventions of classical style is preconditioned on the disorder of natural intuitions produced by romantic composition: the 'essence of classicism is', therefore to always 'come after' such romanticism.[128]

Nietzsche believed that the 'optimistic dialectic' of Socratic science that had driven music out of tragedy demanded a 'music-practicing' or 'artistic Socrates'; Valéry's dialogue on 'Eupalinos, or the Architect' imagines such a possibility.[129] In a dialogue in Hades with the shade of Phaedrus, Socrates speaks of the 'multitude of Socrateses [who] were born with me' and recounts a chance encounter on the seashore with the 'most ambiguous object imaginable', which caused his soul to hesitate between becoming a philosopher and an artist.[130] Valéry imagines this artistic Socrates not as a musician, however, but as an architect, and suggests what is essential to classical practice is not the imitation of nature but the principle of construction embodied in the architecture of Eupalinos. Valéry's Monsieur Teste is, Benjamin similarly proposes, 'the human subject who is ready to cross the historical threshold marking the dividing line between the harmoniously educated, self-sufficient individual and the technician and specialist who is ready', like the artists of the Soviet avant-garde discussed earlier, 'to assume a place within a much larger plan'.[131]

Kurt Weinberg has suggested that in Valéry's *Mon Faust*, a 'third' version of Goethe's play that was first conceived in the mid-1920s and begun around 1940, the resistance of the protagonist to the temptations of the second Fay, Memory, reflects a rejection of Proust's and Bergson's promise of experience, arguing that this Faust is imbued with his author's wisdom that 'to live is to lack something at every moment'.[132] Benjamin illustrates this 'image of the primeval world ... veiled by the tears of nostalgia' with a line from Goethe's poetry – 'Ah, you were in times now past my sister or my wife' – that accounts for the present affinity between two people as the echo of a *past* relationship. Likewise, 'insofar as art aims at the beautiful and, on however a modest scale, "reproduces it"', Benjamin argues, 'it retrieves it (as Faust does Helen) out of the depths of time', and it is this conjuration which makes our 'delight in the beautiful unquenchable'.[133]

Benjamin associates such conjuration of the past with the technique of visualization or making present (*Vergegenwärtigung*) in the works of the American novelist Julien Green, a Paris-based American writer of French literature, whom Benjamin considers 'one of the most important of the younger generation of writers'.[134] For Benjamin, Green's works 'burst the confines of the psychological novel' by representing the subterranean forces of the passions, whose antecedents are found in the Catholic *Trauerspiel* of Calderón and the Stoic philosophy of Seneca, within the modern provinces. The 'silence which is the expression' of Green's retreat to Hell is 'one of his great achievements'.

In a review of Green's work from 1930, Benjamin distinguishes Green's literary technique of visualization from that of naturalism by referring – as he does with respect to critical judgement elsewhere – to its 'magical side' as well as its 'temporal aspect'.[135] Making present involves an act of conjuration, a bringing into presence of that which is absent, achieved through the specific character of its historical index: by imagining people and the conditions of their existence 'in a way that they would never have appeared to a contemporary', Green represents a 'second present' which 'immortalizes what exists'. This effect is in part achieved through Green's stylized use of the simple past tense (*passé simple*), an outmoded literary form which refers to the past action as something finished and completed.[136] The characters conjured in this way appear as if 'apparitions ... compelled to relieve these moments anew', and it is this very temporal representation, Benjamin argues, which renders it a 'magical act'.[137]

But Benjamin also approves of how Green's 'visionary aura' remains distanced from that of dreams by retaining the authentic seal of the here and now of the present ('the here and now is the seal of authenticity that clings to every vision').[138] As a result of this double aspect of presencing, Green's characters and the conditions of their existence 'stand in the twofold darkness of what has only just happened and the unthinkably remote past', housed within a 'temporal space, which is alien to them and which encloses them in a vault of hollow years that echoes back their whispered words and screams'.[139]

Green's *Mont-Cinère* consequently reveals 'a meteorological compromise between a climate of primal history and that of the present day', just as the landscape of *Adrienne Mesurat* 'appears timeless, from the elemental forces at work in its characters to the no less primeval nature of their world'.[140] Benjamin describes this as the 'primal history of the nineteenth century', a glimpse of 'pale and fleeting clearings in history' which occur 'only as the result of catastrophe'.[141] But this reworking of the past necessarily implies a reworking of the present: it is the present that is rendered spectral or ghostly in this diachronic conjunction, and the past which, in contrast, endures as substantial. The emphasis placed upon repetition by Benjamin here therefore falls not so much upon the past as upon the historically actual present which appears as a 'second present' by being magically conjured somewhere else in Green's work[142]: the simple past tense immortalizes that which is represented in a remote past, while the deitic reference to the 'here and now' saturates the present with an ephemeral sense of its own passing away. It is in this 'descent to Hell' that Green's work, like that of Goethe, evades any simplistic ideological support for the bourgeoisie, despite the conformism of his attitude to society.[143]

The process of historical conjuration by which the past is brought into the present concerns what he calls 'the indestructibility of the highest life in all things', the afterlife of cultural works paradoxically predicated on the very possibility of the 'death' of the 'original'.[144] In his illustration of the redemptive 'historical apocatastasis' involved in the critical 'cultural-historical dialectic' of

Convolute N, the non-synthesis of the polarities of past and present brought into a deformative relationship, Benjamin himself invokes Goethe's *Faust*. The reference is not to Goethe's poem, however, but to the tensions embodied in a film of *Faust*: 'Isn't it an affront to Goethe to make a film of *Faust*, and isn't there a world of difference between the poem *Faust* and the film *Faust*? Yes, certainly. But, again, isn't there a whole world of difference between a bad film of *Faust* and a good one?'[145] Benjamin was likely to be thinking of F. W. Murnau's Expressionist production of *Faust: A German Folk Legend* (*Volkssage*), which received its official premiere on 14 October 1926 in Berlin, around the same time as Benjamin's return to Berlin and shortly before his departure to Moscow.[146]

In his discussion of F. W. Murnau's film version of Faust, Matt Erlin argues that Mephisto's magic highlights his function as the film's 'cinematic principle' and that Faust's transaction with the devil therefore 'appears as a self-referential commentary on the way in which the film attempts to transform the Faust legend into cinematic material and thereby infuse it with new life'.[147] This shift from the textual (high culture) to the cinematic (mass entertainment) is signified by Faust's conversion as an 'enthusiastic apostle of the visual', encapsulated by his seduction of the Duchess (using a glowing white orb) and the 'cinematic' framing of the final scene as a film within a film, under Mephisto's 'directorial' intervention. Murnau's deviations from the 'high culture' of Goethe's literary version can be read as his own Faustian pact with the cinematic devil in order to reach out to the masses. But while contemporary historians tended to regard Murnau's work as 'a great film that equals for the first time the great Fausts of literature … audiences and critics in Weimar Germany, however, were less impressed'.[148]

Although Erlin suggests this contrast between the textual and the visual is dialectically superseded in Murnau's concluding focus on Goethe's Gretchen story – such that the self-reflexive cinematic 'tricks' are now psychologized directly into the narrative of the film – this presumption of a positive negation of a negation ('the restoration of a cinematic neoclassicism') depends on a false dichotomy established on the basis of Murnau's 'visual/mass-entertainment' negation of Goethe's 'textual/high-cultural' tradition.[149] This false negation occludes not merely the visual but the cinematic life and afterlife of Goethe's own production of *Faust*.

Although the October 1926 première of Murnau's film version of Faust was a major cultural event, the early French director Georges Méliès had already produced four short films of the Faust legend in the space of seven years in the earliest days of film-making (*Faust and Marguerite* (1897 and 1904), *Damnution of Faust* (1898), *Faust in Hell* (1903)), and Paul Wegener's *Der Student Von Prag* (1913) was one of the first feature-length films of cinema. Méliès, perhaps more than anyone, grasped the phantasmagorical themes in Goethe's version of the legend. Early film-makers' frequent engagement with the Faust legend should be read not as the attempt to reintegrate the textual tradition in response to the artistic devaluation of film, but as the recognition that, especially in the second part of *Faust*, Goethe had already cinematized the literary tradition.

Benjamin's reference to Faust's reproduction of Helen, the classical archetype of beauty, in the second part of Goethe's *Faust*, contrasts two versions of such conjuration. Faust follows Mephistopheles instructions to 'conjure up' Paris and Helen by descending to the Mothers, where 'hover images of all that's been created', and bringing back the tripod which summons them forth, while Mephistopheles directs the performance from the prompter's box, from where the spectres are projected onto the 'smoke-like haze' which engulfs the stage within the stage.[150] Whereas the spectators of the court express an ironic disappointment with these conjured phantoms, Mephistopheles is continually forced to interject when Faust takes them for something real. Faust eventually intervenes upon the phantom scene, causing the figures to dissolve in his attempt to rescue Helen from Paris.

Although the magic produced by the tripod Faust retrieves from the Mothers has been variously associated with necromantic ritual, artistic genius and female procreation, its theatrical necessity should be related instead to the need for the literal technological projection of the phantasmagorical performance that follows. Scholars have pointed to the phantasmagoric reference of this conjuration, arguing that the image of Helen is a metatheatrical act of conjuration: the product of a literal phantasmagoria show. Goethe was familiar with Etienene-Gaspard Robertson's Parisian 'Phantasmagoria', the optical techniques of which had been described in an 1804 scientific article discussed in Goethe's *Theory of Colours*, and appeals to this kind of 'artistic illusion … conjured with a kind of Lanterna Magica' in a letter in which he requests: 'Could you please find out, as soon as possible, who constructs such an apparatus, how could WE obtain it, and what preparations must be made for it?'[151] Goethe's accompanying drawings suggest, Marina Warner explains, that the 'vision of Helen of Troy should also be patterned on optical illusions, with two-way mirrors and changing lighting bringing her image suddenly into focus in the glass'.[152] According to Albrecht Schöne, the whole 'dumb-show of Paris and Helen' therefore represents 'an illusionist spectacle devised by Mephistopheles with the help of a magic lantern that projects images onto a screen or smoke (or incense)'.[153] The 'phantasmagoria show' of Act I masters the situation by playfully ironizing it, utilizing the baroque device of framing the play within a play in order to stage its own continuation, its own immortality. Far from calling the present reality or perspective of the viewer into question, however, the hierarchical layering of this reflective Romantic structure has the effect of reaffirming it. Here, the Emperor's impossible demands for entertainment are met within the theatre by incorporating the emerging possibility of technological spectacle as a 'possible theatre'.

It is important to note, however, that the phantom conjured in Act I is, as John Williams makes clear, not remotely the Helen who appears on stage again in Act III. In contrast to the hierarchical levels of meta-theatricality established in the first phantasmagoria scene, here the dreamlike semblance is immanent and inhabited and its phantasmagoric history *lived*. In Act III, the phantom of Helen has become physically embodied and capable of moving and interacting authentically with the other characters. Writing to Wilhelm von Humboldt after the completion of the third Act in 1826, Goethe emphasizes its peculiar formal structure, citing this as the 'most remarkable thing' about a play he already considers 'as strange and problematic a piece I have ever written'. Goethe's confession to such formal peculiarity reflects what Benjamin, with reference to Konrat Ziegler's 1919 study of the second part of *Faust*, calls the play's fragile and arbitrary composition, which – particularly in the Helen Acts – deviates from the unity of Goethe's overall plan.[154] While the classical Aristotelian unities of place and action are 'most punctiliously observed in the usual way', the unity of time is subverted by being both radically elongated and subjected to a discontinuous rhythmic structure: it 'embraces 3,000 years, from the collapse of Troy to the capture of Missolonghi'.[155] Goethe describes the peculiar and intrusive temporality of Act III as one in which times passes 'as in a phantasmagoria' and in one draft subtitles the act 'a Classico-Romantic Phantasmagoria'.[156] Williams argues that the difference is the result of Faust's 'experience, vicariously and at first hand, [of] the whole primitive pre-classical spectrum of archaic Greek religious myth, the pre-history of Helen herself, as it were'.[157] The second Helen is granted embodiment through the performance of her prehistory, the staged return to her Hellenic past, her flight into the future of Faust's baroque past and their classico-romantic non-synthesis as Goethe's modern future.

This prehistory occurs internal to the momentary present that accompanies Faust's collapse at the end of the conjuration scene, splitting open and expanding the continuity between the end of Act I and the beginning of Act IV. Anthony Phelan suggests that 'the return of some element of antiquity from the past and its reinstatement in the present … gives new meaning to the term representation, which is now a restoration to presence', but one that simultaneously 'destabilizes the personal identity of its central figure by insisting on her allusive character'.[158] "To be sure, it is of the essence of the time structure that it is not clearly differentiated, but that there is an intentional blending of times, a montage, a superimposing of two or more times in an iridescent shimmer of phantasmagoric effect.'[159] If the union of Helen's classicism and Faust's baroque produces, as Kurt Weinberg says, 'his phantasmagoric son Euphorion', this should be grasped not – as Goethe misunderstood it – as Byronic romanticism ('the outer limits of Romantic démsure'), but rather as a phantasmagoric montage of the classical and romantic out of which the untimely – cinematic – modernism of Méliès and Murnau is produced.[160]

Conclusion: All that is ephemeral ... becomes an event

The preceding chapters of this book have sought to construct Benjamin's modernist conception of criticism as a literary transcriticism: a contingent mode of criticism capable of placing the conceptual subsumption of logical and teleological judgement in suspension in order to rescue the sensible and ephemeral contents of experience. The philosophical impetus for the production of such a concept of criticism has been associated with the rise of journalistic criticism and historically located between a crisis of literature in the late 1700s, discussed in Chapter 1, and a crisis of politics in the late 1800s, referred to in Chapter 6.

The former was examined in relation to the rise of public journalism and public art exhibitions that produced a crisis of the classical standards of criticism that was traced across Home's *Elements of Criticism* and Kant's critical philosophy to the development of transcendental criticism, in the sense of a philosophical concern with the conditions of possibility of experience. The latter was encapsulated in Nietzsche's response to the Paris Commune in 1871, whose fall was problematically celebrated as a victory over a political obsession with the ephemerality of now-time (*Jetztzeit*), the egalitarian levelling of distinctions and the masses' abandonment of individual and autonomy style, characteristics also exemplified for Nietzsche in the cultural predominance of journalism.

Kant's concept of criticism developed in Early German Romanticism in ways that enabled a messianic concern with contingency but whose reflective features of singularity, formalism and affirmationism led to a problematic conception of the relation between the particular and the Absolute, one that marked both the Nazarene features of later romantic art and a nationalist politics of the imagination. At the end point of this development, Nietzsche's method of genealogical critique, in rejecting what he regarded as the political legacies of romanticism, turned back to a revitalized classicism, whose pagan influences emphasized a polytheistic multiplicity of content and a chthonic and fatalistic negationism of transcendence.

The modernist concept of criticism examined in this book has been located in the tension between these antinomies: between Kant and Nietzsche, romanticism and classicism, the Nazarene (future) infinitizing of the present and its pagan decomposition into the past. The notion of transcendental critique, developed in Kant's philosophy in the movement between classicism and romanticism, remains central, albeit in a form that replaces Kant's transcendental idealism – and its legacies in the romantic imagination – for an empiricism associated with the sensible Ideals of Goethe's exact sensorial phantasy. As a consequence, such criticism extends the Kantian approach to antinomy beyond the limits of epistemology into a more general concern with the antinomies of experience: a transversal approach that registers the generative and deformative conditions felt within experience itself as a discontinuous multiplicity of possibilities.

Although this genealogical unfolding of Kant is comparable to that performed in Nietzsche, and at times to a vitalist tradition including Klages, Bergson, Sorel and Hulme, Benjamin's project identifies itself with the very political ephemerality and egalitarian levelling down of distinctions that Nietzsche had disdained as an obsession with now-time (*Jetztzeit*), one characteristic in modern literature as journalism and modern politics as socialism. Nietzsche turned back to a vision of the Greeks, albeit one wilder, darker and more tragic than that typically found in neo-classicism, in order to conceptualize a higher concept of art and literature that he also found in the daemonic fatalism practiced by the modern Olympian figure of Goethe. This book has examined the extent to which Benjamin's literary and political project did not abandon the figure of Goethe to the right-wing vitalism of conservative revolutionaries who followed in the wake of Nietzsche but sought to rescue an alternative historical experience from within the very heart of Goethe's writings.

The figures of Goethe and Benjamin, whose lives overlap with the beginning and ending of the historical crises under examination, perform a mediating function in permitting a movement of oscillation between these opposed extremes. The relation established in this book between Benjamin as the great critic of capitalist modernity and Goethe as its great poet facilitates a recognition of the modernism that Benjamin sought to extract from out of Goethe's post-Romantic turn to classicism and, conversely, of the significance of such a post-Romantic classicism for Benjamin's modernism.

In placing Benjamin's thought in relation to that of Goethe, this book has also sought to open up a conceptual interstice between these figures, within which a cluster of concepts have repeatedly surfaced across the preceding chapters, not so much through a generative force of the imagination but, perhaps more accurately, that of the deformative phantasizing of fancy. This deformative violence has been registered in the modern perception of colour as the absolute or pure content of experience, appearing as the deformations of the human visage into the bubble-like heads that populate Grünewald, Turner and Klee's paintings, and in the deformations of language produced through the allegorical fancy of Goethe and Hulme as the modern expression of such pure content.

Similarly, the concept of criticism has, in the oscillation between journalism and philosophical critique, incorporated the contingent ephemerality associated with now-time (*Jetztzeit*), the negative levelling down of distinctions associated with the spatial interplay of the post-auratic and the multiplicity of content associated with technological reproducibility. It therefore takes on certain modernist features of a post-Romantic classicism that preoccupy Benjamin in the 'Work of Art' essay. Finally, the ethical-historical concept of *Lehre*, the collective and contingent multiplicity of possible experiences central to Benjamin's Judeo-messianic transformation of the Kantian and post-Kantian tradition, has come to be conceived as the condition of possibility of experience itself: the transformation of Kant's transcendental idealism into a transcendental empiricism. In its final formulations in Benjamin's work, this is concretized in the contingent possibilities of technology itself, as manifested in the cinematic modernism of Murnau and Eisenstein. It is here, then, in modern technology – and specifically for Benjamin, the deformations of the creative word in the newspaper, the expressive sound in radio and visual perception in cinema – that what Goethe intuitively grasped in the post-romantic classicism of *Faust II* as the ephemeral and the inadequate contents of nature becomes an event: the allegory of redemption.

Notes

Introduction

1 Walter Benjamin, 'One-Way Street', in *Selected Writings*, vol. 1, ed. Marcus Bullock and Michael W. Jennings (Cambridge, MA: Harvard University Press, 1996), 444–5.

2 See, for example, Beatrice Hanssen Andrew Benjamin, eds, *Walter Benjamin and Romanticism* (London: Continuum, 2002).

3 See, for example, Michael Löwy, 'Revolution against "Progress": Walter Benjamin's Romantic Anarchism', *New Left Review*, vol. 1, no. 152 (July/August 1985); Michael Löwy, *Fire Alarm* (London: Verso, 2005); Michael Löwy and Robert Sayre, *Romanticism against the Tide of Modernity* (Durham: Duke University Press, 2001), as well as Marcus Paul Bullock, *Romanticism and Marxism: The Philosophical Development of Literary Theory and Literary History in Walter Benjamin and Friedrich Schlegel* (New York: Peter Lang, 1987).

4 Esther Leslie, *Walter Benjamin: Overpowering Conformism* (London: Pluto Press, 2000); Esther Leslie, *Hollywood Flatlands: Animation, Critical Theory and the Avant-Garde* (London: Verso, 2002); Esther Leslie, *Synthetic Worlds: Nature, Art and the Chemical Industry* (London: Reaktion, 2005); Esther Leslie, *Liquid Crystals: The Science and Art of a Fluid Form* (London: Reaktion, 2016).

5 Andreas Kramer, 'Goethe and the Cultural Project of German Modernism: Steiner, Kandinsky, Friedlaendar, Schwitters and Benjamin', *Publications of the English Goethe Society*, vol. 71, issue 1 (2001): 18–19.

6 Lisa Marie Anderson, *German Expressionism and the Messianism of a Generation* (Amsterdam: Rodopi, 2011), 44; emphasis in the original.

7 Johann Wolfgang von Goethe, *Faust*, Part II, Act V, lines 12104–7; translation amended, based partly on those in Johann Wolfgang von Goethe, *The Collected Works*, vol. 2, ed. Stuart Atkins (Princeton, NJ: Princeton University Press, 1994).

1 Criticism, transdisciplinarity and transcriticism: Walter Benjamin and the Kantian tradition

1 Walter Benjamin, *The Correspondence of Walter Benjamin: 1910–1940*, ed. Gershom Scholem and Theodor W. Adorno (Chicago: University of Chicago Press, 1994), 359.

2　Howard Caygill, *Walter Benjamin: The Colour of Experience* (London: Routledge, 1998), 119.

3　Peter Osborne, 'From Structure to Rhizome: Transdisciplinarity in French Thought (1)', *Radical Philosophy* 165 (January/February 2011): 16. It was Theodor W. Adorno who first described Benjamin's theoretical practice as a 'philosophy directed against philosophy' (Theodor W. Adorno, 'A Portrait of Walter Benjamin', in *Prisms* (Cambridge: MIT Press, 1983), 235). As Peter Osborne notes, Adorno's description of Benjamin's writings characterizes the broader tradition of German critical theory, originating with the Frankfurt School, within which transdisciplinarity 'appears as one way of thinking the conceptual space opened up by the critique of the self-sufficiency of a disciplinary concept of philosophy': the idea that 'philosophy can only be realized outside of philosophy itself' (Osborne, 'From Structure to Rhizome', 15). The other central point of reference for this concept of transdisciplinarity is post-war French theory, more specifically a notion of the transversal found in the practices of Gilles Deleuze and Felix Guattari, which similarly aimed to subvert the foundations of philosophy through the multiplication of and connection across heterogeneous domains (Éric Alliez, 'Rhizome (With No Return)', *Radical Philosophy* 165 (January/February 2011): 38–40). The transdisciplinarity common to both traditions, exemplified in their attempted 'philosophizing about, and out of, non-philosophical experience', aspired to 'both truth and the transformation of experience' (Peter Osborne, 'Philosophy after Theory: Transdisciplinarity and the New', in *Theory After 'Theory'*, ed. Jane Elliott and Derek Attridge (Abingdon: Routledge, 2011), 19–33).

4　See Osborne, 'From Structure to Rhizome', 165.

5　Walter Benjamin, 'On the Program of the Coming Philosophy', in *Selected Writings*, vol. 1, 100.

6　Walter Benjamin, 'Announcement of the Journal *Angelus Novus*', in *Selected Writings*, vol. 1, 296.

7　See Matthew Charles, 'Pedagogy as "Cryptic Politics": Benjamin, Nietzsche, and the End of Education', *boundary 2*, vol. 45, issue 2 (2018): 35–62.

8　Walter Benjamin, 'The Newspaper', in *Selected Writings*, vol. 2, ed. Michael W. Jennings, Howard Eiland and Gary Smith (Cambridge, MA: Harvard University Press, 1999), 742.

9　Walter Benjamin, 'The Life of Students', in *Selected Writings*, vol. 1, 38.

10　See Kojin Karatani, *Transcritique: On Kant and Marx* (Cambridge: MIT Press, 2003), 36–7; and Norman Kemp-Smith, *A Commentary to Kant's Critique of Pure Reason*, 3rd edn (Houndmills: Palgrave Macmillan, 2003), 1.

11　Immanuel Kant, *Lectures on Logic*, ed. J. Michael Young (Cambridge: Cambridge University Press, 1992), 530.

12 Kant, *Lectures on Logic*, 530.

13 Kerr Houston, *An Introduction to Art Criticism: Histories, Strategies, Voices* (Boston: Pearson, 2013), 24.

14 Howard Caygill, *Art of Judgement* (Oxford: Basil Blackwell, 1989), 63, 43, 69.

15 Caygill, *Art of Judgement*, 98, 69.

16 Caygill, *Art of Judgement*, 98, 67.

17 Immanuel Kant, *Critique of Pure Reason*, trans. Werner S. Pluhar (Indianapolis: Hackett, 1996), A15/B29. J. G. Schurman claims that 'it is a significant corroboration of this criticism [of the illegitimacy of Kant's first *Critique*] that while the entire system, in its organization, constitution, and complexion, is determined by the opposition and correlation of sense and understanding, that distinction itself is nowhere established' (J. G. Schurman, 'Kant's Theory of the A Priori Forms of Sense', *The Philosophical Review*, vol. 8, no. 1 (January 1899): 1).

18 Caygill, *Art of Judgement*, 1.

19 Karatani, *Transcritique*, 36–7.

20 Walter Benjamin, 'On Perception', in *Selected Writings*, vol. 1, 94.

21 Benjamin, 'On Perception', *Selected Writings*, vol. 1, 93.

22 Benjamin, 'On Perception', *Selected Writings*, vol. 1, 93; emphasis in the original.

23 Benjamin, 'On Perception', *Selected Writings*, vol. 1, 93–4.

24 Benjamin, 'On Perception', *Selected Writings*, vol. 1, 93–4.

25 Astrid Deuber-Mankowsky, 'Hanging over the Abyss: On the Relation between Knowledge and Experience in Hermann Cohen and Walter Benjamin', in *Hermann Cohen's Critical Idealism*, ed. Reinier Munk (Dordrecht: Springer, 2005), 162–3.

26 Hermann Cohen, 'Das Prinzip der Infinitesimal-Methode und seine Geschichte. Ein Kapitel zur Grundlegung der Erkenntnisskritik', in *Werke*, ed. Helmut Holzhey, vol. 5 (Hildesheim: Olms, 1984), §6, trans. in Andrea Poma, *The Critical Philosophy of Hermann Cohen*, trans. John Denton (Albany: SUNY, 1997), 57–8; emphases in the original.

27 Lydia Patton, 'Hermann Cohen's History and Philosophy of Science' (PhD thesis, McGill University, Montreal, 2004), 75, 22; Hermann Cohen, *Kants Theories der Erfahrung*, in *Werke*, vol. 1 (Hildesheim: Olms, 1987), trans. in Andrea Poma, *The Critical Philosophy of Hermann Cohen*, 8.

28 Cohen, *Kants Theories der Erfahrung*, 48–9, trans. in Poma, *The Critical Philosophy of Hermann Cohen*, 13; emphases in the original.

29 Hermann Cohen, *Logic der reinen Erkenntnis*, in *Werke*, vol. 6 (Hildesheim: Olms, 2005), trans. in Klaus Christian Köhnke, *The Rise of Neo-Kantianism: German Academic Philosophy between Idealism and Positivism* (Cambridge: Cambridge University Press, 1991), 182.

30 Hermann Cohen, *Logic der reinen Erkenntnis*, in *Werke*, vol. 6, 36, trans. in
    Poma, *The Critical Philosophy of Hermann Cohen*, 85–6.

31 While this anticipates Heidegger's own radical reinterpretation of the *Critique
    of Pure Reason*'s 'common tie' in his 1929 study, *Kant and the Problem of
    Metaphysics*, Cohen's 'synthesis' takes the form of a logical rather than ontological
    unifiability and Heidegger is quick to distance his interpretation from neo-
    Kantianism, and in particular from Cohen's *Kant's Theory of Experience*, by
    arguing that 'the intention of the *Critique of Pure Reason*, therefore, remains
    fundamentally misunderstood, if it is interpreted as a "theory of experience"
    or even as a theory of the positive sciences' (Martin Heidegger, *Kant and the
    Problem of Metaphysics*, 5th edn, trans. Richard Taft (Bloomington: Indian
    University Press, 1997), 11). The difference between this concept and Hegelian
    sublation (*Aufhebung*) is emphasized by Cohen, who regards it as rectifying
    what he takes to be the two fundamental errors in Hegel's philosophy of identity,
    as Andrea Poma explains: 'the elimination of the difference between concept
    and being, thought and reality, and the elimination of the difference between
    concept and idea, and thus the elimination of the difference between being and
    what ought to be, between reality and task, for the identity of concept with being'
    (Poma, *The Critical Philosophy of Hermann Cohen*, 77).

32 Hermann Cohen, *Kants Theories der Erfahrung*, 104–5, trans. in Poma, *The
    Critical Philosophy of Hermann Cohen*, 11.

33 Hermann Cohen, 'Zur Kontroverse zwischen Trendelenburg und Kuno Fischer',
    in *Schriften zur Philosophie und Zeitgeschichte*, vol. 1, ed. Albert Görland and
    Ernst Cassirer (Berlin: Akademie Verlag, 1928), 230, trans. in Poma, *The Critical
    Philosophy of Hermann Cohen*, 6; emphasis in the original.

34 Benjamin, 'On Perception', *Selected Writings*, vol. 1, 94.

35 Benjamin, 'On Perception', *Selected Writings*, vol. 1, 95.

36 Benjamin, 'On Perception', *Selected Writings*, vol. 1, 94.

37 Walter Benjamin, 'Review of Hönigswald's *Philosophie und Sprache*', in *Selected
    Writings*, vol. 4, ed. Howard Eiland and Michael W. Jennings (Cambridge,
    MA: Harvard University Press, 2003), 139.

38 Walter Benjamin, 'On the Program of the Coming Philosophy', in *Selected
    Writings*, vol. 1, 103.

39 Benjamin, 'On the Program of the Coming Philosophy', in *Selected Writings*,
    vol. 1, 105; emphasis added.

40 Benjamin, 'On the Program of the Coming Philosophy', in *Selected Writings*,
    vol. 1, 101.

41 Benjamin, 'On Perception', in *Selected Writings*, vol. 1, 94.

42 Benjamin, 'On the Program of the Coming Philosophy', in *Selected Writings*,
    vol. 1, 107.

43 Benjamin, 'On the Program of the Coming Philosophy', in *Selected Writings*, vol. 1, 107.

44 Gershom Scholem, 'Against the Metaphysical Exposition of Space', *MLN*, vol. 127, no. 3 (2012): 456–7.

45 Walter Benjamin, *Gesammelte Schriften*, Bd. 6, ed. Rolf Tiedemann and Hermann Schweppenhäuser (Frankfurt am Main: Suhrkamp, 1991), 32–3.

46 Benjamin, 'On Perception', in *Selected Writings*, vol. 1, 94.

47 Benjamin, 'On the Program of the Coming Philosophy', in *Selected Writings*, vol. 1, 106; Walter Benjamin, 'Theses on the Problem of Identity', in *Selected Writings*, vol. 1, 79.

48 Paul North, 'Apparent Critique: Inferences from a Benjaminian Sketch', *diacritics*, vol. 40, no. 1 (Spring 2012): 71.

49 Karatani, *Transcritique*, 4, 34.

50 Karatani, *Transcritique*, 41, 53, 101, 126.

51 Kojin Karatani, '"Critique Is Impossible without Moves": An Interview of Kojin Karatani by Joel Wainwright', *Dialogues in Human Geography*, vol. 2, issue 1 (2012): 42.

52 Caygill, *Art of Judgement*, 195.

53 Immanuel Kant, *Dreams of a Spirit Seer*, trans. John Manolesco (New York: Vantage Press, 1969), 68, quoted in Caygill, *Art of Judgement*, 195.

54 Kant, *Critique of Pure Reason*, A658/B686.

55 Caygill, *Art of Judgement*, 197; emphasis added.

56 Karatani, *Transcritique*, 34.

57 Slavoj Žižek, *Parallax View* (Cambridge: MIT Press, 2006), 19–21.

58 Karatani, *Transcritique*, 95.

59 Samuel Weber, *Benjamin's -Abilities* (Cambridge, MA: Harvard University Press, 2008), 119–20.

60 Walter Benjamin, *The Origin of German Tragic Drama*, trans. John Osborne (London: Verso, 1998), 41, 47, 35.

61 Benjamin, *The Origin of German Tragic Drama*, 29; translation amended, emphasis added.

62 Rolf Tiedemann, 'Dialectics at a Standstill: Approaches to the *Passengen-Werk*', in Walter Benjamin, *The Arcades Project*, trans. Howard Eiland and Kevin McLaughlin (Cambridge, MA: Harvard University Press, 2002), 929–45; Benjamin, *The Arcades Project*, NIOa,3.

63 Benjamin, *The Arcades Project*, N9,7.

64 Benjamin, 'On the Program of the Coming Philosophy', in *Selected Writings*, vol. 1, 102; emphasis added.

65 Benjamin, 'On the Program of the Coming Philosophy', in *Selected Writings*, vol. 1, 100, translation amended.

66 Benjamin, 'On the Program of the Coming Philosophy', in *Selected Writings*, vol. 1, 105.

67 Deuber-Mankowsky, 'Hanging over the Abyss', 176–9.

68 Immanuel Kant, 'Idea for a Universal History with a Cosmopolitan Purpose', in *Kant: Political Writings*, ed. H. S. Reiss (Cambridge: Cambridge University Press, 1991), 41.

69 Immanuel Kant, *The Conflict of the Faculties*, trans. Mary J. Gregor (Lincoln: University of Nebraska Press, 1992), 151.

70 Deuber-Mankowsky, 'Hanging over the Abyss', 176, 188; emphasis in the original.

71 Deuber-Mankowsky, 'Hanging over the Abyss', 187–9.

72 Deuber-Mankowsky, 'Hanging over the Abyss', 176–9.

73 Deuber-Mankowsky, 'Hanging over the Abyss', 187–9.

74 Deuber-Mankowsky, 'Hanging over the Abyss', 161; emphasis in the original.

75 Kant, *Critique of Pure Reason*, A460/B488.

76 Kant, *Critique of Pure Reason*, A459-60/B488, A610/B638.

77 Immanuel Kant, *Theoretical Philosophy 1755–1770*, ed. David Walford (Cambridge: Cambridge University Press, 1992), 78.

78 Kant, *Theoretical Philosophy 1755–1770*, 76.

79 Cf. Kant, *Theoretical Philosophy 1755–1770*, lvi.

80 Kant, *Critique of Pure Reason*, A458/B486.

81 Philippe Hunemann, 'Purposivenss, Necessity, and Contingency', in *Kant's Theory of Biology*, ed. Eric Watkins and Ina Goy (Berlin: De Gruyter, 2014), 185.

82 Immanuel Kant, *Critique of Judgement*, trans. Werner S. Pluhar (Indianapolis: Hackett, 1987), Ak. 370–3.

83 Kant, *Critique of Judgement*, Ak. 217.

84 Kant, *Critique of Judgement*, Ak. 179.

85 Kant, *Critique of Judgement*, Ak. 180.

86 Kant, *Critique of Judgement*, Ak. 406.

87 Kant, *Critique of Pure Reason*, A606/B634, A609/B637.

88 Kant, *Critique of Pure Reason*, A613/B641.

89 Kant, *Critique of Pure Reason*, A569/B597.

90 Deuber-Mankowsky, 'Hanging over the Abyss', 167.

91 Cohen, *Kants Theories der Erfahrung*, 229, trans. in Poma, *The Critical Philosophy of Hermann Cohen*, 1.

92 Deuber-Mankowsky, 'Hanging over the Abyss', 172; emphases in the original.

93 Benjamin, *The Correspondence of Walter Benjamin: 1910–1940*, 105; Philippe Lacoue-Labarthe, 'Introduction to Walter Benjamin's The Concept of Art Criticism in German Romanticism', in *Walter Benjamin and Romanticism*, ed. Beatrice Hanssen and Andrew Benjamin, 15.

94 Deuber-Mankowsky, 'Hanging over the Abyss', 187; emphasis in the original.

95 Benjamin, 'The Life of Students', in *Selected Writings*, vol. 1, 37.

96 Deuber-Mankowsky, 'Hanging over the Abyss', 182.

97 Kojin Karatani, 'Uses of Aesthetics: After Orientalism', *boundary 2*, vol. 25, no. 2 (summer 1998): 148.

98 Samuel Taylor Coleridge, *Biographia Literaria*, ed. Nigel Leask (London: Everyman, 1997), 50.

99 Coleridge, *Biographia Literaria*, 157; Samuel Taylor Coleridge, *The Book I Value: Selected Marginalia*, ed. H. J. Jackson (Princeton, NJ: Princeton University Press, 2003), 154; see also Samuel Taylor Coleridge, 'Essays on the Principles of Genial Criticism', in *The Collected Works of Samuel Taylor Coleridge*, vol. 11, ed. H. R. Jackson and J. R. de J. Jackson (Princeton, NJ: Princeton University Press, 1995).

100 Karatani, 'Uses of Aesthetics: After Orientalism', 148; Karatani, *Transcritique*, 113; emphasis added.

101 Karatani, 'Uses of Aesthetics: After Orientalism', 148–50.

102 Karatani, 'Uses of Aesthetics: After Orientalism', 150.

103 Clement Greenberg, 'Modernist Painting', in *The Collected Essays and Criticism*, vol. 4, ed. John O'Brian (Chicago: University of Chicago Press, 1995), 85.

104 Nikolaus Lambrianou, 'Neo-Kantianism and Messianism: Origin and Interruption in Hermann Cohen and Walter Benjamin', in *Walter Benjamin: Critical Evaluations in Cultural Theory*, vol. 3, ed. Peter Osborne (London: Routledge, 2005), 93.

2 Weak messianism in German Romanticism

1 Walter Benjamin, *The Correspondence of Walter Benjamin: 1910–1940*, ed. Gershom Scholem and Theodor W. Adorno (Chicago: University of Chicago Press, 1994), 105.

2 Benjamin, *The Correspondence of Walter Benjamin: 1910–1940*, 135–6.

3 Benjamin, 'The Concept of Criticism in German Romanticism', in *Selected Writings*, vol. 1, n.7, 116–17, 185.

4 Philippe Lacoue-Labarthe, 'Introduction to Walter Benjamin's The Concept of Art Criticism in German Romanticism', in *Walter Benjamin and Romanticism*, ed. Beatrice Hanssen and Andrew Benjamin (London: Continuum, 2002), 15.

5 Benjamin, 'The Concept of Criticism in German Romanticism', in *Selected Writings*, vol. 1, 121.

6 Benjamin, *The Correspondence of Walter Benjamin: 1910–1940*, 119.

7 Benjamin, 'The Concept of Criticism in German Romanticism', in *Selected Writings*, vol. 1, 144.

8 Benjamin, 'The Concept of Criticism in German Romanticism', in *Selected Writings*, vol. 1, 146.

9 Benjamin, 'The Concept of Criticism in German Romanticism', in *Selected Writings*, vol. 1, 147.

10 Benjamin, 'The Concept of Criticism in German Romanticism', in *Selected Writings*, vol. 1, 148.

11 Benjamin, 'The Concept of Criticism in German Romanticism', in *Selected Writings*, vol. 1, 129.

12 Friedrich Schlegel, *Philosophical Fragments*, trans. Peter Firchow (Minneapolis: University of Minnesota Press, 1991), 31–2.

13 Schlegel, *Philosophical Fragments*, 32.

14 Friedrich Schlegel, *On the Study of Greek Poetry*, ed. Stuart Barnett (New York: SUNY, 2001), 20; emphases in the original.

15 Hans Eichner, *Friedrich Schlegel* (New York: Twayne, 1970), 35–6.

16 Friedrich Schlegel, 'On Goethe's *Meister*', in *German Aesthetic and Literary Criticism: The Romantic Ironists and Goethe*, ed. Kathleen M. Wheeler (Cambridge: Cambridge University Press, 1984), 69.

17 SofieKluge, 'An Allegory of "Bildung": Friedrich Schlegel's Interpretation of Goethe's *Wilhelm Meisters Lehrjahre*', *Orbis Litterarum*, vol. 62, issue 3 (June 2007): 195.

18 Schlegel, 'On Goethe's *Meister*', 64.

19 Artnd Bohm, 'Goethe and the Romantics', in *The Literature of German Romanticism*, ed. Dennis F. Mahoney (Rochester, NY: Camden House, 2004), 42; emphasis in the original.

20 Schlegel, 'On Goethe's *Meister*', 65.

21 Kluge, 'An Allegory of "Bildung" ', 182.

22 Thijs Lijster, 'The Interruption of Myth: Walter Benjamin's Concept of Critique', in *Conceptions of Critique in Modern and Contemporary Philosophy*, ed. Karin de Boer and Ruth Sonderegger (Houndmills: Palgrave Macmillan, 2012), 157.

23 Benjamin, 'The Concept of Criticism in German Romanticism', in *Selected Writings*, vol. 1, 144–5.

24 Benjamin, 'The Concept of Criticism in German Romanticism', in *Selected Writings*, vol. 1, 177.

25 Benjamin, 'The Concept of Criticism in German Romanticism', in *Selected Writings*, vol. 1, 132, 131.

26 Schlegel, *Philosophical Fragments*, 48, quoted in Benjamin, 'The Concept of Criticism in German Romanticism', in *Selected Writings*, vol. 1, n.3, 185.

27 Marcus Paul Bullock, *Romanticism and Marxism: The Philosophical Development of Literary Theory and Literary History in Walter Benjamin and Friedrich Schlegel* (New York: Peter Lang, 1987), 91–2.

28 Bullock, *Romanticism and Marxism*, 91–2.

29 Kluge, 'An Allegory of "Bildung" ', 196–202.

30 Winfried Menninghaus, 'Walter Benjamin's Exposition of the Romantic Theory of Reflection', in *Walter Benjamin: Critical Evaluation in Cultural Theory*, ed. Peter Osborne (London: Routledge, 2005), vol. 1, 44.

31 Rodolphe Gasché, 'The Sober Absolute: On Benjamin and the Early Romantics', in *Walter Benjamin and Romanticism*, ed. Beatrice Hanssen and Andrew Benjamin (London: Continuum, 2002), 52.

32 Benjamin, 'The Concept of Criticism in German Romanticism', in *Selected Writings*, vol. 1, 145.

33 Novalis, *Schriften* (Berlin: Reimber, 1901), 496, quoted in Benjamin, 'The Concept of Criticism in German Romanticism', in *Selected Writings*, vol. 1, 150.

34 Benjamin, 'The Concept of Criticism in German Romanticism', in *Selected Writings*, vol. 1, 179.

35 Benjamin, 'The Concept of Criticism in German Romanticism', in *Selected Writings*, vol. 1, 168.

36 Benjamin, 'The Concept of Criticism in German Romanticism', in *Selected Writings*, vol. 1, 146.

37 Gasché, 'The Sober Absolute', 57–8.

38 Benjamin, 'The Concept of Criticism in German Romanticism', in *Selected Writings*, vol. 1, 123.

39 Benjamin, 'The Concept of Criticism in German Romanticism', in *Selected Writings*, vol. 1, 179.

40 Benjamin, 'The Concept of Criticism in German Romanticism', in *Selected Writings*, vol. 1, 168.

41 Benjamin, 'The Concept of Criticism in German Romanticism', in *Selected Writings*, vol. 1, 167.

42 Benjamin, 'The Concept of Criticism in German Romanticism', in *Selected Writings*, vol. 1, 159.

43 Gasché, 'The Sober Absolute', 60.

44 Benjamin, 'The Concept of Criticism in German Romanticism', in *Selected Writings*, vol. 1, 154.

45 Benjamin, 'The Concept of Criticism in German Romanticism', in *Selected Writings*, vol. 1, 153.

46 Benjamin, 'The Concept of Criticism in German Romanticism', in *Selected Writings*, vol. 1, 154, 160, 163; emphasis added.

47 Benjamin, 'The Concept of Criticism in German Romanticism', in *Selected Writings*, vol. 1, 154, 164–5.

48 Benjamin, 'The Concept of Criticism in German Romanticism', in *Selected Writings*, vol. 1, 165, 168.

49 Benjamin, 'The Concept of Criticism in German Romanticism', in *Selected Writings*, vol. 1, 152.

50 Benjamin, 'The Concept of Criticism in German Romanticism', in *Selected Writings*, vol. 1, 154.

51 Novalis, *Schriften* (Berlin: Reimber, 1901), vol. 2, 499 and 304, quoted in Benjamin, 'The Concept of Criticism in German Romanticism', in *Selected Writings*, vol. 1, 152–3.

52 Benjamin, 'The Concept of Criticism in German Romanticism', in *Selected Writings*, vol. 1, 152.

53 Benjamin, 'The Concept of Criticism in German Romanticism', in *Selected Writings*, vol. 1, 152, 171.

54 Gasché, 'The Sober Absolute', 63.

55 Gasché, 'The Sober Absolute', 64.

56 Friedrich Schlegel, *Seine prosaischen Jugendschriften*, vol. 2, 427, quoted in Benjamin, 'The Concept of Criticism in German Romanticism', in *Selected Writings*, vol. 1, 171.

57 Charlotte Pingoud, *Grundlinien der äthetischen Doktrin Fr. Schlegels*, 52ff., quoted in Benjamin, 'The Concept of Criticism in German Romanticism', in *Selected Writings*, vol. 1, n.3, 185.

58 Benjamin, 'The Concept of Criticism in German Romanticism', in *Selected Writings*, vol. 1, 145.

59 Walter Benjamin, *The Origin of German Tragic Drama*, trans. John Osborne (London: Verso, 1998), 38; emphasis added.

60 Benjamin, 'The Concept of Criticism in German Romanticism', in *Selected Writings*, vol. 1, 182.

61 Benjamin, 'The Concept of Criticism in German Romanticism', in *Selected Writings*, vol. 1, 182.

62 Benjamin, 'The Concept of Criticism in German Romanticism', in *Selected Writings*, vol. 1, 167.

63 Benjamin, 'The Concept of Criticism in German Romanticism', in *Selected Writings*, vol. 1, 166; emphasis added.

64 Gasché, 'The Sober Absolute', 62–3.

65 Benjamin, 'The Concept of Criticism in German Romanticism', in *Selected Writings*, vol. 1, 182–3.

66 Benjamin, 'The Concept of Criticism in German Romanticism', in *Selected Writings*, vol. 1, 167.

67 Bernadetto Croce, *The Essence of the Aesthetic*, 53, quoted in Benjamin, *The Origin of German Tragic Drama*, 43.

68 Benjamin, *The Origin of German Tragic Drama*, 45.

69 Benjamin, 'The Concept of Criticism in German Romanticism', in *Selected Writings*, vol. 1, 167.

70 Benjamin, 'The Concept of Criticism in German Romanticism', in *Selected Writings*, vol. 1, 153.

71 Benjamin, 'The Concept of Criticism in German Romanticism', in *Selected Writings*, vol. 1, 168.

72 Walter Benjamin, ' "The Regression of Poetry," by C. G. Jochmann', in *Selected Writings*, vol. 4, 361–2.

73 Benjamin, ' "The Regression of Poetry" ', in *Selected Writings*, vol. 4, 361–2.

74 Kojin Karatani, *The Structure of World History: From Modes of Production to Modes of Exchange*, trans. Michael K. Bourdaghs (Durham: Duke University Press, 2014), 216.

75 Howard Caygill, *Art of Judgement* (Oxford: Basil Blackwell, 1989), 62–3.

76 Henry Home of Kames, *Elements of Criticism*, 3rd edn, ed. Abraham Mills (New York: Conner and Cooke, 1836), 15.

77 Home, *Elements of Criticism*, 480.

78 Karatani, *The Structure of World History*, 219.

79 Karatani, *The Structure of World History*, 220.

80 Fabian Lampart, 'The Turn to History and the *Volk*: Brentano, Arnim, and the Grimm Brothers', in *The Literature of German Romanticism*, ed. Dennis F. Mahoney (Rochester, NY: Camden House, 2004), 171–2.

81 Joep Leerssen, 'Notes towards a Definition of Romantic Nationalism', *Romantik: Journal for the Study of Romanticisms*, vol. 2, no. 1 (2013): 22.

82 Walter Benjamin, 'The Philosophy of History of the Late Romantics and the Historical School', in *Selected Writings*, vol. 1, 285.

83 Benjamin, 'The Philosophy of History of the Late Romantics and the Historical School', in *Selected Writings*, vol. 1, 284.

84 Benjamin, 'The Philosophy of History of the Late Romantics and the Historical School', in *Selected Writings*, vol. 1, 284–5.

85 Kir Kuiken, *Imagined Sovereignties: Towards a New Political Romanticism* (New York: Fordham University Press, 2014), 71; see Nigel Leask, *The Politics of the Imagination in Coleridge's Critical Thought* (Basingstoke: Macmillan, 1988), 33.

86 Kuiken, *Imagined Sovereignties*, 3.

87 Kuiken, *Imagined Sovereignties*, 94–7.

88 In his reading of the Japanese cultural scholar Okakura Tenshin, for example, Karatani notes how Okakura similarly endorses the cultural products of

other Asian countries while remaining indifferent to their people, entailing a "Sinicization" as well as Westernization (Kojin Karatani, 'Uses of Aesthetics: After Orientalism', *boundary 2*, vol. 25, no. 2 (Summer 1998): 157, 171): 'the distinctions … between national [Japanese] and foreign (that is, Western) culture … were in effect mapped out by this process' (Seiji M. Lippit, *Topographies of Japanese Modernism* (New York: Columbia University Press, 2002), 7–11). Rather than thinking 'from the unstable position of one who finds himself "between" East and West, seeking refuge in neither pole of the opposition', Okakura advocated a pan-Asianism, founded on the universality of the poetic spirit of the East, that 'was gradually (and against his intentions) made to serve the end of imperialist ideology' (Kojin Karatani, *Origins of Modern Japanese Literature*, trans. Brett de Bary (Durham: Duke University Press, 1993), 44).

89 Karatani, 'Uses of Aesthetics: After Orientalism', 157.
90 Karatani, 'Uses of Aesthetics: After Orientalism', 157, 153.
91 Walter Benjamin, 'The Work of Art in the Age of Its Technological Reproducibility', in *Selected Writings*, vol. 4, 269.
92 Benjamin, 'The Concept of Criticism in German Romanticism', in *Selected Writings*, vol. 1, 178.
93 Benjamin, 'The Concept of Criticism in German Romanticism', in *Selected Writings*, vol. 1, 179.
94 Benjamin, 'The Concept of Criticism in German Romanticism', in *Selected Writings*, vol. 1, 179.

3 Strong aesthetics in Goethe's tender empiricism

1 Benjamin, 'The Concept of Criticism in German Romanticism', *Selected Writings*, vol. 1, 178.
2 Friedrich Schlegel, *Seine prosaischen Jugendschriften*, vol. 1, 123ff, quoted in Benjamin, 'The Concept of Criticism in German Romanticism', in *Selected Writings*, vol. 1, 171.
3 Benjamin, 'The Concept of Criticism in German Romanticism', in *Selected Writings*, vol. 1, 148, n.149, 192; translation amended.
4 Benjamin, 'The Concept of Criticism in German Romanticism', in *Selected Writings*, vol. 1, 148.
5 Johann Wolfgang von Goethe, 'Significant Help Given by an Ingenious Turn of Phrase', in *The Collected Works*, vol. 12, ed. Douglas Miller (Princeton, NJ: Princeton University Press, 1995), 39.
6 Goethe, 'Significant Help Given by an Ingenious Turn of Phrase', in *The Collected Works*, vol. 12, 39.

7 Benjamin, 'The Concept of Criticism in German Romanticism', in *Selected Writings*, vol. 1, n.149, 192, 148.

8 R. H. Stephenson, *Goethe's Conception of Knowledge and Science* (Edinburgh: Edinburgh University Press, 1995), 21.

9 Benjamin, *The Origin of German Tragic Drama*, 38.

10 Joanna Hodge, 'The Timing of Elective Affinity: Walter Benjamin's Strong Aesthetics', in *Walter Benjamin and Art*, ed. Andrew Benjamin (London: Continuum, 2005), 16.

11 Benjamin, 'The Concept of Criticism in German Romanticism', in *Selected Writings*, vol. 1, n.308, 199.

12 Benjamin, *The Origin of German Tragic Drama*, 35–6.

13 Beatrice Hanssen, 'Philosophy at Its Origin: Walter Benjamin's Prologue to the *Ursprung des deutschen Trauerspiels*', *MLN*, vol. 110, no. 4 (September 1995): 825.

14 Benjamin, *The Arcades Project*, N2a, 4.

15 Timothy Lenoir, 'The Eternal Laws of Form: Morphotypes and the Conditions of Existence in Goethe's Biological Thought', *Journal of Social and Biological Structures: Studies in Human Social Biology*, vol. 7, issue 4 (October 1984): 317–18.

16 Johann Wolfgang von Goethe, 'Outline of a General Introduction to Comparative Anatomy, Commencing with Osteology', in *The Collected Works*, vol. 12, 117; Johann Wolfgang von Goethe, 'The Content Prefaced', in *The Collected Works*, vol. 12, 67; Johann Wolfgang von Goethe, *Maxims and Reflections*, trans. Elisabeth Stopp (London: Penguin Books, 1998), #430.

17 Goethe, *Maxims and Reflections*, #1282.

18 Goethe, *Maxims and Reflections*, #607.

19 Goethe, *Maxims and Reflections*, #1286.

20 Johann Wolfgang von Goethe, 'The Formative Impulse', in *The Collected Works*, vol. 12, 35.

21 Goethe, *Maxims and Reflections*, #605.

22 Johann Wolfgang von Goethe, 'Observation on Morphology in General', in *The Collected Works*, vol. 12, 57.

23 Goethe, *Maxims and Reflections*, #419.

24 Goethe, Maxims and Reflections, #419.

25 Goethe, 'Outline of a General Introduction to Comparative Anatomy', in *The Collected Works*, vol. 12, 117.

26 Goethe, 'Outline of a General Introduction to Comparative Anatomy', in *The Collected Works*, vol. 12, 117; Goethe, 'Observation on Morphology in General', in *The Collected Works*, vol. 12, 58.

27 Goethe, 'Outline of a General Introduction to Comparative Anatomy', in *The Collected Works*, vol. 12, 124.

28 Johann Wolfgang von Goethe, 'Formation and Transformation', in *Goethe's Botanical Writings*, trans. Bertha Mueller (Woodbridge, CT: Ox Bow Press, 1989), 24.

29 Johann Wolfgang von Goethe, 'The Purpose Set Forth (From On Morphology)', in *The Collected Works*, vol. 12, 63.

30 Johann Wolfgang von Goethe, 'On Morphology', in *Goethe's Botanical Writings*, 23–4.

31 Goethe, 'On Morphology', in *Goethe's Botanical Writings*, 23.

32 Johann Wolfgang von Goethe, 'Judgement through Intuitive Perception', in *The Collected Works*, vol. 12, 31–2.

33 Kant, *Critique of Pure Reason*, A838/B866.

34 Kant, *Critique of Pure Reason*, A569-70/B597-80.

35 Kant, *Critique of Pure Reason*, A838/B866.

36 Kant, *Critique of Pure Reason*, A570/B598.

37 Kant, *Critique of Judgment*, Ak. 408.

38 Goethe, *Maxims and Reflections*, #1344.

39 Goethe, *Maxims and Reflections*, #468, #411.

40 Goethe, *Maxims and Reflections*, #533, #1226.

41 Johann Wolfgang von Goethe, 'From a Review of Johannes Purkinje's Sight from a Subjective Standpoint', quoted in *The Collected Works*, vol. 12, xxi.

42 Johann Wolfgang von Goethe, 'From a Review of Ernst Stiedenroth's A Psychology in Clarification of Phenomena from the Soul', in *The Collected Works*, vol. 12, 46.

43 Immanuel Kant, *Anthropology from a Pragmatic Point of View*, trans. Robert B. Louden (Cambridge: Cambridge University Press, 2006), Ak. 167.

44 Kant, *Critique of Judgment*, Ak. 314; Kant, *Anthropology from a Pragmatic Point of View*, Ak. 167–8.

45 Kant, *Critique of Judgment*, Ak. 314.

46 Kant, *Critique of Judgment*, Ak. 314; translation amended.

47 Kant, *Critique of Judgment*, Ak. 313–14.

48 Kant, *Critique of Judgment*, Ak. 317–18.

49 Monika Class, *Coleridge and Kantian Ideas in England, 1796–1817: Coleridge's Response to German Philosophy* (London: Bloomsbury, 2012), 156–7.

50 Kant, *Critique of Judgment*, Ak. 314.

51 Kant, *Critique of Judgment*, Ak. 316.

52 Kant, *Critique of Judgment*, Ak. 351–2.

53 Kant, *Critique of Judgment*, Ak. 314.

54 Johann Wolfgang von Goethe, *Materialien zur Geschichte der Farbenlehre*, quoted in Benjamin, *The Origin of German Tragic Drama*, 27.

55 Elaine P. Miller, 'Nietzsche on Individuation and Purposiveness in Nature', in *A Companion to Nietzsche*, ed. Keith Ansell Pearson (Chichester: Blackwell, 2009), 65, 63.

56 Friedrich Nietzsche, *The Birth of Tragedy*, trans. Clifton P. Fadiman (New York: Dover Publications, 1995), 50–5.

57 Friedrich Nietzsche, *Twilight of the Idols*, trans. Antony M. Ludovici (London: Wordsworth, 2007), 81; emphases in the original.

58 Walter Benjamin, 'Socrates', in *Selected Writings*, vol. 1, 52; translation amended.

59 Benjamin, 'The Concept of Criticism in German Romanticism', in *Selected Writings*, vol. 1, 179.

60 Benjamin, *The Origin of German Tragic Drama*, 35, 29.

61 Johann Wolfgang von Goethe, *Faust*, Part II, Act I, trans. Walter Arndt (New York: Norton, 2001), lines 6287–90; translated amended.

62 John F. Cornell, 'Faustian Phenomena: Teleology in Goethe's Interpretation of Plants and Animals', *The Journal of Medicine and Philosophy: A Forum for Bioethics and Philosophy of Medicine*, vol. 15, issue 5 (October 1990): 490.

63 Arthur Schopenhauer, *On the Fourfold Root of the Principle of Sufficient Reason*, trans. E. F. J. Payne (La Salle, IL: Open Court, 1974), 56.

64 Schopenhauer, *On the Fourfold Root of the Principle of Sufficient Reason*, 233.

65 Arthur Schopenhauer, 'On the Will in Nature', in *On the Fourfold Root of the Principle of Sufficient Reason* (New York: Cosimo, 2007), 216–17.

66 Schopenhauer, *On the Fourfold Root of the Principle of Sufficient Reason*, 5.

67 Arthur Schopenhauer, *The World as Will and Idea*, vol. 3, trans. R. B. Haldane and J. Kemp (London: Kegan Paul, 1909), 79.

68 Schopenhauer, *The World as Will and Idea*, vol. 3, 382.

69 Schopenhauer, *The World as Will and Idea*, vol. 3, 380.

70 Schopenhauer, *The World as Will and Idea*, vol. 3, 373.

71 Friedrich Nietzsche, 'On the Concept of the Organic since Kant', trans. Paderborn Nawrath in *The Agonist*, vol. 3, issue 1 (Spring 2010): 93.

72 Miller, 'Nietzsche on Individuation and Purposiveness in Nature', 68–70.

73 Miller, 'Nietzsche on Individuation and Purposiveness in Nature', 65.

74 Nietzsche, 'On the Concept of the Organic since Kant', 98.

75 Miller, 'Nietzsche on Individuation and Purposiveness in Nature', 64.

76 Miller, 'Nietzsche on Individuation and Purposiveness in Nature', 64.

77 Miller, 'Nietzsche on Individuation and Purposiveness in Nature', 66.

78 Goethe, 'The Purpose Set Forth', in *The Collected Works*, vol. 12, 64.

79 Johann Wolfgang von Goethe, 'Epirrhema', in *The Collected Works*, vol. 1, ed. Christopher Middleton (Princeton, NJ: Princeton University Press, 1983), 158–9; translation amended.

80　Goethe, 'The Purpose Set Forth', in *The Collected Works*, vol. 12, 63.

81　Miller, 'Nietzsche on Individuation and Purposiveness in Nature', 62.

82　Miller, 'Nietzsche on Individuation and Purposiveness in Nature', 67–8.

83　Walter Benjamin, 'Goethe's Elective Affinities', in *Selected Writings*, vol. 1, 333.

84　Benjamin, 'Goethe's Elective Affinities', in *Selected Writings*, vol. 1, 334.

85　Benjamin, 'Goethe's Elective Affinities', in *Selected Writings*, vol. 1, 350–1.

86　Benjamin, *The Origin of German Tragic Drama*, 34.

87　Benjamin, *The Origin of German Tragic Drama*, 43.

88　Plato, *The Republic*, ed. G. R. F. Ferrari (Cambridge: Cambridge University Press, 2000), 339.

89　Graham Gilloch, *Walter Benjamin: Critical Constellations* (Cambridge: Polity, 2002), 71.

90　David Lowe and Simon Sharp, *Goethe and Palladio* (Barrington, MA: Lindisfarne, 2005), 29, 34, 37.

91　Friederike von Schwerin-High, 'Blank Verse Theatre Texts and Weimar Classicism', in *Weimar Classicism: Studies in Goethe, Schiller, Foster, Berlepsch, Wieland, Herder, and Stein*, ed. David Gallagher (Lewiston, NY: Mellen, 2011), 65, 94.

92　T. J. Reed, 'Weimar Classicism: Goethe's Alliance with Schiller', in *Weimar Classicism: Studies in Goethe, Schiller, Foster, Berlepsch, Wieland, Herder, and Stein*, 27.

93　Theodor W. Adorno, *Notes to Literature*, vol. 2, ed. Rolf Tiedemann (New York: Columbia University Press, 1991), 155–7.

4　Pure content: the ephemerality of colour

1　Caygill, *Walter Benjamin: The Colour of Experience*, 82.

2　Kant, *Critique of Pure Reason*, A29/B45-A30/B45.

3　Kant, *Critique of Pure Reason*, A29/B45-A30/B45, A166/B208-A167-B209.

4　Walter Benjamin, 'Dialogue on the Rainbow', in *Early Writings, 1910–1917*, trans. Howard Eiland (Cambridge, MA: Harvard University Press, 2011), 217; Pope Pius IX, 'Ineffabilis Deus', Apostolic Constitution issued on 8 December 1854, http://www.newadvent.org/library/docs_pi09id.htm.

5　Benjamin, 'Socrates', in *Selected Writings*, vol. 1, 53.

6　Walter Benjamin, 'A Child's View of Colour', in *Selected Writings*, vol. 1, 50–2.

7　Walter Benjamin, 'Painting, or Signs and Marks', in *Selected Writings*, vol. 1, 84–5.

8　Walter Benjamin, *Gesammelte Schriften*, Bd. 6, ed. Rolf Tiedemann and Herman Schweppenhäuser (Frankfurt am Main: Suhrkamp, 1991), 69–71.

9 Benjamin, *Gesammelte Schriften*, Bd. 6, 121–2.

10 Caygill, *Walter Benjamin: The Colour of Experience*, 83–4.

11 Benjamin, 'The Concept of Criticism in German Romanticism', in *Selected Writings*, vol. 1, 180.

12 Benjamin, 'Goethe's Elective Affinities', in *Selected Writings*, vol. 1, 297–300.

13 Benjamin, 'A Child's View of Colour', in *Selected Writings*, vol. 1, 50–1; Benjamin, *Gesammelte Schriften*, Bd. 7, ed. Rolf Tiedemann and Hermann Schweppenhäuser (Frankfurt am Main: Suhrkamp, 1991), 25.

14 Benjamin, 'Socrates', in *Selected Writings*, vol. 1, 52.

15 Benjamin, *Gesammelte Schriften*, Bd. 6, 144.

16 Caygill, *Walter Benjamin: The Colour of Experience*, xiv.

17 Leslie, *Hollywood Flatlands*, 263–4.

18 Johann Wolfgang von Goethe, 'Contribution to Optics', in *Goethe's Theory of Colour*, ed. Maria Schindler (Sussex: New Knowledge Books, 1964), ¶8; Leslie, *Hollywood Flatlands*, 268–9; Benjamin, *Gesammelte Schriften*, Bd. 4, ed. Tillman Rexroth (Frankfurt am Main: Suhrkamp, 1991), 614.

19 Goethe, 'Contribution to Optics', in *Goethe's Theory of Colour*, ¶67.

20 Goethe, 'Contribution to Optics', in *Goethe's Theory of Colour*, ¶38.

21 Goethe, *Maxims and Reflections*, #430.

22 Johann Wolfgang von Goethe, 'Research into the Elements of a Theory of Colours', in *Goethe's Theory of Colour*, ¶14.

23 Goethe, *Maxims and Reflections*, #430.

24 Goethe, 'Research into the Elements of a Theory of Colours', *Goethe's Theory of Colour*, ¶56, ¶67.

25 Goethe, 'Research into the Elements of a Theory of Colours', *Goethe's Theory of Colour*, ¶66.

26 Éric Alliez, *The Brain-Eye: New Histories of Modern Painting*, trans. Robin Mackay (London: Rowman and Littlefield, 2016), 18.

27 Johann Wolfgang von Goethe, 'Colours in the Sky', in *The Collected Works*, vol. 12, 151.

28 Johann Wolfgang von Goethe, 'Theory of Colour', in *The Collected Works*, vol. 12, 159.

29 Johann Wolfgang von Goethe, 'Except from "Toward a Theory of Weather"', in *The Collected Works*, vol. 12, 148.

30 Alliez, *The Brain-Eye*, 19.

31 Alliez, *The Brain-Eye*, 11–12.

32 Gilles Deleuze, *Kant's Critical Philosophy*, trans. Hugh Tomlinson and Barbara Habberjam (London: Althone, 1984), 48–9.

33 Deleuze, *Kant's Critical Philosophy*, 49.

34 Gilles Deleuze, *Difference and Repetition*, trans. Paul Patton
(New York: Columbia University Press, 1994), 146–7.

35 Gilles Deleuze, *Nietzsche and Philosophy*, trans. Hugh Tomlinson
(London: Continuum, 1986), 48.

36 Deleuze, *Kant's Critical Philosophy*, 53–5.

37 Deleuze, *Kant's Critical Philosophy*, 56; emphasis added.

38 Deleuze, *Kant's Critical Philosophy*, 54; Kant, *Critique of Judgment*, Ak. 302.

39 Deleuze, *Kant's Critical Philosophy*, 57.

40 Alliez, *The Brain-Eye*, 13, 1.

41 Gilles Deleuze, *The Logic of Sense*, ed. Constantin V. Boundas
(London: Continuum, 2004), 8–12, 24–5.

42 Deleuze, *The Logic of Sense*, 128.

43 Deleuze, *The Logic of Sense*, 73.

44 Deleuze, *The Logic of Sense*, 11, 158, 137. Indeed, humour is often characterized
by the grammatical form of the 'fourth person singular' that Deleuze in *The
Logic of Sense* also associates with the pure event (118). While the fourth-person
singular is used in some languages to distinguish the obviate third person, a third
person (he/she/it) even further removed from the speaker, it can be found more
colloquially in English when referring to a nonspecific or indefinite third person,
found in its purest form in jokes: 'Man walks into a bar'.

45 Slavoj Žižek, *Organs without Bodies: On Deleuze and Consequences*
(New York: Routledge, 2004), 68.

46 Deleuze, *The Logic of Sense*, 118.

47 Deleuze, *Difference and Repetition*, 57.

48 Deleuze, *The Logic of Sense*, 23, 105.

49 Deleuze, *Difference and Repetition*, 57.

50 Alliez, *The Brain-Eye*, 2–4; emphasis in the original.

51 Alliez, *The Brain-Eye*, 7.

52 Alliez, *The Brain-Eye*, 8, xxiv.

53 Benjamin, *Gesammelte Schriften*, Bd. 6, 122–3.

54 Benjamin, *Gesammelte Schriften*, Bd. 6, 280.

55 Walter Benjamin, 'The Rainbow: A Conversation about Imagination', in *Early
Writings, 1910-1917*, 220.

56 Sigrid Weigel, 'The Flash of Knowledge and the Temporality of Images: Walter
Benjamin's Image-Based Epistemology and Its Preconditions in Visual Arts
and Media History', trans. Chadwick Truscott Smith and Christine Kutschbach,
Critical Inquiry, vol. 41, no. 2 (winter 2015): 356.

57 Walter Benjamin, 'Aphorisms on Imagination and Colour', in *Selected Writings*,
vol. 1, 48–9.

58 Alliez, *The Brain-Eye*, 16.

59 Benjamin, *Gesammelte Schriften*, Bd. 6, 113–14.

60 Peter Selz, *German Expressionist Painting* (Berkeley: University of California Press, 1974), 29; Dietmar Elger, *Expressionism: A Revolution in German Art* (Köln: Taschen, 2007), 94.

61 Benjamin, *The Origin of German Tragic Drama*, 54.

62 Benjamin, *The Origin of German Tragic Drama*, 139.

63 Walter Benjamin, *Gesammelte Briefe*, Bd. 1 (Frankfurt am Main: Suhrkamp, 1978), 143; Gershom Scholem, *Walter Benjamin: The Story of a Friendship*, trans. Harry Zohn (New York: New York Review Books, 1981), 37.

64 Martin Rodan, 'Matthias Grünewald, «le plus forcené» des peintres selon Joris-Karl Huysmans', in *Bulletin du Centre de recherche français à Jérusalem*, vol. 24 (2013): 7.

65 J.-K. Huysmans, *La Bas*, trans. Robert Irwin (Cambridge: Dedalus, 1986), 12–13.

66 J.-K. Huysmans, *Grünewald: With an Essay by J.-K. Huysmans*, trans. Robert Baldick (Oxford: Phaidon Press, 1976), 12.

67 Mary Rasmussen, 'Viols, Violists and Venus in Grünewald's Isenheim Altar', *Early Music*, vol. 29, no. 1 (February 2001): 70–2.

68 Walter Benjamin, 'Notes for a Study of the Beauty of Colored Illustrations in Children's Books', in *Selected Writings*, vol. 1, 265; translation amended.

69 Selz, German Expressionist Painting, 25.

70 André Domnrowski, 'The Untimely Classicism of Hans von Marées', in *Modern Art and the Idea of the Mediterranean*, ed. Vojtěch Jirat-Wasiutyński (Toronto: University of Toronto Press, 2007), 87.

71 Nikolaus Pevsner, 'Some Thoughts on German Painting', in *Pevsner: The Complete Broadcast Talks, Architecture and Art on Radio and Television, 1945–1977*, ed. Stephen Games (London: Routledge, 2016), 327.

72 Fritz Novotny, *Painting and Sculpture in Europe, 1780–1880* (New Haven: Yale University Press, 1995), 324–5.

73 Novotny, *Painting and Sculpture in Europe*, 324.

74 Setz, *German Expressionist Painting*, 28–9.

75 Domnrowski, 'The Untimely Classicism of Hans von Marées', in *Modern Art and the Idea of the Mediterranean*, 86.

76 Domnrowski, 'The Untimely Classicism of Hans von Marées', in *Modern Art and the Idea of the Mediterranean*, 87, 102–3.

77 Michael F. Marra, *Essays on Japan: Between Aesthetics and Literature* (Leiden: Brill, 2010), 133–4.

78 Marra, *Essays on Japan*, 135.

79 Walter Benjamin, 'Program for a Proletarian Children's Theatre', in *Selected Writings*, vol. 2, 204.

80 Conrad Fielder, *On Judging Works of Visual Art*, trans. Henry Schaefer-
    Simmern and Fulmer Mood (Berkeley: University of California Press, 1978),
    57–8. The Japanese philosopher Nishida Kitaro, who became acquainted with
    Fiedler's work in 1912, further associates Fiedler's Goethean 'pure seeing' with
    his own concept of 'pure experience' developed in *An Inquiry into the Good*: the
    basic form of every sensuous and intellectual experience that precedes the split
    into a subject–object duality and therefore any conceptual judgement about the
    colour seen or sound heard (Nishida Kitaro, *An Inquiry into the Good*, trans.
    Masao Abe and Christopher Ives (New Haven: Yale University Press, 1990), 3).

81 Fiedler, *On Judging*, 80.

82 Domnrowski, 'The Untimely Classicism of Hans von Marées', in *Modern Art
    and the Idea of the Mediterranean*, 101, 104.

83 Domnrowski, 'The Untimely Classicism of Hans von Marées', in *Modern Art
    and the Idea of the Mediterranean*, 94.

84 Selz, *German Expressionist Painting*, 16–17.

85 Martin Jay, 'Chromophilia: *Der Blaue Reiter*, Walter Benjamin, and the
    Emancipation of Color', *positions: asia critique*, vol. 26, no. 1 (February
    2018): 14.

86 Benjamin, *Gesammelte Briefe*, Bd. 1, 394, translated in Weigel, 'The Flash of
    Knowledge and the Temporality of Images', 352–3.

87 Benjamin, *The Correspondence of Walter Benjamin: 1910–1940*, 156.

88 Jay, 'Chromophilia: *Der Blaue Reiter*, Walter Benjamin, and the Emancipation of
    Color', 21–2.

89 John Gage, *Colour and Culture: Practice and Meaning from Antiquity
    to Abstraction* (Berkeley: University of California Press, 1999), 207; Jay,
    'Chromophilia: *Der Blaue Reiter*, Walter Benjamin, and the Emancipation of
    Color', 14.

90 Paul Klee, *Paul Klee* (New York: Parkstone, 2012), 115.

91 Paul Klee, *Notebooks*, vol. 1, ed. Jürg Spiller (London: Lund Humphries,
    1961), 3–4.

92 Malika Maskarinec, 'Paul Klee and the Genesis of Form', *Word & Image*, vol. 32,
    issue 2 (2016): 208.

93 Klee, *Notebooks*, vol. 1, 17.

94 Klee, *Notebooks*, vol. 1, 69.

95 Klee, *Notebooks*, vol. 1, 237.

96 Klee, *Notebooks*, vol. 1, 266.

97 Klee, *Notebooks*, vol. 1, 264–5.

98 Gilles Deleuze, 'Postscript on the Societies of Control', *October*, vol. 59 (winter
    1992): 5–7.

99 Klee, *Notebooks*, vol. 1, 468.

100 Klee, *Notebooks*, vol. 1, 468–9.

101 Alliez, *The Brain-Eye*, 14–15.

102 Klee, *Notebooks*, vol. 1, 468–9.

103 Goethe, 'Theory of Colour', in *The Collected Works*, vol. 12, ¶50.

104 Gerald Finley, *Angel in the Sun: Turner's Vision of History* (Montreal: McGill-Queens University Press, 1999), 202.

105 Gerald Finley, 'The Deluge Pictures: Reflections on Goethe, J. M. W. Turner and Early Nineteenth-Century', *Zeitschrift für Kunstgeschichte*, Bd. 60, H. 4 (1997): 532.

106 Jerrold Ziff, 'John Langhorne and Turner's "Fallacies of Hope"', *Journal of the Warburg and Courtauld Institutes*, vol. 27 (1964): 340–2.

107 Finley, *Angel in the Sun*, 205.

108 Finley, *Angel in the Sun*, 205.

109 Finley, 'The Deluge Pictures', 538.

110 David Jasper, 'J. M. W. Turner: Interpreter of the Bible', in *Biblical Studies/Cultural Studies: The Third Sheffield Colloquium*, ed. J. Cheryl Exum and Stephen D. Moore (Sheffield: Sheffield Academic Press, 1998), 312.

111 Jonathan Crary, *Techniques of the Observer: On Vision and Modernity in the Nineteenth Century* (Cambridge: MIT Press, 1992), 138.

112 Finley, *Angel in the Sun*, 206.

113 W. J. T. Mitchell, 'Metamorphoses of the Vortex: Hogarth, Turner and Blakes', in *Articulate Images: The Sister Arts from Hogarth to Tennyson*, ed. Richard Wendorf (Minneapolis: University of Minnesota Press, 1983), 147.

114 Mitchell, 'Metamorphoses of the Vortex', in *Articulate Images*, 147–50.

115 A. Wilton, 'Turner and Colour', in *Art/Neuroscience Series in Front of 'Bright Stone of Honour'* (Ashmolean Museum: Oxford University, 2008); Rachel Teukolsky, *The Literate Eye: Victorian Art Writing and Modernist Aesthetics* (Oxford: Oxford University Press, 2009), 59.

116 Caygill, *Walter Benjamin: The Colour of Experience*, 47; emphases in the original.

117 Caygill, *Walter Benjamin: The Colour of Experience*, 149.

118 Caygill, *Walter Benjamin: The Colour of Experience*, 149, 152.

119 Caygill, *Walter Benjamin: The Colour of Experience*, 150.

5 Pure expression: the critical violence of language

1 Goethe, 'Theory of Colour', in *The Collected Works*, vol. 12, 159; Caygill, *Walter Benjamin: The Colour of Experience*, 22.

2 Benjamin, 'Socrates', in *Selected Writings*, vol. 1, 52–3.

3 Walter Benjamin, 'The Metaphysics of Youth', in *Selected Writings*, vol. 1, 7.

4   Benjamin, *Gesammelte Schriften*, Bd. 6, 71. For a translation and discussion of Benjamin's fragment 'On Shame', see Jacob Bard-Rosenberg, 'Walter Benjamin on Blushing: New Translations of Fragments on Colour and Some Inflationary Reading Notes', *Academia.edu* (December 2017), https://www.academia.edu/35350866/Walter_Benjamin_on_Blushing_New_translations_of_fragments_on_colour_and_some_inflationary_reading_notes_draft_.

5   Deuber-Mankowsky, 'Hanging over the Abyss', 184–5.

6   Walter Benjamin, 'On Language as Such and on the Language of Man', in *Selected Writings*, vol. 1, 62–3.

7   Benjamin, 'On Language as Such and the Language of Man', in *Selected Writings*, vol. 1, 65.

8   Benjamin, *On the Origin of German Tragic Drama*, 166.

9   Benjamin, *On the Origin of German Tragic Drama*, 38.

10   Walter Benjamin, 'The Task of the Translator', in *Selected Writings*, vol. 1, 261.

11   Benjamin finds confirmation for this thesis in 'The Ground of Intentional Immediacy', in the neo-Kantian realism of Alois Adolf Riehl. See Walter Benjamin, 'The Ground of Intentional Immediacy', in *Selected Writings*, vol. 1, 88.

12   Benjamin, 'The Concept of Criticism in German Romanticism', in *Selected Writings*, vol. 1, 154.

13   Benjamin, 'The Task of the Translator', in *Selected Writings*, vol. 1, 262.

14   Benjamin, 'The Task of the Translator', in *Selected Writings*, vol. 1, 261.

15   Benjamin, 'The Task of the Translator', in *Selected Writings*, vol. 1, 261.

16   Benjamin, 'The Task of the Translator', in *Selected Writings*, vol. 1, 257.

17   Benjamin, 'The Task of the Translator', in *Selected Writings*, vol. 1, 262.

18   Johann Wolfgang von Goethe, 'Note and Queries for a Better Understanding' (from *West-Easterly Divan*), trans. Jorg Waltje, *Other Voices*, vol. 2, no. 2 (March 2002); translation amended.

19   Benjamin, 'The Task of the Translator', in *Selected Writings*, vol. 1, 260.

20   Benjamin, 'Goethe's *Elective Affinities*', in *Selected Writings*, vol. 1, 317.

21   Benjamin, 'Goethe's *Elective Affinities*', in *Selected Writings*, vol. 1, 333.

22   Benjamin, *On the Origin of German Tragic Drama*, 160.

23   Goethe, *Maxims and Reflections*, #1112; Benjamin, *On the Origin of German Tragic Drama*, 161–2.

24   Benjamin, 'Goethe's *Elective Affinities*', in *Selected Writings*, vol. 1, 349–50

25   Benjamin, 'Goethe's *Elective Affinities*', in *Selected Writings*, vol. 1, 350.

26   Benjamin, 'Goethe's *Elective Affinities*', in *Selected Writings*, vol. 1, 340.

27   Benjamin, 'Goethe's *Elective Affinities*', in *Selected Writings*, vol. 1, 340.

28   Benjamin, *On the Origin of German Tragic Drama*, 182; translated amended.

29 In notes associated with the writing of the 'Critique of Violence', Benjamin describes such a position, with some reservations, as an ethical anarchism and makes clear that it stands in opposition to Herbart Vorwerk's assumption, in his juridical analysis of the legal right to use force, that only the state has such a right (Walter Benjamin, 'The Right to Use Force', in *Selected Writings*, vol. 1, 231–4).

30 Jürgen Habermas, 'Consciousness-Raising or Redemptive Criticism: The Contemporaneity of Walter Benjamin', in *New German Critique*, no. 17 (1979): 30–59.

31 Walter Benjamin, 'Critique of Violence', in *Selected Writings*, vol. 1, 250–2; Georges Sorel,*Reflections on Violence*, ed. Jeremy Jennings (Cambridge: Cambridge University Press, 2004), 28.

32 Benjamin, 'Critique of Violence', in *Selected Writings*, vol. 1, 250–2.

33 Benjamin, *The Correspondence of Walter Benjamin: 1910–1940*, 94.

34 Walter Benjamin, 'Comments on Gundolf's Goethe', in *Selected Writings*, vol. 1, 97–9; Benjamin, *The Correspondence of Walter Benjamin: 1910–1940*, 196.

35 Benjamin, 'Goethe's *Elective Affinities*', in *Selected Writings*, vol. 1, 305, 307, 339.

36 Benjamin, 'Goethe's *Elective Affinities*', in *Selected Writings*, vol. 1, 339, 330.

37 Benjamin, 'Goethe's *Elective Affinities*', in *Selected Writings*, vol. 1, 307; cf. Friedrich Nietzsche, *The Gay Science*, trans. Walter Kaufmann (New York: Vintage, 1974), 273.

38 Benjamin, 'Goethe's *Elective Affinities*', in *Selected Writings*, vol. 1, 309–10, 339.

39 Benjamin, 'Goethe's *Elective Affinities*', in *Selected Writings*, vol. 1, 317, 322.

40 Friedrich Nietzsche, *Beyond Good and Evil*, ed. Rolf-Peter Horstmann and Judith Norman (Cambridge: Cambridge University Press, 2002), 59, quoted in Walter Benjamin, 'Fate and Character', in *Selected Writings*, vol. 1, 202. Nietzsche's aphorism refers to Heraclitus's Fragment 247: *ethos anthropoi daimon* (the character of a human is their *daimon*).

41 Benjamin, 'Fate and Character', in *Selected Writings*, vol. 1, 203–4.

42 Benjamin, 'Fate and Character', in *Selected Writings*, vol. 1, 203.

43 Benjamin, 'Fate and Character', in *Selected Writings*, vol. 1, 327–8.

44 Johann Wolfgang von Goethe, *Elective Affinities*, trans. R. J. Hollingdale (Harmondsworth, Middlesex: Penguin Books, 1971), 300.

45 Rochelle Tobias, 'Irreconcilable: Ethics and Aesthetics for Hermann Cohen and Walter Benjamin', *MLN*, vol. 127, no. 3 (April 2012): 665–80.

46 Benjamin, 'Goethe's *Elective Affinities*', in *Selected Writings*, vol. 1, 333, 340.

47 Tobias, 'Irreconcilable: Ethics and Aesthetics for Hermann Cohen and Walter Benjamin', *MLN*, vol. 127, no. 3 (April 2012): 667–8.

48 Walter Benjamin, 'The Meaning of Time in the Moral Universe', in *Selected Writings*, vol. 1, 286.

49 Tobias, 'Irreconcilable: Ethics and Aesthetics for Hermann Cohen and Walter Benjamin', *MLN*, vol. 127, no. 3 (April 2012): n.15, 273.

50 Gasché, 'The Sober Absolute', 64.

51 Gasché, 'The Sober Absolute', 67–8.

52 Benjamin, *On the Origin of German Tragic Drama*, 78, 62; Tobias, 'Irreconcilable: Ethics and Aesthetics for Hermann Cohen and Walter Benjamin', *MLN*, vol. 127, no. 3 (April 2012): 667.

53 Benjamin, 'Goethe's *Elective Affinities*', in *Selected Writings*, vol. 1, 342–3.

54 Benjamin, 'Goethe's *Elective Affinities*', in *Selected Writings*, vol. 1, 332.

55 Benjamin, *On the Origin of German Tragic Drama*, 223–4.

56 Benjamin, *On the Origin of German Tragic Drama*, 176.

57 Benjamin, *On the Origin of German Tragic Drama*, 232.

58 Benjamin, 'Goethe's *Elective Affinities*', in *Selected Writings*, vol. 1, 340.

59 Benjamin, 'Goethe's *Elective Affinities*', in *Selected Writings*, vol. 1, 352.

60 Benjamin, 'Goethe's *Elective Affinities*', in *Selected Writings*, vol. 1, 345.

61 Benjamin, 'Goethe's *Elective Affinities*', in *Selected Writings*, vol. 1, 355.

62 Benjamin, 'Goethe's *Elective Affinities*', in *Selected Writings*, vol. 1, 354–5.

63 Caygill, *Walter Benjamin: The Colour of Experience*, 50; emphasis in the original.

64 Walter Benjamin, 'Literary History and the Study of Literature', in *Selected Writings*, vol. 2, 459.

65 Walter Benjamin, 'Comments on Gundolf's Goethe', in *Selected Writings*, vol. 1, 98.

66 Benjamin, *The Arcades Project*, N1, 8.

67 Benjamin, 'Comments on Gundolf's Goethe', in *Selected Writings*, vol. 1, 98.

68 G. G. Gervinus, quoted in Gordon A. Craig, 'Georg Gottfried Gervinus: The Historian as Activist', *Pacific Historical Review*, vol. 41, no. 1 (February 1972): 1–14.

69 Walter Benjamin, 'Curriculum Vitae (III)', in *Selected Writings*, vol. 2, 78.

70 Benjamin, *On the Origin of German Tragic Drama*, 45–6.

71 Benjamin, *On the Origin of German Tragic Drama*, 45–7.

72 Benjamin, 'The Concept of Criticism in German Romanticism', in *Selected Writings*, vol. 1, 181.

73 Benjamin, *The Arcades Project*, N3, 1.

74 Walter Benjamin, 'Theory of Knowledge', in *Selected Writings*, vol. 1, 277.

75 Edward P. Comentale and Andrzej Gasiorek, 'On the Significance of Hulmean Modernism', in *T.E. Hulme and the Question of Modernism*, ed. Edward P. Comentale and Andrzej Gasiorek (Aldershot: Ashgate, 2006), 2–3.

76 Comentale and Gasiorek, 'On the Significance of Hulmean Modernism', in *T.E. Hulme and the Question of Modernism*, 7.

77 T. E. Hulme, 'Modern Art and Its Philosophy', in *Selected Writings*, ed. Patrick McGuiness (New York: Routledge, 2003), 97–8.

78 T. E. Hulme, 'German Chronicle', in *Selected Writings*, ed. Patrick McGuiness (New York: Routledge, 2003), 89.

79 Wilhelm Worringer, *Abstraction and Empathy: A Contribution to the Psychology of Style*, trans. Michael Bullock (Chicago: Elephant, 1997), 8.

80 Worringer, *Abstraction and Empathy*, 16–17.

81 Hulme, 'Modern Art and Its Philosophy', in *Selected Writings*, 96–7.

82 Hulme, 'Modern Art and Its Philosophy', in *Selected Writings*, 108.

83 T. E. Hulme, 'A Lecture on Modern Poetry', in *Selected Writings*, ed. Patrick McGuiness (New York: Routledge, 2003), 63.

84 T. E. Hulme, 'Bergson's Theory of Art', in *The Collected Writings of T. E. Hulme*, ed. Karen Csengeri (Oxford: Clarendon, 1994), 191–204.

85 Mary Ann Gillies, 'The Curious History of Imagism: Of Hulme, Bergson, Worringer, and Imagism's Readers. A Response to Andrew Hay', *Connotations*, vol. 23, no. 1 (2013): 145.

86 Joseph Frank, *The Idea of Spatial Form* (New Brunswick: Rutgers University Press, 1991), 58.

87 T. E. Hulme, 'Romanticism and Classicism', in *Selected Writings*, ed. Patrick McGuiness (New York: Routledge, 2003), 75.

88 T. S. Eliot, '*Ulysses*, Order and Myth', in *Selected Prose*, ed. Frank Kermode (London: Faber and Faber, 1975), 177–8.

89 Hulme, 'Modern Art and Its Philosophy', in *Selected Writings*, 104.

90 Miriam Hansen, 'T. E. Hulme, Mercenary of Modernism, or, Fragments of Avantgarde Sensibility in Pre-World War I Britain', *ELH*, vol. 47, no. 2 (summer 1980): 369.

91 T. E. Hulme, 'Notes on Language and Style', in *Selected Writings*, ed. Patrick McGuiness (New York: Routledge, 2003), 44.

92 Hansen, 'T. E. Hulme, Mercenary of Modernism', 376, 369.

93 Hansen, 'T. E. Hulme, Mercenary of Modernism', 377.

94 Hulme, 'A Lecture on Modern Poetry', in *Selected Writings*, 64; Alun R. Jones, *The Life and Opinions of T. E. Hulme* (Boston: Beacon, 1960), 23; T. E. Hulme, 'Cinders', in *Selected Writings*, 22.

95 T. E. Hulme, 'Cinders', *Selected Writings*, 36.

96 Hulme, 'Notes on Language and Style', in *Selected Writings*, 47.

97 Hulme, 'Cinders', in *Selected Writings*, 36.

98 Edward P. Comentale, 'Hulme's Feelings', in *T. E. Hulme and the Question of Modernism*, 210; for Hulme's Nietzscheanism, cf. Elizabeth Kuhn, 'Toward an Anti-humanism of Life: The Modernism of Nietzsche, Hulme and Yeats', *Journal of Modern Literature*, vol. 34, no. 4 (summer 2011): 11; Hansen, 'T. E. Hulme,

Mercenary of Modernism', 364; Helen Carr, 'T.E. Hulme and the 'Spiritual Dread of Space', in *T. E. Hulme and the Question of Modernism*, 96–8.

99   Hulme, 'Cinders', in *Selected Writings*, 19–22.

100 Hulme, 'Cinders', in *Selected Writings*, 18–21.

101 Hulme, 'Notes on Language and Style', in *Selected Writings*, 39.

102 Hulme, 'Notes on Language and Style', in *Selected Writings*, 56.

103 Hulme, 'Cinders', in *Selected Writings*, 28.

104 Kant, for example, mentions 'wastelands lying in deep shadow and inviting melancholy meditation' in his examples of the judgement of the sublime, which induce an imagined feeling of 'amazement bordering on terror' (Kant, *Critique of Judgment*, Ak. 269). But his deduction of such a judgement implicates it in a moral vocation that surpasses any subjugation to empirical nature, not a realization which trivializes all human values to the cindery reality beneath. Hulme's experience of the formlessness of the flat open spaces and wide horizons fails to meet Kant's definition of the disinterested pleasure in pure judgements of free natural beauty, such as flowers and birdsong, which are based on the free lawfulness of the imagination in relation to the represented form of the object, or his description of the charm that arises from the view of distant and indistinct objects, which provide the imagination with an occasion to entertain itself in play with fantasies and engage in fictions (*dichten*).

105 Kant, *Critique of Judgment*, Ak. 276.

106 Although, as Alison Ross observes, Kant's aesthetic account of the wasteland nonetheless remains connected to a regulative teleological assumption rejected by Hulme, that even 'things that we find disagreeable and contrapurposive' such as 'wilderness areas of America' appear to be beneficial to humans, since they provide an incentive to colonize such areas (Kant, Critique of Judgment, Ak. 259, quoted in Alison Ross, *The Aesthetic Paths of Philosophy: Presentation in Kant, Heidegger, Lacoue-Labarthe, and Nancy* (Stanford, CA: Stanford University Press, 2007), 52).

107 Kuhn, 'Toward an Anti-humanism of Life', 11; Hansen, 'T. E. Hulme, Mercenary of Modernism', 376, 364.

108 Hulme, 'Romanticism and Classicism', in *Selected Writings*, 69–71.

109 Coleridge, *Biographia Literaria*, chapter 13.

110 Alan P. R. Gregory, *Coleridge and the Conservative Imagination* (Macon, GA: Mercer University Press, 2003), 62 and 57.

111 Samuel Taylor Coleridge, *Coleridge's Notebooks: A Selection*, ed. Seamus Perry (Oxford: Oxford University Press, 2002), 124.

112 Theresa M. Kelley, 'Romanticism's Errant Allegory', in *The Cambridge Companion to Allegory*, ed. Rita Copeland and Peter Struck (Cambridge: Cambridge University Press, 2010), 217–18.

113 Tom Sutcliffe, 'In Defence of Shakespeare's Difficult Bits', *Guardian*, 5 January 2016, https://www.theguardian.com/commentisfree/2016/jan/05/shakespeare-globe-theatre-language; cf. E. Charles Nelson, 'Shakespeare Has Missed the Dandelion', *Shakespeare*, vol. 12, no. 2 (2016): 175–84.

114 Hulme, 'Romanticism and Classicism', in *Selected Writings*, 78, 75.

115 Hulme, 'Romanticism and Classicism', in *Selected Writings*, 68.

116 Hulme, 'Romanticism and Classicism', in *Selected Writings*, 74–5.

117 Hulme, 'Romanticism and Classicism', in *Selected Writings*, 78.

118 T. E. Hulme, 'Poems and Fragments', in *Selected Writings*, ed. Patrick McGuiness (New York: Routledge, 2003), 1.

119 Paul Edwards, 'The Imagery of Hulme's Poems and Notebooks', in *T. E. Hulme and the Question of Modernism*, ed. Edward P. Comentale and Andrzej Gasiorek (Aldershot: Ashgate, 2006), 32–3.

120 Hulme, 'Poems and Fragments', in *Selected Writings*, 2.

121 Hulme, 'Poems and Fragments', in *Selected Writings*, 3.

122 Hulme, 'Poems and Fragments', in *Selected Writings*, 3.

123 Hulme, 'Poems and Fragments', in *Selected Writings*, 1.

124 Hulme, 'Poems and Fragments', in *Selected Writings*, 2.

125 Hulme, 'Poems and Fragments', in *Selected Writings*, 3.

6 Pure history: the untimeliness of technology

1 Uwe Steiner, 'The True Politician: Walter Benjamin's Concept of the Political', *New German Critique*, no. 83 (spring/summer 2001): 61.

2 Thomas O. Haakenson, '"The Merely Illusory Paradise of Habits": Salomo Friedländer, Walter Benjamin, and the Grotesque', *New German Critique*, vol. 36, no. 1 (106) (winter 2009): 120, n.144, 147.

3 Scholem, *Walter Benjamin: The Story of a Friendship*, 123–4; Steiner, 'The True Politician'; see also Anson Rabinbach, 'Between Apocalypse and Enlightenment: Benjamin, Bloch and modern German Jewish Messianism', in *Walter Benjamin: Critical Evaluation in Cultural Theory*, ed. Peter Osborne (London: Routledge, 2005), vol. 3, 141.

4 Salomo Friedländer, *Gesammelte Schriften*, Bd. 10, ed. Detlef Thiel (Wartaweil: Waitawhile, 2009), 98, trans. Alice Lagaay, 'Minding the Gap of Indifference: Approaching Performance Philosophy with Salomo Friedlaender', *Performance Philosophy*, vol. 1 (2015): 68.

5 Weber, *Benjamin's Abilities*, 179; Brendan Moran, 'Politics of Creative Indifference', *Philosophy Today*, vol. 55, no. 3 (2011): 307.

6 Steiner, 'The True Politician', 63.

7 Lagaay, 'Minding the Gap of Indifference', 65.

8 Salomo Friedländer, 'Moderner Sieg der Goethischen Farbenlehre', in *Deutsches Literaturarchiv in Marbach* 60.870, trans. Haakenson, ' "The Merely Illusory Paradise of Habits" ', 134.

9 Haakenson, ' "The Merely Illusory Paradise of Habits" ', 121. Haakenson associates Friedländer's literary grotesques with a radical deployment of the Kantian imagination (*Einbildungskraft*) to examine human norms and exclusions through the use of unusual juxtapositions, although – in part because of the problems, discussed in Chapter 2, associated with a concept of the imagination that emphasizes its synthesizing power – such a practice might be better associated with the deformations Benjamin identifies with a distinct understanding of phantasy (a distinction also employed by Friedländer). As Haakenson later implies, this might be connected to the differing political projects of Friedländer and Benjamin as encapsulated in their distinct conceptions of the grotesque: Friedländer sought a moment of critical reflection within sense perception itself as a way of engendering communicability between the imagination and the understanding and thus of a 'fundamental unity of humanity despite perceived differences', whereas in his discussion of Chaplin's *Groteskfilme*, Benjamin 'sought to hold on to the collective as the promise of destruction and redemption' (Haakenson, ' "The Merely Illusory Paradise of Habits" ', 144, 128, 141); that is, to the dividual in its collective sense, as opposed to the individual.

10 Benjamin, *The Correspondence of Walter Benjamin: 1910–1940*, 313, 311.

11 Benjamin, *The Correspondence of Walter Benjamin: 1910–1940*, 313.

12 Benjamin, *The Arcades Project*, N2a, 4.

13 Walter Benjamin, 'Eduard Fuchs, Collector and Historian', in *Selected Writings*, vol. 3, 262; Benjamin, *The Arcades Project*, N2a, 4.

14 Friedrich Nietzsche, *Unpublished Writings from the Period of* Unfashionable Observations, trans. Richard T. Gray (Stanford, CA: Stanford University Press, 1995), 66; emphasis in the original.

15 Nietzsche, *Unpublished Writings*, 403.

16 Johann Wolfgang von Goethe, *Autobiographische Schriften* II, Vol. 9, 417, trans. in Diane Morgan, 'Goethe's "Enhanced Praxis" and the Emergence of a Cosmopolitical Future', in *Cosmopolitics and the Emergence of a Future*, ed. Gary Banham and Diane Morgan (Basingstoke: Palgrave Macmillan, 2007), 238–41; emphasis in the original.

17 Friedrich Nietzsche, *Untimely Meditations*, ed. Daniel Breazeale and trans. R. J. Hollingdale (Cambridge: Cambridge University Press, 1997), 116, 59.

18 Nietzsche, *Untimely Meditations*, 64.

19 Reinhart Koselleck, *Sediments of Time: On Possible Histories*, ed. Sean Franzel and Stefan-Ludwig Hoffmann (Stanford, CA: Stanford University Press, 2018), 120.

20 Koselleck, *Sediments of Time*, 124.

21 Koselleck, *Sediments of Time*, 122–3, 125.

22 Koselleck, *Sediments of Time*, 127.

23 Koselleck, *Sediments of Time*, 128–9.

24 Koselleck, *Sediments of Time*, 131–3.

25 Koselleck, *Sediments of Time*, 129, 125–6.

26 Koselleck, *Sediments of Time*, 130–1.

27 Koselleck, *Sediments of Time*, 139–40.

28 Koselleck, *Sediments of Time*, 133–4.

29 Morgan, 'Goethe's "Enhanced Praxis"', 41; Gary Banham, 'Introduction: Cosmopolitics and Modernity', in *Cosmopolitics and the Emergence of a Future*, ed. Gary Banham and Diane Morgan (Basingstoke: Palgrave Macmillan, 2007), xv.

30 Friedrich Nietzsche, trans. in Georg Lukács, *The Destruction of Reason* (Atlantic Highlands, NJ: Humanities Press, 1981), 235.

31 Friedrich Nietzsche, 'The Greek State', in *On the Genealogy of Morality*, ed. Keith Ansell-Pearson and trans. Carol Diethe (Cambridge: Cambridge University Press, 2007), 166.

32 Nietzsche, *Twilight of the Idols*, 81.

33 Nietzsche, *Untimely Meditations*, 87–8.

34 Nietzsche, *Untimely Meditations*, 112, 120.

35 Steiner, 'The True Politician', 61–2.

36 Nietzsche, 'The Greek State', in *On the Genealogy of Morality*, 166.

37 Walter Benjamin, *Moscow Diary*, ed. Gary Smith (Cambridge, MA: Harvard University Press, 1986), 39.

38 Walter Benjamin, 'Goethe', in *Selected Writings*, vol. 2, 187.

39 Benjamin, 'Goethe', in *Selected Writings*, vol. 2, 182–3.

40 Benjamin, 'Goethe', in *Selected Writings*, vol. 2, 187.

41 Benjamin, 'Goethe', in *Selected Writings*, vol. 2, 182, 187.

42 Benjamin, 'Goethe', in *Selected Writings*, vol. 2, 182.

43 Benjamin, *Moscow Diary*, 39.

44 Benjamin, 'Eduard Fuchs', in *Selected Writings*, vol. 3, 262.

45 Benjamin, *The Arcades Project*, N2, 3.

46 Walter Benjamin, 'Criticism as the Fundamental Discipline of Literary History', in *Selected Writings*, vol. 2, 415.

47 Benjamin, 'Eduard Fuchs', in *Selected Writings*, vol. 3, 262.

48 Walter Benjamin, 'On Some Motifs in Baudelaire', in *Selected Writings*, vol. 4, n.63, 352.

49 Nietzsche, *Unpublished Writings*, 247.

50 Benjamin, 'Goethe's *Elective Affinities*', in *Selected Writings*, vol. 1, 316.

51 Benjamin, 'Goethe's *Elective Affinities*', in *Selected Writings*, vol. 1, 326.

52 Benjamin, 'Goethe's *Elective Affinities*', in *Selected Writings*, vol. 1, 327.

53 Benjamin, 'Goethe's *Elective Affinities*', in *Selected Writings*, vol. 1, 307–8.

54 Benjamin, 'Goethe's *Elective Affinities*', in *Selected Writings*, vol. 1, 326.

55 Benjamin, *On the Origin of German Tragic Drama*, 36.

56 Benjamin, 'The Concept of Criticism in German Romanticism', in *Selected Writings*, vol. 1, 181.

57 Benjamin, 'The Concept of Criticism in German Romanticism', in *Selected Writings*, vol. 1, 180.

58 Benjamin, 'The Concept of Criticism in German Romanticism', in *Selected Writings*, vol. 1, 181.

59 Benjamin, 'The Concept of Criticism in German Romanticism', in *Selected Writings*, vol. 1, 184.

60 Walter Benjamin, 'News about Flowers', in *Selected Writings*, vol. 2, 156.

61 Benjamin, 'The Concept of Criticism in German Romanticism', in *Selected Writings*, vol. 1, 180.

62 Walter Benjamin, 'Little History of Photography', in *Selected Writings*, vol. 2, 520.

63 Howard Caygill, 'Stelarc and the Chimera: Kant's Critique of Prosthetic Judgement', *Art Journal*, vol. 56, issue 1 (spring 1997): 50.

64 Goethe, *Maxims and Reflections*, #706, #502.

65 Benjamin, 'News about Flowers', in *Selected Writings*, vol. 2, 156.

66 Benjamin, 'News about Flowers', in *Selected Writings*, vol. 2, 157.

67 Benjamin, 'News about Flowers', in *Selected Writings*, vol. 2, 156–7.

68 Walter Benjamin, 'The Work of Art in the Age of Its Technological Reproducibility (Third Version)', in *Selected Writings*, vol. 4, 266.

69 Walter Benjamin, 'Outline of the Psycho-physical Problem', in *Selected Writings*, vol. 1, 395.

70 Walter Benjamin, 'One-Way Street', in *Selected Writings*, vol. 1, 451, 486–7.

71 Alberto Toscano, *Fanaticism: On the Use of an Idea* (London: Verso, 2010), 123.

72 Georg Simmel, *The Philosophy of Money*, ed. David Frisby (London: Routledge, 2004), 488.

73 Benjamin, *The Correspondence of Walter Benjamin: 1910–1940*, 599.

74 Ludwig Klages, *Science of Character*, trans. by Walter Henry Johnston (London: George Allen & Unwin, 1929), 70.

75 Ludwig Klages, *Der Geist als Widersacher der Seele*, 6th unabridged ed. (Bonn: Bouvier Verlag Herbert Grundmann, 1981), 7, trans. in Herbert

Schnädelbach, *Philosophy in Germany, 1831–1933*, trans. Eric Matthews (Cambridge: Cambridge University Press, 1984), 149–50.

76 Klages, *Der Geist als Widersacher der Seele*, 89.

77 Klages, *Science of Character*, 172–3.

78 Ludwig Klages, 'Vom Traumbewusstsein', in *Sämtliche Werke*, Bd. 3, ed. Ernst Frauchiger (Bonn: Bouvier, 1973), 185, trans. in John McCole, *Walter Benjamin and the Antinomies of Tradition* (Ithaca, NY: Cornell University Press, 1993), 238.

79 Ludwig Klages, *Vom kosmogonischen Eros* (Bonn: Bouvier, 1963), 92.

80 Klages, *Der Geist als Widersacher der Seele*, trans. in Paul Bishop, *The Archaic: The Past in the Present* (London: Routledge, 2012), 29–30.

81 Klages, *Science of Character*, 169.

82 Benjamin, *The Arcades Project*, K1a, 3.

83 Irving Wohlfarth, 'Walter Benjamin and the Idea of a Technological Eros: A Tentative Reading of *Zum Planetarium*', *Benjamin Studies/Studien*, vol. 1, no. 1 (2002): 79, 84.

84 Benjamin, 'One-Way Street', in *Selected Writings*, vol. 1, 487.

85 Walter Benjamin, 'The Work of Art in the Age of Its Technological Reproducibility (Second Version)', in *Selected Writings*, vol. 3, 107.

86 Benjamin, 'The Work of Art in the Age of Its Technological Reproducibility (Second Version)', in *Selected Writings*, vol. 3, n.10, 124; Benjamin, 'One-Way Street', in *Selected Writings*, vol. 1, 486–7.

87 Karl Marx, 'Economic and Philosophical Manuscripts', in *Early Writings*, trans. Rodney Livingstone and Gregor Benton (London: Penguin, 1992), 355.

88 Wohlfarth, 'Walter Benjamin and the Idea of a Technological Eros', 74–5.

89 Benjamin, *Moscow Diary*, 132.

90 Christine Lodder, *Russian Constructivism* (New Haven: Yale University Press, 1983), 3.

91 Alexander Rodchenko, 'Puti sovremennoi fotografii', *Novyi lef*, 9, 38–9, trans. in Lodder, *Russian Constructivism*, 202.

92 Lodder, *Russian Constructivism*, 199.

93 Sergei Eisenstein, 'A Dialectic Approach to Film Form', in *Film Form: Essays in Film Theory*, ed. Jay Leyda (London: Dobson, 1963), 47; Friedrich Engels, *Dialectics of Nature* (New York: International, 1940), 30.

94 Michael Cowan, 'The Heart Machine: "Rhythm" and Body in Weimar Film and Fritz Lang's *Metropolis*', *Modernism/Modernity*, vol. 14, no. 2 (2007): 234.

95 Matthew Vollgraff, 'Postscript: Intersecting Lines; Sergei Eisenstein Writes to Ludwig Klages', *Critical Quarterly*, vol. 59, no. 1 (2017): 114.

96 Walter Benjamin, 'Epic Theatre', in *Selected Writings*, vol. 2, 584.

97 Benjamin, 'One-Way Street', in *Selected Writings*, vol. 1, 466; translation amended.

98 Benjamin, 'On Some Motifs in Baudelaire', in *Selected Writings*, vol. 4, 336.

99 Walter Benjamin, 'Johann Jakob Bachofen', in *Selected Writings*, vol. 3, 14.

100 Benjamin, 'On Some Motifs in Baudelaire', in *Selected Writings*, vol. 4, 314.

101 Benjamin, 'On Some Motifs in Baudelaire', in *Selected Writings*, vol. 4, n.63, 353.

102 Goethe, *Faust*, Part II, Act V, lines 12104–7; translation amended, based partly on those in Johann Wolfgang von Goethe, *The Collected Works*, vol. 2, ed. Stuart Atkins (Princeton, NJ: Princeton University Press, 1994).

103 Deleuze, *Logic of Sense*, 12.

104 István Mészáros, *Marx's Theory of Alienation* (Merlin Press: London, 1970), 298.

105 Goethe, *Faust*, Part I, lines 1699–702; translation amended.

106 Irving Wohlfarth, 'The Messianic Structure of Benjamin's Last Reflections', in *Walter Benjamin: Critical Evaluation in Cultural Theory*, ed. Peter Osborne (London: Routledge, 2005), vol. 1, 175.

107 Walter Benjamin, 'On the Concept of History', in *Selected Writings*, vol. 4, 392.

108 Walter Benjamin, 'Announcement of the Journal Angelus Novus', in *Selected Writings*, vol. 1, 296.

109 Wolfharth, 'The Messianic Structure of Benjamin's Last Reflections', 175.

110 Benjamin, 'On the Concept of History', in *Selected Writings*, vol. 4, 393.

111 Löwy, *Fire Alarm*, 69.

112 Benjamin, *The Arcades Project*, K1, 1; emphasis added.

113 Walter Benjamin, 'Paralipomena to "On the Concept of History"', in *Selected Writings*, vol. 4, 404.

114 Benjamin, 'On the Concept of History', in *Selected Writings*, vol. 4, 395, 390.

115 Deuber-Mankowsky, 'Hanging over the Abyss', 187–9.

116 Friedrich Engels, 'Ludwig Feuerbach and the End of Classical German Philosophy', in *Marx-Engels Collected Works*, vol. 26 (London: Lawrence and Wishart, 1990), 359; Karl Marx, *The Eighteenth Brumaire of Louis Bonaparte* (New York: International Publishers, 1963), 21.

117 Karl Marx and Friedrich Engels, *The Communist Manifesto* (London: Penguin, 1985), 83; translation amended.

118 Martin Puchner, *Poetry of the Revolution: Marx, Manifestos, and the Avant-Gardes* (Princeton, NJ: Princeton University Press, 1996), 53–4.

119 Benjamin, 'On the Concept of History', in *Selected Writings*, vol. 4, 392; translation amended.

120 Karl Marx, *Grundrisse: Foundations of the Critique of Political Economy*, trans. Martin Nicholaus (London: Penguin, 1993), 361.

121 Benjamin, 'On the Concept of History', in *Selected Writings*, vol. 4, 396.

122 Walter Benjamin, 'Theological-Political Fragment', in *Selected Writings*, vol. 3, 306.

123 Benjamin, 'Theological-Political Fragment', in *Selected Writings*, vol. 3, 305–6.

124 Benjamin, *The Arcades Project*, N8, 1.

125 Benjamin, 'Theological-Political Fragment', in *Selected Writings*, vol. 3, 306.

126 Löwy, *Fire Alarm*, 26.

127 Walter Benjamin, 'Das Problem des Klassischen und die Antike', in *Gesammelte Schriften*, Bd. 3, ed. Hella Tiedemann-Bartels (Frankfurt am Main: Suhrkamp, 1991), 291, 293.

128 Paul Valéry, 'The Position of Baudelaire', in *The Collected Works of Paul Valéry*, vol. 8, trans. Malcolm Cowley and James R. Lawler (Princeton, NJ: Princeton University Press, 2015), 201.

129 Nietzsche, *The Birth of Tragedy*, 50–5.

130 Paul Valéry, 'Eupalinos, or The Architect', in *The Collected Works of Paul Valéry*, vol. 4, ed. Jackson Mathew (Princeton, NJ: Princeton University Press, 1989), 110.

131 Walter Benjamin, 'The Present Social Situation of the French Writer', in *Selected Writings*, vol. 2, 757.

132 Kurt Weinberg, *The Figure of Faust in Valéry and Goethe: An Exegesis of 'Mon Faust'* (Princeton, NJ: Princeton University Press, 1976), 212–13.

133 Benjamin, 'On Some Motifs in Baudelaire', in *Selected Writings*, vol. 4, 338.

134 Benjamin, 'The Present Social Situation of the French Writer', in *Selected Writings*, vol. 2, 753.

135 Walter Benjamin, 'Julien Green', in *Selected Writings*, vol. 2, 333.

136 Annie Brudo, *Rêve et fantastique chez Julien Green* (Paris: Presses Universitaires de France, 1995), 237; The Editors of Encyclopaedia Britannica, 'Julien Green', *Encyclopædia Britannica Online* (September 2018): http://www.britannica.com/EBchecked/topic/244888/Julien-Green.

137 Benjamin, 'Julien Green', in *Selected Writings*, vol. 2, 333.

138 Benjamin, 'Julien Green', in *Selected Writings*, vol. 2, 333.

139 Benjamin, 'Julien Green', in *Selected Writings*, vol. 2, 335, 333.

140 Walter Benjamin, 'The Fireside Saga', in *Selected Writings*, vol. 2, 151; Walter Benjamin, 'Review of Green's Adrienne Mesurat', in *Selected Writings*, vol. 2, 160.

141 Benjamin, 'The Fireside Saga', in *Selected Writings*, vol. 2, 151–2.

142 Benjamin, 'Julien Green', in *Selected Writings*, vol. 2, 333.

143 Benjamin, 'The Present Social Situation of the French Writer', in *Selected Writings*, vol. 2, 753.

144 Benjamin, *The Arcades Project*, N1a, 4, <O°, 1>.

145 Benjamin, *The Arcades Project*, N1a, 4.

146 Cf. Benjamin, *The Correspondence of Walter Benjamin 1910–1940*, 307.

147 Matt Erlin, 'Tradition as Intellectual Montage: F.W. Murnau's Faust (1926)', in *Weimar Cinema: An Essential Guide to Classic Films of the Era*, ed. Noah Isenberg (New York: Columbia University Press, 2009), 163.

148 Erlin, 'Tradition as Intellectual Montage', 155.

149 Erlin, 'Tradition as Intellectual Montage', 165–6.

150 Goethe, *Faust*, Part II, Act I, lines 6380–565; cf. Neil M. Flax, 'Goethe's Faust II and the Experimental Theatre of His Time', *Comparative Literature*, vol. 31, no. 2 (spring 1979).

151 Marina Warner, *Phantasmagoria: Spirit Visions, Metaphors, and Media in the Twenty-First Century* (Oxford: Oxford University Press, 2006), 154.

152 Warner, *Phantasmagoria*, 154.

153 Albrecht Schöne specially emphasizes its technical aspect in his *Frankfurter Ausgabe* 1994 edition of *Faust*; cf. Flax, 'Goethe's Faust II and the Experimental Theatre of His Time'.

154 Benjamin, *Gesammelte Schriften*, Bd. 3, 69–71.

155 Siegfried Unseld, *Goethe and His Publishers*, trans. Kenneth J. Northcott (Chicago: University of Chicago Press, 1996), 324.

156 Johann Wolfgang von Goethe, 'Second Sketch for the Announcement of the Helena', in Goethe, *Faust*, 523.

157 John R. Williams, 'The Problem of the Mothers', in *A Companion to Goethe's Faust: Parts I and II*, ed. Paul Bishop (Rochester, NY: Camden House, 2001), 141.

158 Anthony Phelan, 'The Classical and the Medieval in *Faust II*', ed. Paul Bishop (Rochester, NY: Camden House, 2001), 162.

159 Harold Stein Jantz, *The Form of "Faust": The Work of Art and Its Intrinsic Structures* (Baltimore: John Hopkins University Press, 1978), 153.

160 Weinberg, *The Figure of Faust in Valéry and Goethe*, 160.

Bibliography

Adorno, Theodor W. *Notes to Literature*, vol. 2, edited by Rolf Tiedemann and translated by Shierry Weber. Nicholsen. New York: Columbia University Press, 1991.

Alliez, Éric. 'Rhizome (With No Return)'. *Radical Philosophy*, vol. 165 (January/February 2011): 36–42.

Alliez, Éric. *The Brain-Eye: New Histories of Modern Painting*, translated by Robin Mackay. London: Rowman and Littlefield, 2016.

Anderson, Lisa Marie. *German Expressionism and the Messianism of a Generation*. Amsterdam: Rodopi, 2011.

Banham, Gary. 'Introduction: Cosmopolitics and Modernity'. In *Cosmopolitics and the Emergence of a Future*, ed. Gary Banham and Diane Morgan, viii–xiii. Basingstoke: Palgrave Macmillan, 2007.

Bard-Rosenberg, Jacob. 'Walter Benjamin on Blushing: New Translations of Fragments on Colour and Some Inflationary Reading Notes'. *Academia.edu* (December 2017): https://www.academia.edu/35350866/Walter_Benjamin_on_Blushing_New_translations_of_fragments_on_colour_and_some_inflationary_reading_notes_draft_.

Benjamin, Walter. *Gesammelte Briefe*, Bd. 1. Frankfurt am Main: Suhrkamp, 1978.

Benjamin, Walter. *Moscow Diary*, edited by Gary Smith. Cambridge, MA: Harvard University Press, 1986.

Benjamin, Walter. *Gesammelte Schriften*, Bd. 3, edited by Hella Tiedemann-Bartels. Frankfurt am Main: Suhrkamp, 1991.

Benjamin, Walter. *Gesammelte Schriften*, Bd. 4, edited by Tillman Rexroth. Frankfurt am Main: Suhrkamp, 1991.

Benjamin, Walter. *Gesammelte Schriften*, Bd. 6, edited by Rolf Tiedemann and Hermann Schweppenhäuser. Frankfurt am Main: Suhrkamp, 1991.

Benjamin, Walter. *Gesammelte Schriften*, Bd. 7, edited by Rolf Tiedemann and Hermann Schweppenhäuser. Frankfurt am Main: Suhrkamp, 1991.

Benjamin, Walter. *The Correspondence of Walter Benjamin: 1910–1940*, edited by Gershom Scholem and Theodor W. Adorno. Chicago: University of Chicago Press, 1994.

Benjamin, Walter. *Selected Writings*, vol. 1, edited by Marcus Bullock and Michael W. Jennings. Cambridge, MA: Harvard University Press, 1996.

Benjamin, Walter. *The Origin of German Tragic Drama*, translated by John Osborne. London: Verso, 1998.

Benjamin, Walter. *Selected Writings*, vol. 2, edited by Michael W. Jennings, Howard Eiland and Gary Smith. Cambridge, MA: Harvard University Press, 1999.

Benjamin, Walter. *The Arcades Project*, translated by Howard Eiland and Kevin McLaughlin. Cambridge, MA: Harvard University Press, 2002.

Benjamin, Walter. *Selected Writings*, vol. 4, edited by Howard Eiland and Michael W. Jennings. Cambridge, MA: Harvard University Press, 2003.

Benjamin, Walter. *Early Writings, 1910–1917*, translated by Howard Eiland. Cambridge, MA: Harvard University Press, 2011.

Bishop, Paul. *The Archaic: The Past in the Present*. London: Routledge, 2012.

Bohm, Artnd. 'Goethe and the Romantics'. In *The Literature of German Romanticism*, edited by Dennis F. Mahoney, 35–60. Rochester, NY: Camden House, 2004.

Bullock, Marcus Paul. *Romanticism and Marxism: The Philosophical Development of Literary Theory and Literary History in Walter Benjamin and Friedrich Schlegel*. New York: Peter Lang, 1987.

Caygill, Howard. *Art of Judgement*. Oxford: Basil Blackwell, 1989.

Caygill, Howard. 'Stelarc and the Chimera: Kant's Critique of Prosthetic Judgement'. *Art Journal*, vol. 56, issue 1 (spring 1997): 46–51.

Caygill, Howard. *Walter Benjamin: The Colour of Experience*. London: Routledge, 1998.

Charles, Matthew. 'Pedagogy as "Cryptic Politics": Benjamin, Nietzsche, and the End of Education'. *boundary 2*, vol. 45, issue 2 (2018): 35–62.

Class, Monika. *Coleridge and Kantian Ideas in England, 1796–1817: Coleridge's Response to German Philosophy*. London: Bloomsbury, 2012.

Cohen, Hermann. *Schriften zur Philosophie und Zeitgeschichte*, vol. 1, edited by Albert Görland and Ernst Cassirer. Berlin: Akademie Verlag, 1928.

Cohen, Hermann. *Werke*, edited by Helmut Holzhey. Hildesheim: Olms, 1977ff.

Coleridge, Samuel Taylor. *The Collected Works of Samuel Taylor Coleridge*, vol. 11, edited by H. R. Jackson and J. R. de J. Jackson. Princeton, NJ: Princeton University Press, 1995.

Coleridge, Samuel Taylor. *Biographia Literaria*, edited by Nigel Leask. London: Everyman, 1997.

Coleridge, Samuel Taylor. *Coleridge's Notebooks: A Selection*, edited by Seamus Perry. Oxford: Oxford University Press, 2002.

Coleridge, Samuel Taylor. *The Book I Value: Selected Marginalia*, edited by H. J. Jackson. Princeton, NJ: Princeton University Press, 2003.

Comentale, Edward P. and Andrzej Comentale, eds. *T.E. Hulme and the Question of Modernism*. Aldershot: Ashgate, 2006.

Cornell, John F. 'Faustian Phenomena: Teleology in Goethe's Interpretation of Plants and Animals'. *The Journal of Medicine and Philosophy: A Forum for Bioethics and Philosophy of Medicine*, vol. 15, issue 5 (October 1990): 481–92.

Cowan, Michael. 'The Heart Machine: "Rhythm" and Body in Weimar Film and Fritz Lang's *Metropolis*'. *Modernism/Modernity*, vol. 14, no. 2 (2007): 225–48.

Craig, Gordon A. 'Georg Gottfried Gervinus: The Historian as Activist'. *Pacific Historical Review*, vol. 41, no. 1 (February 1972): 1–14.

Crary, Jonathan. *Techniques of the Observer: On Vision and Modernity in the Nineteenth Century*. Cambridge: MIT Press, 1992.

Deleuze, Gilles. *Kant's Critical Philosophy*, translated by Hugh Tomlinson and Barbara Habberjam. London: Althone, 1984.

Deleuze, Gilles. *Nietzsche and Philosophy*, translated by Hugh Tomlinson. London: Continuum, 1986.

Deleuze, Gilles. 'Postscript on the Societies of Control'. *October*, vol. 59 (winter 1992): 3–7.

Deleuze, Gilles. *Difference and Repetition*, translated by Paul Patton. New York: Columbia University Press, 1994.

Deleuze, Gilles. *The Logic of Sense*, edited by Constantin V. Boundas and translated by Mark Lester. London: Continuum, 2004.

Deuber-Mankowsky, Astrid. 'Hanging over the Abyss: On the Relation between Knowledge and Experience in Hermann Cohen and Walter Benjamin'. In *Hermann Cohen's Critical Idealism*, edited by Reinier Munk, 161–92. Dordrecht: Springer, 2005.

Domnrowski, André. 'The Untimely Classicism of Hans von Marées'. In *Modern Art and the Idea of the Mediterranean*, edited by Vojtěch Jirat-Wasiutyński, 84–115. Toronto: University of Toronto Press, 2007.

Eichner, Hans. *Friedrich Schlegel*. New York: Twayne, 1970.

Eisenstein, Sergei. 'A Dialectic Approach to Film Form'. In *Film Form: Essays in Film Theory*, edited by Jay Leyda, 45–63. London: Dobson, 1963.

Elger, Dietmar. *Expressionism: A Revolution in German Art*. Köln: Taschen, 2007.

Eliot, T. S. *Selected Prose*, edited by Frank Kermode. London: Faber and Faber, 1975.

Engels, Friedrich. *Dialectics of Nature*. New York: International, 1940.

Engels, Friedrich. 'Ludwig Feuerbach and the End of Classical German Philosophy'. In *Marx-Engels Collected Works*, vol. 26, 353–98. London: Lawrence and Wishart, 1990.

Fielder, Conrad. *On Judging Works of Visual Art*, translated by Henry Schaefer-Simmern and Fulmer Mood. Berkeley: University of California Press, 1978.

Finley, Gerald. 'The Deluge Pictures: Reflections on Goethe, J. M. W. Turner and Early Nineteenth-Century'. *Zeitschrift für Kunstgeschichte*, Bd. 60, H. 4 (1997): 530–48.

Finley, Gerald. *Angel in the Sun: Turner's Vision of History*. Montreal: McGill-Queens University Press, 1999.

Frank, Joseph. *The Idea of Spatial Form*. New Brunswick: Rutgers University Press, 1991.

Friedländer, Salomo. *Gesammelte Schriften*, Bd. 10, edited by Detlef Thiel. Wartaweil: Waitawhile, 2009.

Gage, John. *Colour and Culture: Practice and Meaning from Antiquity to Abstraction*. Berkeley: University of California Press, 1999.

Gasché, Rodolphe. 'The Sober Absolute: On Benjamin and the Early Romantics'. In *Walter Benjamin and Romanticism*, edited by Beatrice Hanssen and Andrew Benjamin, 51–68. London: Continuum, 2002.

Gillies, Mary Ann. 'The Curious History of Imagism: Of Hulme, Bergson, Worringer, and Imagism's Readers. A Response to Andrew Hay'. *Connotations*, vol. 23, no. 1 (2013): 140–52.

Gilloch, Graham. *Walter Benjamin: Critical Constellations*. Cambridge: Polity, 2002.

Goethe, Johann Wolfgang von. *Elective Affinities*, translated by R. J. Hollingdale. Harmondsworth, Middlesex: Penguin Books, 1971.

Goethe, Johann Wolfgang von. *The Collected Works*, vol. 1, edited by Christopher Middleton. Princeton, NJ: Princeton University Press, 1983.

Goethe, Johann Wolfgang von. *Goethe's Botanical Writings*, translated by Bertha Mueller. Woodbridge, CT: Ox Bow Press, 1989.

Goethe, Johann Wolfgang von. *The Collected Works*, vol. 2, edited and translated by Stuart Atkins. Princeton, NJ: Princeton University Press, 1994.

Goethe, Johann Wolfgang von. *The Collected Works*, vol. 12, edited and translated by Douglas Miller. Princeton, NJ: Princeton University Press, 1995.

Goethe, Johann Wolfgang von. *Maxims and Reflections*, translated by Elisabeth Stopp. London: Penguin Books, 1998.

Goethe, Johann Wolfgang von. *Faust*, parts I and II, translated by Walter Arndt, edited by Cyrus Hamlin. New York: Norton, 2001.

Goethe, Johann Wolfgang von. 'Note and Queries for a Better Understanding' (from *West-Easterly Divan*), trans. Jorg Waltje. *Other Voices*, vol. 2, no. 2 (March 2002).

Greenberg, Clement. *The Collected Essays and Criticism*, vol. 4, edited by John O'Brian. Chicago: University of Chicago Press, 1995.

Gregory, Alan P. R. *Coleridge and the Conservative Imagination*. Macon, GA: Mercer University Press, 2003.

Haakenson, Thomas O. '"The Merely Illusory Paradise of Habits": Salomo Friedländer, Walter Benjamin, and the Grotesque'. *New German Critique*, vol. 36, no. 1 (106) (winter 2009): 119–47.

Habermas, Jürgen. 'Consciousness-Raising or Redemptive Criticism: The Contemporaneity of Walter Benjamin'. *New German Critique*, no. 17 (1979): 30–59.

Hansen, Miriam. 'T. E. Hulme, Mercenary of Modernism, or, Fragments of Avantgarde Sensibility in Pre-World War I Britain'. *ELH*, vol. 47, no. 2 (summer 1980): 355–85.

Hanssen, Beatrice. 'Philosophy at Its Origin: Walter Benjamin's Prologue to the Ursprung des deutschen Trauerspiels'. *MLN*, vol. 110, no. 4 (September 1995): 809–33.

Hanssen, Beatrice and Andrew Benjamin, eds. *Walter Benjamin and Romanticism*. London: Continuum, 2002.

Heidegger, Martin. *Kant and the Problem of Metaphysics*, 5th edn, translated by Richard Taft. Bloomington: Indian University Press, 1997.

Hodge, Joanna. 'The Timing of Elective Affinity: Walter Benjamin's Strong Aesthetics'. In *Walter Benjamin and Art*, edited by Andrew Benjamin, 14–31. London: Continuum, 2005.

Home, Henry (Lord Kames). *Elements of Criticism*, 3rd edn, edited by Abraham Mills. New York: Conner and Cooke, 1836.

Houston, Kerr. *An Introduction to Art Criticism: Histories, Strategies, Voices*. Boston: Pearson, 2013.

Hulme, T. E. *Selected Writings*, edited by Patrick McGuiness. New York: Routledge, 2003.

Hulme, T. E. *The Collected Writings of T. E. Hulme*, edited by Karen Csengeri. Oxford: Clarendon, 1994.

Hunemann, Philippe. 'Purposivenss, Necessity, and Contingency'. In *Kant's Theory of Biology*, edited by Eric Watkins and Ina Goy, 185–202. Berlin and Boston: De Gruyter, 2014.

Huysmans, J.-K. *Grünewald: With an Essay by J-K. Huysmans*, translated by Robert Baldick. Oxford: Phaidon Press, 1976.

Huysmans, J.-K. *La Bas*, translated by Robert Irwin. Cambridge: Dedalus, 1986.

Jasper, David. 'J. M. W. Turner: Interpreter of the Bible'. In *Biblical Studies/Cultural Studies: The Third Sheffield Colloquium*, edited by J. Cheryl Exum and Stephen D. Moore, 299–314. Sheffield: Sheffield Academic Press, 1998.

Jay, Martin. 'Chromophilia: Der Blaue Reiter, Walter Benjamin, and the Emancipation of Color', *positions: asia critique*, vol. 26, no. 1 (February 2018): 13–33.

Kant, Immanuel. *Dreams of a Spirit Seer*, translated by John Manolesco. New York: Vantage Press, 1969.

Kant, Immanuel. *Critique of Judgement*, translated by Werner S. Pluhar. Indianapolis: Hackett, 1987.

Kant, Immanuel. *Kant: Political Writings*, edited by H. S. Reiss. Cambridge: Cambridge University Press, 1991.

Kant, Immanuel. *Lectures on Logic*, translated and edited by J. Michael Young. Cambridge: Cambridge University Press, 1992.

Kant, Immanuel. *The Conflict of the Faculties*, translated by Mary J. Gregor. Lincoln: University of Nebraska Press, 1992.

Kant, Immanuel. *Theoretical Philosophy 1755–1770*, translated and edited by David Walford. Cambridge: Cambridge University Press, 1992.

Kant, Immanuel. *Critique of Pure Reason*, translated by Werner S. Pluhar. Indianapolis: Hackett, 1996.

Kant, Immanuel. *Anthropology from a Pragmatic Point of View*, translated by Robert B. Louden. Cambridge: Cambridge University Press, 2006.

Karatani, Kojin. *Origins of Modern Japanese Literature*, translated by Brett de Bary. Durham: Duke University Press, 1993.

Karatani, Kojin. 'Uses of Aesthetics: After Orientalism', *boundary 2*, vol. 25, no. 2 (summer 1998): 145–60.

Karatani, Kojin. *Transcritique: On Kant and Marx*, translated by Sabu Kohso. Cambridge: MIT Press, 2003.

Karatani, Kojin. 'Critique Is Impossible without Moves': An Interview of Kojin Karatani by Joel Wainwright'. *Dialogues in Human Geography*, vol. 2, issue 1 (2012): 30–52.

Karatani, Kojin. *The Structure of World History: From Modes of Production to Modes of Exchange*, translated by Michael K. Bourdaghs. Durham: Duke University Press, 2014.

Kelley, Theresa M. 'Romanticism's Errant Allegory'. In *The Cambridge Companion to Allegory*, edited by Rita Copeland and Peter Struck, 211–28. Cambridge: Cambridge University Press, 2010.

Kemp-Smith, Norman. *A Commentary to Kant's Critique of Pure Reason*, 3rd edn. Houndmills: Palgrave Macmillan, 2003.

Kitaro, Nishida. *An Inquiry into the Good*, translated by Masao Abe and Christopher Ives. New Haven: Yale University Press, 1990.

Klages, Ludwig. *Science of Character*, translated by Walter Henry Johnston. London: George Allen & Unwin, 1929.

Klages, Ludwig. *Vom kosmogonischen Eros*. Bonn: H. Bouvier, 1963.

Klages, Ludwig. 'Vom Traumbewusstsein'. In *Sämtliche Werke*, vol. 3. Bonn: Bouvier, 1973.

Klages, Ludwig. *Der Geist als Widersacher der Seele*, 6th unabridged edn. Bonn: Bouvier Verlag Herbert Grundmann, 1981.

Klee, Paul. *Notebooks*, vol. 1, edited by Jürg Spiller. London: Lund Humphries, 1961.

Klee, Paul. *Paul Klee*. New York: Parkstone, 2012.

Kluge, Sofie. 'An Allegory of "Bildung". Friedrich Schlegel's Interpretation of Goethe's *Wilhelm Meisters Lehrjahre*'. *Orbis Litterarum*, vol. 62, issue 3 (June 2007): 177–209.

Köhnke, Klaus Christian. *The Rise of Neo-Kantianism: German Academic Philosophy between Idealism and Positivism*. Cambridge: Cambridge University Press, 1991.

Koselleck, Reinhart. *Sediments of Time: On Possible Histories*, edited Sean Franzel and Stefan-Ludwig Hoffmann. Stanford, CA: Stanford University Press, 2018.

Kramer, Andreas. 'Goethe and the Cultural Project of German Modernism: Steiner, Kandinsky, Friedlaendar, Schwitters and Benjamin'. *Publications of the English Goethe Society*, vol. 71, issue 1 (2001): 18–36.

Kuhn, Elizabeth. 'Toward an Anti-humanism of Life: The Modernism of Nietzsche, Hulme and Yeats'. *Journal of Modern Literature*, vol. 34, no. 4 (summer 2011): 1–20.

Kuiken, Kir. *Imagined Sovereignties: Towards a New Political Romanticism*. New York: Fordham University Press, 2014.

Lacoue-Labarthe, Philippe. 'Introduction to Walter Benjamin's The Concept of Art Criticism in German Romanticism'. In *Walter Benjamin and Romanticism*, edited by Beatrice Hanssen and Andrew Benjamin, 9–18. London: Continuum, 2002.

Lagaay, Alice. 'Minding the Gap of Indifference: Approaching Performance Philosophy with Salomo Friedlaender'. *Performance Philosophy*, vol. 1 (2015): 65–73.

Lambrianou, Nikolaus. 'Neo-Kantianism and Messianism: Origin and Interruption in Hermann Cohen and Walter Benjamin'. In *Walter Benjamin: Critical Evaluations in Cultural Theory*, vol. 3, edited by Peter Osborne, 82–103. London: Routledge, 2005.

Lampart, Fabian. 'The Turn to History and the Volk: Brentano, Arnim, and the Grimm Brothers'. In *The Literature of German Romanticism*, edited by Dennis F. Mahoney, 171–90. Rochester, NY: Camden House, 2004.

Leask, Nigel. *The Politics of the Imagination in Coleridge's Critical Thought*.
    Basingstoke: Macmillan, 1988.

Leerssen, Joep. 'Notes towards a Definition of Romantic Nationalism'.
    Romantik: *Journal for the Study of Romanticisms*, vol. 2, no. 1 (2013): 9–35.

Lenoir, Timothy. 'The Eternal Laws of Form: Morphotypes and the Conditions of
    Existence in Goethe's Biological Thought'. In *Journal of Social and Biological
    Structures: Studies in Human Social Biology*, vol. 7, issue 4 (October 1984):
    317–24.

Leslie, Esther. *Walter Benjamin: Overpowering Conformism*. London: Pluto
    Press, 2000.

Leslie, Esther. *Hollywood Flatlands: Animation, Critical Theory and the Avant-
    Garde*. London: Verso, 2002.

Leslie, Esther. *Synthetic Worlds: Nature, Art and the Chemical Industry*. London:
    Reaktion, 2005.

Leslie, Esther. *Liquid Crystals: The Science and Art of a Fluid Form*. London:
    Reaktion, 2016.

Lijster, Thijs. 'The Interruption of Myth: Walter Benjamin's Concept of Critique'. In
    Conceptions of Critique in Modern and Contemporary Philosophy, edited by Karin
    de Boer and Ruth Sonderegger, 156–74. Houndmills: Palgrave Macmillan, 2012.

Lippit, Seiji M. *Topographies of Japanese Modernism*. New York: Columbia
    University Press, 2002.

Lodder, Christine. *Russian Constructivism*. New Haven: Yale University Press, 1983.

Lowe, David and Simon Sharp. *Goethe and Palladio*. Barrington, MA:
    Lindisfarne, 2005.

Löwy, Michael. 'Revolution against "Progress": Walter Benjamin's Romantic
    Anarchism'. *New Left Review*, vol. 1, no. 152 (July/August 1985): 42–59.

Löwy, Michael. *Fire Alarm*. London: Verso, 2005.

Löwy, Michael and Robert Sayre. *Romanticism against the Tide of Modernity*.
    Durham: Duke University Press, 2001.

Lukács, Georg. *The Destruction of Reason*. Atlantic Highlands, NJ: Humanities
    Press, 1981.

Marx, Karl. *The Eighteenth Brumaire of Louis Bonaparte*. New York: International
    Publishers, 1963.

Marx, Karl. 'Economic and Philosophical Manuscripts'. In *Early Writings*, translated
    by Rodney Livingstone and Gregor Benton, 279–400. London: Penguin, 1992.

Marx, Karl. *Grundrisse: Foundations of the Critique of Political Economy*, translated
    by Martin Nicholaus. London: Penguin, 1993.

Marx, Karl and Friedrich Engels. *The Communist Manifesto*. London: Penguin, 1985.

Maskarinec, Malika. 'Paul Klee and the Genesis of Form'. *Word & Image*, vol. 32, issue 2 (2016): 207–17.

McCole, John. *Walter Benjamin and the Antinomies of Tradition*. Ithaca, NY: Cornell University Press, 1993.

Menninghaus, Winfried. 'Walter Benjamin's Exposition of the Romantic Theory of Reflection'. In *Walter Benjamin: Critical Evaluation in Cultural Theory*, vol 1, edited by Peter Osborne, 25–62. London: Routledge, 2005.

Mészáros, István. *Marx's Theory of Alienation*.London: Merlin Press, 1970.

Miller, Elaine P. 'Nietzsche on Individuation and Purposiveness in Nature'. In *A Companion to Nietzsche*, edited by Keith Ansell Pearson, 58–75. Chichester: Blackwell, 2009.

Mitchell, W. J. T. 'Metamorphoses of the Vortex: Hogarth, Turner and Blakes'. In *Articulate Images: The Sister Arts from Hogarth to Tennyson*, edited by Richard Wendorf, 125–68. Minneapolis: University of Minnesota Press, 1983.

Moran, Brendan. 'Politics of Creative Indifference'. *Philosophy Today*, vol. 55, no. 3 (2011): 307–22.

Morgan, Diane. 'Goethe's "Enhanced Praxis" and the Emergence of a Cosmopolitical Future'. In *Cosmopolitics and the Emergence of a Future*, edited by Gary Banham and Diane Morgan, 235–55. Basingstoke: Palgrave Macmillan, 2007.

Nelson, E. Charles. 'Shakespeare Has Missed the Dandelion'. *Shakespeare*, vol. 12, no. 2 (2016): 175–84.

Nietzsche, Friedrich. *The Gay Science*, translated by Walter Kaufmann. New York: Vintage, 1974.

Nietzsche, Friedrich. *The Birth of Tragedy*, translated by Clifton P. Fadiman. New York: Dover Publications, 1995.

Nietzsche, Friedrich. *Unpublished Writings from the Period of* Unfashionable Observations, translated by Richard T. Gray. Stanford, CA: Stanford University Press, 1995.

Nietzsche, Friedrich. *Untimely Meditations*, edited by Daniel Breazeale and translated by R. J. Hollingdale. Cambridge: Cambridge University Press, 1997.

Nietzsche, Friedrich. *Beyond Good and Evil*, edited by Rolf-Peter Horstmann and Judith Norman. Cambridge: Cambridge University Press, 2002.

Nietzsche, Friedrich. *On the Genealogy of Morality*, edited by Keith Ansell-Pearson and translated by Carol Diethe. Cambridge: Cambridge University Press, 2007.

Nietzsche, Friedrich. *Twilight of the Idols*, translated by Antony M. Ludovici. London: Wordsworth, 2007.

Nietzsche, Friedrich. 'On the Concept of the Organic since Kant', trans. Paderborn Nawrath. *The Agonist*, vol. 3, issue 1 (spring 2010): 90–110.

North, Paul. 'Apparent Critique: Inferences from a Benjaminian Sketch'. *Diacritics*, vol. 40, no. 1 (spring 2012): 70–97.

Novotny, Fritz. *Painting and Sculpture in Europe, 1780–1880*. New Haven: Yale University Press, 1995.

Osborne, Peter. 'From Structure to Rhizome: Transdisciplinarity in French Thought (1)'. *Radical Philosophy*, vol. 165 (January/February 2011): 15–16.

Osborne, Peter. 'Philosophy after Theory: Transdisciplinarity and the New'. In *Theory After 'Theory'*, edited by Jane Elliott and Derek Attridge, 19–33. Abingdon: Routledge, 2011.

Patton, Lydia. 'Hermann Cohen's History and Philosophy of Science'. PhD thesis, McGill University, Montreal, 2004.

Pevsner, Nikolaus. 'Some Thoughts on German Painting'. In *Pevsner: The Complete Broadcast Talks, Architecture and Art on Radio and Television, 1945–1977*, edited by Stephen Games, 325–8. London: Routledge, 2016.

Plato, *The Republic*, edited by G. R. F. Ferrari. Cambridge: Cambridge University Press, 2000.

Poma, Andrea. *The Critical Philosophy of Hermann Cohen*, translated by John Denton. Albany: SUNY, 1997.

Puchner, Martin. *Poetry of the Revolution: Marx, Manifestos, and the Avant-Gardes*. Princeton, NJ: Princeton University Press, 1996.

Rabinbach, Anson. 'Between Apocalypse and Enlightenment: Benjamin, Bloch and modern German Jewish Messianism'. In *Walter Benjamin: Critical Evaluations in Cultural Theory*, vol. 3, edited by Peter Osborne, 116–61. London: Routledge, 2005.

Rasmussen, Mary. 'Viols, Violists and Venus in Grünewald's Isenheim Altar'. *Early Music*, vol. 29, no. 1 (February 2001): 60–74.

Reed, T. J. 'Weimar Classicism: Goethe's Alliance with Schiller'. In *Weimar Classicism: Studies in Goethe, Schiller, Foster, Berlepsch, Wieland, Herder, and Stein*, edited by David Gallagher, 21–38. Lewiston, NY: Mellen, 2011.

Rodan, Martin. 'Matthias Grünewald, «le plus forcené» des peintres selon Joris-Karl Huysmans'. *Bulletin du Centre de recherche français à Jérusalem*, no. 24 (2013): 7.

Ross, Alison. *The Aesthetic Paths of Philosophy: Presentation in Kant, Heidegger, Lacoue-Labarthe, and Nancy*. Stanford, CA: Stanford University Press, 2007.

Schlegel, Friedrich. 'On Goethe's Meister'. In *German Aesthetic and Literary Criticism: The Romantic Ironists and Goethe*, edited by Kathleen M. Wheeler, 59–72. Cambridge: Cambridge University Press, 1984.

Schlegel, Friedrich. *Philosophical Fragments*, translated by Peter Firchow. Minneapolis: University of Minnesota Press, 1991.

Schlegel, Friedrich. *On the Study of Greek Poetry*, edited and translated by Stuart
  Barnett. New York: SUNY, 2001.

Schnädelbach, Herbert. *Philosophy in Germany, 1831–1933*, translated by Eric
  Matthews. Cambridge: Cambridge University Press, 1984.

Scholem, Gershom. *Walter Benjamin: The Story of a Friendship*, translated by Harry
  Zohn. New York: New York Review Books, 1981.

Scholem, Gershom. 'Against the Metaphysical Exposition of Space'. *MLN*, vol. 127,
  no. 3 (2012): 456–61.

Schopenhauer, Arthur. *The World as Will and Idea*, vol. 3, translated by R. B.
  Haldane and J. Kemp. London: Kegan Paul, 1909.

Schopenhauer, Arthur. *On the Fourfold Root of the Principle of Sufficient Reason*,
  translated by E. F. J. Payne. La Salle, IL: Open Court, 1974.

Schopenhauer, Arthur. 'On the Will in Nature'. In *On the Fourfold Root of the
  Principle of Sufficient Reason*. New York: Cosimo, 2007.

Schurman, J. G. 'Kant's Theory of the A Priori Forms of Sense'. *The Philosophical
  Review*, vol. 8, no. 1 (January 1899): 1–22.

Schwerin-High, Friederike von. 'Blank Verse Theatre Texts and Weimar
  Classicism'. In *Weimar Classicism: Studies in Goethe, Schiller, Foster, Berlepsch,
  Wieland, Herder, and Stein*, edited by David Gallagher, 65–98. Lewiston, NY:
  Mellen, 2011.

Selz, Peter. *German Expressionist Painting*. Berkeley: University of California
  Press, 1974.

Steiner, Uwe. 'The True Politician: Walter Benjamin's Concept of the Political'. *New
  German Critique*, no. 83 (spring/summer 2001): 43–88.

Stephenson, R. H. *Goethe's Conception of Knowledge and Science*. Edinburgh:
  Edinburgh University Press, 1995.

Sutcliffe, Tom. 'In Defence of Shakespeare's Difficult Bits'. *Guardian* (5 January
  2016): https://www.theguardian.com/commentisfree/2016/jan/05/
  shakespeare-globe-theatre-language.

Teukolsky Rachel. *The Literate Eye: Victorian Art Writing and Modernist Aesthetics*.
  Oxford: Oxford University Press, 2009.

Tobias, Rochelle. 'Irreconcilable: Ethics and Aesthetics for Hermann Cohen and
  Walter Benjamin'. *MLN*, vol. 127, no. 3 (April 2012): 665–80.

Toscano, Alberto. *Fanaticism: On the Use of an Idea*. London: Verso, 2010.

Weber, Samuel. *Benjamin's – abilities*. Cambridge, MA: Harvard University
  Press, 2008.

Weigel, Sigrid. 'The Flash of Knowledge and the Temporality of Images: Walter
  Benjamin's Image-Based Epistemology and Its Preconditions in Visual Arts and

Media History', translated by Chadwick Truscott Smith and Christine Kutschbach. *Critical Inquiry*, vol. 41, no. 2 (winter 2015): 344–66.

Wilton, A. 'Turner and Colour'. In *Art/Neuroscience Series in Front of 'Bright Stone of Honour'*. Ashmolean Museum: Oxford University, 2008.

Wohlfarth, Irving. 'Walter Benjamin and the Idea of a Technological Eros: A Tentative Reading of *Zum Planetarium'*. *Benjamin Studies/Studien*, vol. 1, no. 1 (2002): 65–109.

Wohlfarth, Irving. 'The Messianic Structure of Benjamin's Last Reflections'. In *Walter Benjamin: Critical Evaluation in Cultural Theory*, vol. 1, edited by Peter Osborne, 169–231. London: Routledge, 2005.

Worringer, Wilhelm. *Abstraction and Empathy: A Contribution to the Psychology of Style*, translated by Michael Bullock. Chicago: Elephant, 1997.

Ziff, Jerrold. 'John Langhorne and Turner's "Fallacies of Hope"'. *Journal of the Warburg and Courtauld Institutes*, vol. 27 (1964): 340–2.

Žižek, Slavoj. *Organs without Bodies: On Deleuze and Consequences*. New York: Routledge, 2004.

Žižek, Slavoj. *Parallax View*. Cambridge: MIT Press, 2006.

Index

Lightning Source UK Ltd.
Milton Keynes UK
UKHW020626160621
385597UK00003B/90